Explorations in Navajo Poetry and Poetics

Explorations in Navajo Poetry and Poetics

Anthony K. Webster

University of New Mexico Press
Albuquerque

© 2009 by the University of New Mexico Press
All rights reserved. Published 2009
Printed in the United States of America

Library of Congress Cataloging-in-Publication Data

Webster, Anthony K., 1969–
  Explorations in Navajo poetry and poetics / Anthony K. Webster.
    p. cm.
  Includes bibliographical references and index.
  ISBN 978-0-8263-4801-2 (pbk. : alk. paper)
  1. Navajo poetry. I. Title.

PM2009.W43 2009
897.2′61009—dc22

2009029683

Cover illustration courtesy of Barbara Haines
Cover design by Barbara Haines

CONTENTS

Preface vii

INTRODUCTION Navajo Poetry and Poetics 1
ONE Poetic Devices in Navajo Oral and Written Poetry 16
TWO Poetics and Politics of Navajo Ideophony 51
THREE Language, Language Ideology, and Navajo Poetry 80
FOUR Performance, the Individual, and Feelingful Iconicity 122
FIVE Narratives of Navajoness and Indigenous Articulations 152
SIX Intercultural Performances and the Dynamics of Place 185
CONCLUSION Multiplying Glimpses of Navajo Poetics 218

Appendix A 227
Appendix B 229
Notes 231
Bibliography 239
Index 269

PREFACE

The original research for this book was done as part of my dissertation research on the emergence of written Navajo poetry on the Navajo Nation. Fieldwork on the Navajo Nation was conducted under a Historic Preservation Office (HPO) permit from June 2000 through August 2001. More recent research, also conducted under permits from HPO, was done in the summers of 2007 and 2008. One simply cannot do research on the Navajo Nation without a permit. I especially want to thank Ronald P. Maldonado for his help with HPO over the years.

I am not an English professor, nor am I a literary critic. I am a linguistic anthropologist. My training at the University of Texas at Austin was in both linguistics and anthropology. My concerns also differ from traditional readings of Native American literature. I am less interested in reading these poems as literature (they are), than I am in understanding the performances and poetics of these poems as cultural phenomenon. Understanding something of the poetics of Navajo poetry also means understanding something of the linguistics of the Navajo language and the ethnography of speaking of Navajos. In particular, it means understanding Navajos' social and aesthetic uses of the Navajo and English languages. One goal of this book is to make an extended argument about the need to understand literature from ethnographic and linguistic perspectives.

The aspects of language that I take up here are often considered marginal in much of the linguistics literature. Code-mixing, punning, ideophony, and the felt attachments to language are, however, central to the research of ethnopoetics and a discourse-centered approach to language and culture. A second goal of this book is to show the value in applying ethnopoetic and discourse-centered approaches to contemporary poetry.

That such poetry is also performed is of keen import. Contemporary Navajo poetry is not merely written and then read silently. Rather, Navajo poets perform their poetry before a variety of audiences. A third goal of this book is to show that a performance focus on contemporary Navajo poetry is more than warranted, it is essential.

Much of what I learned about Navajo poetry came from talking to a number of Navajo poets over the years. Here I wish to thank those who have wanted their names made public: the late Shonnie Allen, Rutherford Ashley, Tacey Atsitty, Martha Austin-Garrison, Shonto Begay, Esther Belin, Timothy Benally, Zoey Benally, Sherwin Bitsui, Vee Browne, Norla Chee, Tina Deschenie, Gloria Emerson, Nia Francisco, Rex Lee Jim, Hershman John, Blackhorse Mitchell, the late Alyse Neundorf, Luci Tapahonso, Laura Tohe, Orlando White, and Venaya Yazzie. There are numerous others who wished to remain anonymous. I especially want to thank Blackhorse Mitchell and Laura Tohe. Much of what I know about the Navajo language is because of Blackhorse Mitchell's patience. Much of what I know about Navajo poetry as performance is because of Laura Tohe. Without them, this book could not have been written. Thank you. I also want to thank Navajo filmmaker Bennie Klain for being a good friend. Thanks also to Karen Halona and William Riddle for being there.

I also want to thank various colleagues who have guided my thinking over the years. My interest in linguistic anthropology was first sparked by undergraduate courses at Purdue University with Myrdene Anderson. Since then, she has continued to provide perspective and support. I want to thank Scott Rushforth for nurturing my interest in things Athabaskan and things ethnopoetic. I also want to thank Elizabeth Keating, Ward Keeler, the late Carlota Smith, and Anthony Woodbury at the University of Texas at Austin for influencing my thinking in one way or another (always for the better). Thanks to Pauline Turner Strong and Joel Sherzer for being outstanding dissertation advisors. I continue to owe them both so much. To Polly, apparently I was wrong about not wanting to write a book. Colleagues in things Navajo have also been supportive. I thank James Faris, Ted Fernald, Margaret Field, Charlotte Frisbie, Madeline Iris, Joyce McDonough, Daniel McLaughlin, William Nichols, Clay

Slate, Barre Toelken, and Oswald Werner for guidance and/or kind words at various times. Thanks especially to my friend Leighton C. Peterson. It is no exaggeration that this book could not have been written without his help. I hope it lives up to his high standards. I especially thank him for taking the time to read through the manuscript and make detailed comments. I also want to thank Adam Frank, Sean O'Neill, David Samuels, Janis Nuckolls, Eleanor Nevins, Barbara Johnstone, Anthony Stocks, Chris Loether, Paul Kroskrity, and Jason Jackson for conversations about issues and topics taken up in this book. Some of your ideas have certainly found their way here.

Portions of this book were first begun at Wesleyan University, while I was an Andrew Mellon Postdoctoral Fellow at the Center for the Americas. I want to thank all in the center for making my time there so enjoyable. I especially thank Ann Wightman for making my stay at Wesleyan so productive. Thanks also to Michelle Reid who occupied the office next to mine. It was during that time at Wesleyan that I had the chance to visit with the late David P. McAllester and talk of things Navajo. I also want to thank my colleagues at Southern Illinois University, Carbondale. The Department of Anthropology has been a supportive and congenial place to work and write. I especially thank Jane Adams, Janet Fuller, Jonathan Hill, C. Andrew Hofling, and David Sutton. Gray Whaley in the History Department and Jo Nast in Art & Design have patiently listened to me ramble about topics found in here. Hong Zhang and Juan Luis Rodriguez were research assistants during research undertaken in Carbondale. I thank them both. Funding for this research was aided by a Wenner-Gren Foundation grant, two Philips Fund grants from the American Philosophical Society, a Jacobs Fund grant from the Whatcom Museum, various grants from the University of Texas at Austin, and a faculty seed grant from Southern Illinois University at Carbondale. Much thanks. I also thank Lisa Pacheco at the University of New Mexico Press for helping guide this book to fruition and two anonymous readers for UNM Press for a number of very useful suggestions. I further thank Rosemary Carstens for many useful suggestions about the form of this book.

I want to thank my brothers Frank, Joe, and Chris for being brothers and for keeping me in my place when I needed it (and sometimes when I did not). I dedicate this book to the memory of my father, Frank A.

Webster (March 30, 1930–January 17, 2009), for being the kind of father who taught me that a shortcut has absolutely nothing to do with distance or a length of time, but with the experience of taking a different path. Sadly, he was unable to see this book finally published. I also dedicate this book to the memory of my late mother, Ann Webster (July 4, 1930–May 10, 1995), for cultivating in me a love of language and literature. Thanks also to my in-laws Tony and Pat Hosemann for their continued support on getting this book done. I especially want to thank Hunter and Cassee for making my life profoundly more meaningful and enjoyable than I knew it could be. And finally, to my wife, Aimee, thank you. I am simply better for having known you.

Introduction
Navajo Poetry and Poetics

A verbal art like poetry is reflective; it stops to think.
W. H. Auden

The What and How of the Story

People tell stories. If ethnopoetics has taught us anything, it is that while the "what" of a story (the content) is important, the "how" of the story (the poetic structuring) is of equal importance. This book is about the ways that the how of the story and the what of the story are intertwined. The stories here are Navajo poetry, both written and performed orally.

Fairly early in my ethnographic and linguistic research on the Navajo Nation on the emergence of written Navajo poetry, I attempted to elicit indigenous Navajo terms for poetry. The most common response that I was able to elicit was: *hane'* (story, narrative). Diné College (the tribally controlled college with its main campus located in Tsaile, Arizona) promotes the phrase *hane' naach'ąąh* (designed stories). However, in general, Navajos I talked with used *hane'*. Poetry was, then, a kind of story or narrative. Poetry, like *hane'*, is meant to be publicly shared (see also Peterson 2006). There are a number of very good reasons to approach Navajo poetry as a kind of storytelling. That is one of the focuses of this book: The ways that Navajo poetry is a kind of story-telling. I argue that it is through a number of poetic devices that Navajo written poetry is linked with Navajo oral traditions. Navajo poetry is also linked with other traditions as well. I further argue that these poetic forms reveal something about the felt attachments to language that Navajo poets have. I believe it is important to understand such felt attachments to language, especially—as in the case of Navajo—when the language is threatened. Young Navajos are not learning the language at a rate that will ensure its continued persistence. It is also the case that many Navajos have developed felt attachments to English as well. That is also worthy of investigation.

In the spring of 2000, I drove up to the Navajo Nation to begin fieldwork on the emergence of Navajo written poetry. I was a graduate student at the University of Texas at Austin, and I was going there to do my dissertation fieldwork. I would live for a time in Chinle, Arizona (three months), and then, for a longer period of time (twelve months), outside Lukachukai, Arizona. I left the Navajo Nation in August of 2001. Since that time, I have corresponded frequently with Navajo poets and, in the summers of 2007 and 2008, I again conducted ethnographic and linguistic research on the Navajo Nation. This time, I lived north of Shiprock, New Mexico.

When I originally began my research on contemporary Navajo poetry, I had hoped to focus exclusively on Navajo-language poetry. This was such a colossal mistake that I am embarrassed now to write about it. However, I think there is a lesson here. My bias was and is not an uncommon one. I was interested in some "authentic" Navajo poetry. To be "authentic" it must, by default, be in Navajo. I had confused being Navajo with speaking Navajo. Not all Navajos speak Navajo and not all Navajos that speak Navajo write poetry in Navajo. By excluding poetry written in English, I would have excluded the great majority of poetry currently being written and performed on the Navajo Nation. In fact, poets like Rex Lee Jim, Nia Francisco, and Laura Tohe write poetry in both English and Navajo. Jim once told me that the motivation behind which language to write in had more to do with his personal aesthetics and the content of the poem than with anything else.

My embarrassment is mitigated somewhat by the realization that such stereotyping of particular Navajo poets as solely poets in Navajo was not and is not unique to me. Writing in Navajo can also be typecast to individuals. In 2000, on an evening drive down to Gallup, New Mexico, to get dinner, Jim told me about a book of poetry he had submitted to a university press. When the reviews came back—and Jim later showed me the review—one reviewer knowing Jim was the author recommended publication when Jim included the Navajo counterparts. The poems were all in English. There were no Navajo counterparts, and Jim was not inclined to write Navajo counterparts. Jim had wanted to write a book of poetry in English. The book was not published (for an example of the poetry from this book see Webster 2004). Jim had become stereotyped as the Navajo poet who writes in Navajo.

Other poets, like Esther Belin, have written eloquently about the fact that they do not speak Navajo. As Belin writes, "A degree from UC Berkeley will never change the fact that I cannot understand my grandfather when he asks for more coffee" (Belin 1999:43). Literacy in Navajo is still relatively rare on the Navajo Nation. Many Navajos speak Navajo, but they cannot always write Navajo. One Navajo poet told me that he would write in Navajo when the Navajo writing system did not look like English. A goal of this book is to focus on what Navajos are actually doing with their languages. One thing that they are doing is writing and performing poetry.

Watching Navajo poets perform their poetry in Navajo and English suggests that the use of language was an important aspect of their performances. Poets like Sherwin Bitsui, who writes primarily in English, would still open his performances in Navajo. Poets like Luci Tapahonso and Laura Tohe would extend the sections in Navajo beyond what was in the written versions of those poems. Such uses of Navajo were heightened affective expressions (they called attention to the expressive moment). This was a way of connecting with Navajo-speaking audience members. Yet English language poems also connected with Navajo audiences.

My focus on Navajo poetry emerged one day in March 2000 when I was talking with Rex Lee Jim at the Inn of the Navajo Nation (now Diné Restaurant), Window Rock, Arizona. As I listened to Jim talk about poetry and the importance of language in poetry, I began to sense the outlines of a dissertation. In an interview with Jim in early 2001, I would ask him why he wrote poetry. His response was classic Jim: "so that anthropologists have something to study." When Bitsui would perform his poem "Northern Sun," he would often turn to me and smile as he said, "Is this what I deserve: A white anthropologist sitting next to me at a winter ceremony?" He would draw me, the anthropologist, into the performance of the poem through his teasing. Esther Belin once told me that she hoped that her book of poetry, *From the Belly of My Beauty*, would be stocked in the anthropology section of bookstores. If we think of poetry as a kind of storytelling then this makes perfect sense. Her poems are stories about being, among other things, Navajo. These examples suggest that Navajo poets are quite aware of the anthropological representations of Navajos. I took these examples as reminders that they (Navajo poets) would be reading what I did.

One of the arguments that I make in this book is that much of Navajo poetry is also narratives of Navajoness. Navajo poets, I argue throughout the final chapters, reckon and express their identity through narratives. Deborah House (2002) and Jennifer Nez Denetdale (2007b) have both discussed the importance of narratives in Navajo identity formation. House (2002) is primarily concerned with the content of narratives of Navajoness. Denetdale, a Navajo and a historian, on the other hand approaches these stories from a different direction. For Denetdale, the crucial point is the ways that Navajo narratives differ from Western narratives about Navajos. Denetdale (2007b) points out, for example, that many Navajo narratives about the Long Walk (a singular historic moment in Navajo history) focus on the maintenance of clan relations (Navajos are primarily matrilineal and descent is traced through one's mother). Such Navajo historical narratives are less interested in the larger sociopolitical narratives often told in Western history books. Narratives become a way of expressing and creating identity.

This perspective on identity—that identity is a kind of narrative—resonates with the work of Edward Spicer. Spicer was an anthropologist who worked primarily with the Yaqui of the American Southwest and Sonora, Mexico. Late in his career he began to contemplate what he called "persistent identity systems" (Spicer 1971:796). Spicer (1975:46) understood identity this way:

> Identity is a conception of and feelings about the events which a people have lived through in the course of their history... It is the meanings of events in which their ancestors took part, in ways that they are proud of, which differentiates peoples into what we call ethnic groups... It is in the telling and retelling of the events from a particular people's point of view that ethnic difference is rooted.

I like this definition of identity because it matches what Navajos are doing and saying. Identity is a kind of storytelling, a way of recounting the past. As I show in later chapters, many of the poems being written today relate to events in Navajo history. They are history from a Navajo perspective. There are a number of poems about the Long Walk, for example. It also reminds us that identity is a feeling, and these feelings can be expressed and evoked by poetic resources. This definition is also in concert with the work of contemporary linguistic anthropology, which attempts to understand the dynamics of language as both an index and an icon of identity (see Errington 1998; Kroskrity 1993; Kuipers 1998; Van Vleet 2008).

Poetry and Poetics

Another reason that I prefer this working definition of identity is because one can investigate it empirically. It locates identity in the circulation of narratives or discourse. Poetry and poetry performances are kinds of discourse. They are public, in the sense that they are actively shared. Joel Sherzer (1987:295), an anthropologist who has worked primarily with the Kuna of Panama, has argued for a "discourse-centered approach to language and culture." According to Sherzer (296):

> It is discourse which creates, recreates, modifies, and fine tunes both culture and language and their intersection, and it is especially in verbally artistic discourse such as poetry, magic, verbal dueling, and political rhetoric that the potentials and resources provided by grammar, as well as cultural meanings and symbols, are exploited to the fullest and the essence of language-culture relationships becomes salient.

Greg Urban (1991:1), another anthropologist in the discourse-centered tradition, who has worked with indigenous peoples in South America, states the matter succinctly when he says, "culture is localized in concrete, publicly accessible signs, the most important of which are actually occurring instances of discourse." This book is discourse-centered as well. In many of the chapters that follow, I will focus on specific performances of Navajo poetry and suggest ways that such performances help to circulate frameworks of meaning that—in English—we might term "Navajo."

There is a distinction here that needs to be made. When I talk about Navajo poetry, what I am talking about is a recognized genre of expression by Navajos. Navajos talk of "Navajo poetry," and there are named and recognizable "Navajo poets." Some of this poetry has been published. Some of it has not been. I met a number of Navajos who wrote poetry but had no aspirations of having their poetry published. Instead, for some, they hoped to pass their poetry on to their grandchildren. Others wanted to publish their poetry but had not yet found a venue. Others wrote poetry for classes at Diné College. Still others, like Zoey Benally, perform their poetry at poetry slams. This is contemporary Navajo written poetry. Most written poetry can also be performed.

On the other hand, when I am discussing Navajo poetics, I mean something very different than I do when I discuss Navajo poetry. When I write of poetics I mean something very similar to both definitions of the poetic function given by Roman Jakobson (1960). His first definition is that the poetic function focuses on the message over content (1960:356). His second definition (358) notes that, "the poetic function projects the principle of equivalence from the axis of selection into the axis of combination." This is the way the choices of sounds, lexical items, syntactic structures, and the like are combined to create expressive alignment. This is the *how* of storytelling. It should be clear that poetics does not reside only in something we might term "poetry." Paul Friedrich (1986, 1996, and 2006), a linguistic anthropologist whose work defies easy reduction, has argued that poetic language is pervasive in all language use.

Friedrich (1986:17) goes on to argue that, "poetic language . . . is the locus of the most interesting differences between languages and should be the focus of the study of such differences." Friedrich (53) terms this "poetic indeterminacy." This book builds on the concern with the differences between languages based on poetic languages, by also looking at the ways languages—poetic languages—are intermingled. Poetic languages are also the places where languages are combined, through punning, code-switching, or code-mixing.

There is a tradition here that Friedrich is tapping into. It is a tradition that links back to Franz Boas (1966) and Edward Sapir (1921, 1985). It finds potent expression in Boas's (1966:58) claim:

> When the question arises, for instance, of investigating the poetry of the Indians, no translation can possibly be considered as an adequate substitute for the original. The form of rhythm, the treatment of language, the adjustment of text to music, the imagery, the use of metaphors, and all the numerous problems involved in any thorough investigation of the style of poetry, can be interpreted only by the investigator who has equal command of the ethnographical traits of the tribe and of their language.

It is this tradition that Sherzer (1990:18) taps into when he discusses "the poeticization of grammar." Sherzer (18) defines this as the use of "an element or feature of grammar either losing its grammatical function as it takes on a poetic function or adding a poetic function to its already existing referential and grammatical function." Such a process of the poeticization of grammar would, most likely, be language and discursive community specific. It is also related to what linguist Anthony Woodbury (1998:238) terms "form-dependent expression." For Woodbury (238) form-dependent expressions entail "any situation where the arbitrary patterns of a lexicogrammatical code are harnessed to constitute, shape, or model communicative purpose or content, expression is crucially dependent on form." This is the way that linguistic forms are interwoven through use in social practices. There is a feedback loop here, though. As such form-dependent expressions are repeatedly used, they accrue felt connections that make them feel as if they are not arbitrary. They are, following Friedrich (1979:44), relatively nonarbitrary. As Sherzer (1987:296) argues, language "is motivated from the point of view of the meaningfulness and appropriateness that individuals feel about their language as it is used in actual social and cultural contexts."

This tradition also finds expression in the work of Dell Hymes (1981, 2000, 2003) and Dennis Tedlock (1983) concerning ethnopoetics. At its most basic, ethnopoetics is the study of the ways that narratives are structured into "lines" and are thus poetic (Hymes 1981). Lines fit both of Jakobson's definitions of the poetic function. First, the creation of lines calls attention to the form over the content. Second, such structured units as the line are the sites for the playing out of the paradigmatic axis on the syntagmatic axis. Rhyme, in some English-language poetry, creates lines and is also the playing out of phonological choices on a distributional axis. Navajo poets are less concerned with rhyme than many English language poets. However, because of the influence of English poetry on Navajo poets, there are some poems that use rhyme in Navajo English-language poems. Vee Browne (2000:30, 32), for example, has experimented with limericks in both English and Navajo.

Navajo poets are engaged with world poetic traditions in other ways, as well. Luci Tapahonso, for example, has written a poem titled "Leda and the Cowboy" that explicitly links with William Butler Yeats's poem "Leda and the Swan." Yeats's poem was inspired by Greek mythology (as passed on in Western literary traditions), and Tapahonso's poem is a Navajo response to Greek myth as mediated through Yeats. Navajo poetry and Navajo poets are engaged with the larger world around them. It is no longer fair, if it ever was, to say that Navajos are isolated from global discourses. They are not. They are, instead, active participants in that world. In 2000, Rex Lee Jim told me about his poetry reading in Navajo to Māori audiences in New Zealand. Jim told me that no one in the audience understood what he said, but that they wanted him to read in Navajo and not in English. His reading in Navajo indexed—or pointed to—a shared indigeneity. Indeed, one of Rex Lee Jim's (1998) books of poetry, *Dúchas Táá Kóó Diné*, is a trilingual collection with poetry in Navajo, English, and Gaelic and was published in Ireland. A number of Navajo poets have performed internationally.

Ethnopoetics is—or should be—concerned with more than simply poetic lines. Ethnopoetics has been concerned with individual creativity and the careful attention to linguistic details. Friedrich (2006) and Jan Blommaert (2006) have offered useful evaluations of ethnopoetics. As Blommaert (259) writes, "ethnopoetic work is one way of addressing the main issue in ethnography: to describe (and reconstruct) languages not in the sense of stable, closed and internally homogeneous units characterizing mankind..., but as ordered complexes of genres, styles, registers and forms of use." Such a perspective must engage individual poets, but also the languages they use and the connections they make. Related to that, as Blommaert (266) adds, "ultimately, what ethnopoetics does is to show voice, to visualize the particular ways—often deviant from hegemonic norms—in which subjects produce meaning." I see the recognition of voice as central to this book. As Friedrich (2006:228) notes in his own review of ethnopoetics, "ethnopoetics tends to relativize knowledge, to recognize its subtlety."

Note, also, that both ethnopoetics and a discourse-centered approach focus in on "performance" and understanding "verbal art as performance" (see Bauman 1984, 1986). According to Richard Bauman (1984:11), performance can be understood, "as a mode of spoken verbal communication [that] consists in the assumption of responsibility to an audience for a display of communicative competence." Performance is a "constitutive" use of language (Bauman 1984:11; see also Taylor 2006). A performance-centered perspective, like a discourse-centered approach and ethnopoetics, attends to language as action and not language as an abstraction. I will return to this point in Chapter 4 when I discuss the performances of contemporary Navajo poetry.

Another concept that I will discuss more fully in Chapter 4, but that animates much of the discussion of this book, is the idea of "feelingful iconicity." Let me sketch out here what I mean by that turn of phrase. By feelingful iconicity, I follow David Samuels (2004b), Steven Feld (1988) and Friedrich (1986:16–53), and understand feelingful iconicity as the felt attachments that accrue to expressive forms. This is what Sapir (1921) termed "the feeling-tones of words." As Samuels (2004b:11) argues for multiple genres of Apache music, feelingful iconicity is the "emotional attachment to aesthetic forms." Such emotional attachments create a sense of "continuity." Influencing Samuels has been the work of Feld. Feld (1988:132; emphasis in original) describes the Kaluli aesthetic for "lift-up-over sounding" as "an icon of what Sapir, Whorf, and others spoke of as an *intuitive* nature of a felt worldview, what Paul Friedrich (1986) has described as the emotionally satisfying dimensions of poetic indeterminacy." As Samuels (2004b:11) states, this is "the continuity of the *feeling* evoked by expressive forms." Feelingful iconicity is part of the poetic function of language, where there is a felt naturalness to the expressive dimension—a felt naturalness that has accrued over time and thus creates a sense of continuity. This feelingful iconicity is not bound only to expressive forms in Navajo, however.

In the rush to analyze and document the last speakers of dying indigenous languages, linguists and linguistic anthropologists have overlooked the Englishes that indigenous peoples have been speaking and the ways such Englishes have been shaped for poetic purposes (see Seaburg 2007; Riddington and Riddington 2006; Bartelt 2001; Leap 1993a). We have also missed the ways that indigenous peoples have linguistically played with the contact between languages, seeing, for example, English as ripe for punning opportunities in Navajo. Navajo poets, as I discuss in Chapter 3, are also selective in their representations of the kinds of "Navajo language" in their poetry. A truly discourse-centered approach to Navajo and a truly ethnopoetic perspective on Navajo poetry should look at all the languages that Navajo poets do or do not employ.

Navajos and Navajo

The Navajo Nation, covering parts of Arizona, New Mexico, and Utah, is roughly the size of West Virginia (for useful histories see Iverson 2002; Denetdale 2007b; Parman 1994). The Navajo language is a Southern Athabaskan language, related to other Apachean languages spoken in the Southwest such as Western Apache, Chiricahua Apache, and Jicarilla Apache. It is more distantly related to Athabaskan languages like Tolowa and Hupa that are spoken on the West Coast of the United States and languages like Chipewyan, Slavey, and Koyukon, which are spoken in Canada and Alaska. According to the 2000 U.S. Census, there are nearly 300,000 people who identify as Navajo. In the Census, 178,014 people identified themselves as speakers of Navajo, with roughly 120,000 of those identifying themselves as speakers of Navajo and as residents of the Navajo Nation. Rough numbers, then, give an impression that the Navajo language is widely spoken (in fact, it is spoken in every state in the United States) by a significant number of speakers. However, as Navajo scholars such as Tiffany Lee (2007) and Ancita Benally (Benally and Viri 2005) point out, the Navajo language is a threatened language. It is threatened in the sense that young Navajos are not learning the language at a rate that will ensure its continued use. Also, despite a number of efforts over the years, literacy in Navajo is still rather limited (see Spicer 1962:456–457; McLaughlin 1992; Spolsky 2002). There has been a great deal of literature on the status of the Navajo language as a threatened language. One aspect of this book is to highlight certain poetic features to which Navajos have felt attachments. Language is more than mere reference. It is more than a lexicogrammatical system. Rather, it is something that individuals over time build attachments to. This is, again, the feelingful iconicity that adheres to a language in use. A focus on the poetic uses of the Navajo language and English, will, I believe shed light on the ways that individuals orient to language. This focus treats languages as more than a grammatical system, but rather as something that people inhabit and that inhabits them as well.

Poetry is an emerging and important voice for individual Navajos. Indeed, an understanding of how Navajo poets perform and circulate their poetry seems of crucial importance to an understanding of the felt and lived realities of both Navajo poets and Navajo audiences. This book is based on both linguistic and ethnographic fieldwork on the Navajo Nation (2000–2001, 2007, 2008). There are very few venues on the Navajo Nation for performing Navajo poetry. Gloria Emerson's coffee shop is one new venue (though how long it stays one is an open question). It was not there when I did fieldwork in 2000–2001. At that time, an open-microphone night at Diné College in Tsaile, Arizona, seemed to be the only regular venue for young Navajos to perform poetry in public settings. Many of the poetry events described in this book have an ad hoc quality to them, precisely because they were not regularly performed. One Navajo friend had a poetry reading at his house in the winter of 2000 (Rex Lee Jim, Sherwin Bitsui, and Orlando White all read their poetry that night). Many Navajo poets often used my interviewing them as a chance to perform their poetry as well. In Appendix B, I list some of the more regularly scheduled events that include Navajo poetry performances (or have included Navajo poets).

This book focuses on Navajo poetry performances and poetics as a part of the circulation of assertions and displays of narratives of Navajoness. Rather than dealing with narratives of Navajoness as an abstraction, this book focuses on specific instances and performances of narratives of

Navajoness and on the linguistic and poetic resources brought to bear in those performances. This book differs from Deborah House's *Language Shift Among the Navajo* (2002), in that it pays particular attention to the poetic forms of narratives of Navajoness. Thus, I am concerned with the linguistic devices that Navajo poets use in achieving a sense of Navajoness through their poetry and poetry performances.

Daniel McLaughlin (1992) provides a sociolinguistic perspective on Navajo literacy practices. McLaughlin argues against a "special diglossia" where Navajo is used in oral communication and English is the language of written communication. While this distinction is generally true, written Navajo can be found in sites of power such as schools, missions, and the government; more importantly, Navajo is also "in traditional domains, to record ceremonial procedures, for example, and in the home, to write letters, lists, journals, and notes" (McLaughlin 1992:151). It is also used in emails that I receive from various Navajo poets and friends and written Navajo can be found on the Internet as well (for example, on social networking sites). Several poets I interviewed kept journals that included their poetry in Navajo. Poets would often take these journals out and show them to me, and then read various poems from them. McLaughlin (1992) also notes a general shift in attitudes occurring among the Navajos of Mesa Valley. No longer is written Navajo seen simply as an aid to record "traditional culture"; rather, written Navajo is also becoming associated with "thinking it useful primarily for the promotion of self-understanding" (McLaughlin 1992:156). Nowhere, perhaps, can this be better seen than in the emergence of Navajo poetry. In such ways, as McLaughlin argues, literacy is an empowering practice for Navajos.

The research that this book is based on was done under permits by the Navajo Nation Historic Preservation Department. I received permits to conduct research on Navajo poetry on the Navajo Nation in 2000, 2001, 2007, and again in 2008. It is no longer the case that anthropologists can simply pull up on the Navajo Nation and begin to do research. Today, instead, researchers have to apply to the Navajo Nation for a permit. This, I might add, is as it should be. Research should be done in consultation with Native peoples. I have, for example, presented papers to Navajo audiences at the Navajo Studies Conference (Albuquerque, New

Mexico, 2006; Tsaile, Arizona, 2007), the Athabaskan Language Conference (Tsaile, Arizona, 2007), and at the Northwestern Ethnographic Field school (McGaffey, New Mexico, 2001) where I worked as a consultant. Hearing feedback from Navajo audience members acts as a check on my research; it also makes my research public.

Throughout this book, I will use a number of real names for people. I do this because many of the people I worked with wanted to be recognized as poets. Some people did not. For them I use pseudonyms. Some readers may notice that I am not consistent in the spelling of Navajo words. This is true. When I quote Navajo poets I write the words the way they spell them. Navajo poets spell Navajo words in a variety of ways. My job is to document such usage. It is not my job to promote a standard. I believe an over reliance on "the standard" and a diminishing of the ways that Navajos actually write their language limits the potential for creativity and subtly undermines notions of incommensurability between Navajo and English. In my experience with Navajo poets, many have been more concerned with evoking the feelingful relationship with Navajo than they have been with getting the orthography right. Vernacular orthographies of Navajo continue to reproduce an idealized Navajo, whereas, as I argue in Chapter 3, code-mixed Navajo challenges an oppositional ideology between Navajo and English.

Outline of Book

A number of years ago, Howard Bahr (1994) suggested that the study of change in Navajo social life should be understood as "multiplying glimpses." This book applies a perspective that attempts to glimpse—in the sense that I claim no omnipotent and unobscured view—Navajo poetry and poetic practices. It is an exploration, not an authoritative statement. In presenting a number of glimpses, or chapters, concerning poetic practices among Navajos, I hope to suggest something of the diversity of social work Navajo poets are attempting to accomplish through their poetry.

Many of the following chapters have appeared in one form or another as published articles in a number of journals. Here I wish to acknowledge those journals. Portions of Chapter 1 appeared in *Anthropological*

Linguistics; parts of Chapter 2 appeared in *Language & Communication*; portions of Chapter 3 found home in *Pragmatics*; an earlier version of Chapter 4 was published in *Language in Society*; and portions of Chapter 6 will appear in *Semiotica*. While research for this book was partly done for my dissertation in linguistic anthropology at the University of Texas at Austin, very little of my dissertation has found its way into this book. A very different version of Chapter 4 can be found in my dissertation, as can a substantially different version of Chapter 5.

The first two chapters of this book concern poetic devices in Navajo. Chapter 1 investigates the poetic devices found in Navajo written and oral poetic traditions as well as the languages of those poetic devices. This chapter uses an ethnopoetic perspective to understand language shift and the felt connections to language that Navajos express and explore through their use of poetic devices in oral and written poetry. It documents a number of examples where Navajo oral poetic devices in Navajo are not transferred or translated into Navajo written poetry in English.

Chapter 2 focuses on a neglected aspect of Navajo poetics. This chapter looks at the use of ideophony (sound symbolism) in a variety of Navajo poetic genres. Examples are given from Navajo place-names, narratives, and songs. Final examples involve the use of ideophony in contemporary written Navajo poetry. While it is often argued that ideophones appear to be a relatively fragile poetic form, their degree of use by Navajo poets may indicate the indexing of resistance toward Western literary traditions. Poetic devices such as ideophones are often devalued by a Western linguistic ideology that marginalizes iconic linguistic forms. Yet it is precisely such linguistic forms that create felt attachments to languages, making them more than mere reference.

In Chapter 3, I take up the issue of the choices of what images "a" Navajo language may take in contemporary poetry and the ideological underpinnings of such choices. I suggest that much of the use of the Navajo language in contemporary Navajo written poetry, especially English-dominant poetry, serves as an icon of proper Navajo usage. It is a purist view of the Navajo language. Navajo poetry is implicated, even if tacitly, in a discourse of linguistic purism that is tied to an oppositional linguistic ideology that sees Navajo and English as discrete and distinct "objects." Navajo poetry erases the contemporary sociolinguistic diversity—including bilingual Navajo—on the Navajo Nation. And in so doing, it closes off parts of Navajo sociolinguistic realities and in its stead creates an imagined Navajo language community. In Appendix A, I list a number of Navajo books of poetry analyzed in Chapter 3.

In Chapter 4, the focus turns to the oral performances of Navajo written poetry. This chapter pays close attention to the subtle shifts in language found in two oral performances of Laura Tohe's "Cat or Stomp" and the written version. The chapter argues for understanding these performances as "narratives of Navajoness." It also argues for understanding the poetics of Tohe's performance both as an individual achievement as well as in its linguacultural milieu. In this chapter, I argue that there is a feelingful connection to both Navajo and English and, as such, both languages can be brought to bear in performances of narratives of Navajoness.

In Chapter 5, I focus on a long narrative poem by Navajo poet Laura Tohe that concerns the Long Walk and on two public performances of that poem. Here I discuss the ways that Tohe's poem is an indigenous articulation that valorizes certain aspects of the Navajo past and Navajo oral tradition. This discussion is framed by a consideration of events that were occurring around the Navajo Nation in 2000–2001. I also suggest something of the intertextual links that Tohe engages in through her use of Navajo poetic devices.

Chapter 6 analyzes portions of a poetry performance by Navajo poet Laura Tohe to a non-Navajo audience in rural Illinois. By analyzing Tohe's metalinguistic commentaries about the use of Navajo, as well as her actual uses of Navajo in her performance, it is argued that Tohe presents a metasemiotic stereotype of Navajo users. These are based on a certain set of linguistic ideologies about the felt connection to language. Paying close attention to the uses of Navajo language place-names also reveals how Tohe connects her performance with larger concerns about Navajo claims to place.

ONE

Poetic Devices in Navajo Oral and Written Poetry

Wherever we go we are impressed by the fact that pattern is one thing, the utilization of pattern quite another.

Edward Sapir, *Language*

Introduction

In this chapter, I outline the poetic devices found in Navajo oral narratives and compare them to poetic devices found in Navajo written poetry. One goal of this chapter is to give specific examples wherein Navajo oral poetic devices are used in Navajo orthographic poetry. It has often been assumed that Navajo written poetry is influenced by Navajo oral poetry (Brill de Ramirez 1999). Here I wish to delimit just which devices can be found in both written and oral poetry. I take seriously the statements made by many Navajo poets concerning the oral tradition and its influences on their poetry. Most of the Navajo poets I interviewed stated that one of their primary influences was the "oral tradition," or the "stories" they heard growing up, or what their grandparents had told them. To take Navajo poetry seriously, we must take these influences seriously as well.

A second goal is to compare the languages of that transference across mediums. I will be concerned with which language various Navajo poetic devices use in written poetry. A special concern will be opening narrative framing devices, as well as other ethnopoetic organizing devices. Such framing devices seem markedly salient to native speakers and are therefore of special interest in attempting to identify the influence of the oral tradition on written poetry, as well as the commensurability those devices might have in transferences from Navajo to English. Are rhetorical poetic devices transferred from Navajo to English? Which devices can be transferred and which are not transferred across codes? This chapter gives several examples of both.

Navajo Language Shift

Henry Shonerd (1990:193), in a review of historical documents about the relationship between Navajo and Euro-Americans concerning language policy, argues that Navajo language persistence "is best understood in light of an almost 400-year history of attempts to suppress language varieties indigenous to the culture." Today Navajo is a threatened language. This language shift has been reported by a number of scholars (Slate 1993; Holm and Holm 1995; Dick and McCarty 1997; Dick 1998; Field 2001; Lee and McLaughlin 2001; House 2002; Spolsky 2002; Benally and Viri 2005).[1] Most of these studies report on the social nature of the language shift. Many follow the lead of Slate (1993) and posit ways of "reversing Navajo language shift." Indeed, Slate has argued that supporting—what Woodbury (1998) called "secured domains"—where Navajo is used, such as the traditional formulaic introduction via clan names, will help strengthen Navajo but will also foster the family and community "nexus of Navajo" (Slate 1993:35). Thus, we might argue that clan names, kinship terms, mythic names, and place names are secured domains. House (2002:100) critiques Slate's position by arguing (correctly) that there will never be pan-Navajo agreement concerning which domains are "secure" and which are not. Secured domains can be defined as those language domains in which "their habitual use reinforces existing social network structure and provides for them a privileged social space in which shared ways can be retained, continued, and reworked" (Woodbury 1993:111).

In a review of the published poetry by Navajos we cannot, for example, say that poetry is a completely "secured domain" for Navajo. There are Navajo poems in English and in Navajo. Certainly, following Bonnie Urciuoli (1996), poetry is a nonthreatening domain where the Navajo language might be deemed "aesthetically" pleasing and "nonthreatening" by a non-Navajo dominant society that seems reactionary against language use in "the workplace." Indeed, conflicts do arise when Navajo is used in the workplace (see Zachary 2005).

Poetry is more likely to be written in English than Navajo. This is because literacy in Navajo is still limited (see Dick and McCarty 1997; Lockard 1995; McLaughlin 1992). However, poetry is a partially secured domain, because Navajo code-switching (switching from an English-language dominant poem to Navajo) does occur and clusters around certain lexical domains such as place names, clan names, terms of references, and mythic names. In other words, while Navajos may not agree which domains should be secured, in written poetry there does seem to be a clustering of lexical domains that seem more likely to be represented in Navajo. I use code-switching in a rather broad sense and include any instance where the Navajo language is used (be it lexical, morphological, or syntactic) (see Webster 2006a). I exclude certain forms such as "hogan," which were, according to Washington Matthews (1994:55), already an "adopted English word in the Southwest" by 1897.

It is also worth noting that House's (2002) counter argument suffers from the same problem she raises for Slate's work. House wants to follow the Diné College model based on *Sa'ąh Naagháí Bik'eh Hózhóón* (often known at Diné College by the acronym SNBK), but in doing so, she seems to imply that this phrase—central to much in Navajo philosophy—is understood everywhere the same.[2] Diné College teaches a particular approach to this philosophy and, indeed, not all Navajos I have spoken with can agree on its meaning or a "good" English translation. House (2002) also seems comfortable talking about "traditional" education and curriculum. Diné College, for all that is good and empowering about it, is after all based on—and certified by—Western educational regimes of knowledge.

While House (2002) and Slate (1993) offer useful suggestions for "reversing Navajo language shift," they, like other writers (Lee and McLaughlin 2001; Spolsky 2002), have relatively little to say about the actual linguistic details of that shift. To give one brief example, most writers concur with Slate (1993) when he discusses the importance of kinship systems being used in Navajo. The terms *shimá* (my mother), *shinálí* (my paternal grandparent), and *shimásání* (my maternal grandmother) are ubiquitous on the Navajo Nation. They are used by both non-Navajo and Navajo speakers alike. Today *shimásání* has taken on a more general meaning of "elder woman" and is often the expected form to be used with elder Navajo women. However, it is interesting to note certain ways that kinship terms and the first-person possessive *sh(i)-* (my) are used in instances of code-switching. Navajo humorist Vincent Craig often uses the term *shiheart* in his routines. This form is recognizable as the code-mixed form for "my heart." Norla Chee (2001:6) titles one of her poems "Shí Buddy" (my buddy). For many Navajos, Navajos who speak Navajo and those who do not, *shi-* as the first person possessive form is salient.

In each chapter of this volume, I have interspersed consecutively numbered examples, drawn from my recordings, video-tapes, and my notes, as well as from other sources to illustrate each language usage discussed. The following examples address the use of shi-:

(1) "I learned this from my nálí ..."
 "This is about my shinálí ..."
 "Shimásání taught me this ..."
 "My shimásání used to say ..."

The variation concerns whether or not the speaker uses both the first-person Navajo possessive form *shi-* and the English first-person possessive "my" or if they use only the English possessive form and the Navajo lexical item. That is, does the speaker treat *shimásání* as an unanalyzable unit or does the speaker treat *shimásání* as a segmentable unit with the attendant first-person possessive morpheme that can then be removed to avoid redundancy? The question here is of the saliency of the Navajo first-person possessive morpheme for some Navajos. In Navajo, kinship terms are inalienable and thus must have a possessive marking. The form *-nálí* cannot occur alone. The possessive marking can, of course, be a code-mixed form such as *my-nálí*. But "my *shinálí*" is redundant and can be compared to James Collins's (1985) examples from Tolowa where the distinction between alienable and inalienable is being lost, and the third-person form is becoming the default form that one then attaches the first- or second-person possessive to. The above examples could be evidence of the loss by some non-Navajo speakers of the alienable/inalienable distinction. However, the point here is that much of the work on language shift from Navajo to English has been on macrolevel social processes and not about specific microlevel linguistic details.

The work by AnCita Benally and Denis Viri (2005), Galena Dick (1998), and Galena Dick and Teresa McCarty (1997) offer Navajo perspectives on the current language shift situation. Dick (1998) focuses on a lingual autobiography of Navajo educator Galena Sells Dick and stresses the role of education, especially at Rough Rock, in language maintenance. Like the article by Dick and McCarty (1997), this work also stresses the role of literacy in Navajo language maintenance programs. That resources should be used for Navajo literacy is, of course, important. It is also important to note that literacy—in and of itself—is not a panacea for language shift. Today there are more documents written in Navajo than at any time in the past, and yet the language is still shifting toward English. Likewise, Benally and Viri (2005) offer a complicated and nuanced picture of the state of the Navajo language. They argue that Navajo language is at a "crossroads," where the potentials for renewal and decline both loom large. Again the focus is on macrolevel analysis at the expense of microlevel usage. Though they do note that certain lexical items are being replaced by English-language forms (see Chapter 3).

The pessimism reflected in some of Benally and Viri (2005) can also be found in Spolsky's (2002) reassessment of the state of the Navajo language. On Navajo literacy, Spolsky (2002:157) states, it "never managed to challenge the usefulness and appropriateness of English literacy . . . vernacular literacy, too, was co-opted into a force for language shift to English." He does, however, note that there are other media available to Navajos. For example, KTNN (the Navajo radio station located in the Navajo Nation capital Window Rock, Arizona) often has programming in Navajo. Likewise, a number of CDs and CD-ROMs have become available in Navajo, and texts written in Navajo are being published on the Internet. As Lee and McLaughlin (2001) note, the potential for new technologies in the maintenance and renewal of Navajo is there. As with literacy, however, new technologies cannot be seen as a panacea for all that ails the Navajo language (Webster 2006b). The question, as Benally and Viri (2005:107) point out, is this:

> On several levels, extinction seems to be looming for the Navajo language, but on other levels, the language appears strong and viable. Ultimately, the future of the Navajo language lies with its

speakers. The language is theirs. The stories, songs, and prayers that come with the language are for them . . . the Navajo language can survive if the speakers choose to keep it alive.

One point that needs to also be addressed concerns the transference of "ways of speaking" that can and do survive the shift from one lexicogrammatical code to another (Hymes 1990; Kwachka 1992; Field 2001). To this end Margaret Field provides a microlevel analysis of Navajo interactive language practices. Field (2001) has suggested that triadic directives, a form of indirect request through a third party, may be more resistant to change than the concomitant shift from Navajo to English. Thus, even as Navajo shifts to English, certain discourse routines may persist. For example, while the preferred way for Navajo poets to introduce themselves is in Navajo and by clans, some younger Navajo poets introduce themselves in English with the English glossing of clan names (this is surprisingly rare). In this way, a discourse routine (the formulaic introduction by clans) is maintained even in the face of a lexicogrammatical shift.

This seems a fruitful avenue of investigation, and it is to that kind of investigation that I will turn in the next section. However, I wish to make certain assumptions more explicit about this line of investigation. First, it is important when comparing discourse routines (and here I am talking about poetics) that a baseline for comparison is set. Thus, I will describe a number of poetic devices found in Navajo verbal art and compare them with poetic devices found in Navajo orthographic poetry. In this book, I will look primarily at published examples of Navajo verbal art. Many of the features can be found in contemporary verbal art but, in line with the desires of consultants I have worked with, I have refrained from publishing new traditional narratives. Since many poets stated that they based their poetry on the oral tradition, it seems important to understand the poetic devices used in the oral tradition. In this way, we can see both what is transferred from oral poetics to orthographic poetics as well as what can and does remain in Navajo and what can and does get transferred into English.

This leads to the second point (here I follow Woodbury [1993, 1998]) and argue that while the work of Field (2001) is illuminating, there is an impression left that all interactive routines and perhaps poetics can be transferred across codes. The problem is that some of this work does not directly address what cannot be or is not transferred across codes (Woodbury 1993). For example, certain Navajos were quite adamant with me that clan names or place names, or both, could not be translated into English; they had to be stated in Navajo. For these speakers, any translation of a clan name into English was a loss and not commensurate. Also, while *jiní* (they say, it is said) is often noted as a crucial poetic device in Navajo narratives (Toelken and Scott 1981; Webster 2004), when I asked a Navajo poet (Blackhorse Mitchell) to translate some narratives for me, he left out the translation of this device into English. Because, he said, it was too cumbersome. It is not enough, then, to say that some devices (i.e., the use of four repetitions) can be transferred from one lexico-grammatical code to another. We must also point to places where the transfer is resisted, incomplete, or incommensurate.

Finally, as Anne Goodfellow (2003) notes concerning Kʷakʷala (an indigenous language of the Northwest Coast), we need to document both the language shift that is occurring and also the new languages that are emerging through sustained contact between languages and speakers. Field's work is an important corrective to views that see language and language loss in absolute terms. Navajos do often consider language loss in absolute terms. This is an attitude that many Navajos feel and feel deeply. During my fieldwork, there was a proposition (Proposition 203 "English for the Children") on the ballot in Arizona that would have severely limited bilingual education (the measure passed, but was not implemented on the Navajo Nation). I attended several community meetings where people spoke passionately about the importance of their language and the meaning that their language had to them. The matter was about more than a lexico-grammatical code, it was about what it meant to be Navajo. Elder Navajo men and women, standing before community members, wept as they spoke about the Navajo language or, as they phrased it, *Diné bizaad* or *Dinék'ehjí yálti'* (he/she is talking the Diné way). They referred to the Navajo language in Navajo, even when there was code-switching from Navajo to English at other places, and they used *Diné bizaad* or *Dinék'ehjí yálti'* to refer to Navajo. This use was an affective display, indicating the felt attachment to the Navajo language. The use of

Dinék'ehjí yáłti (he/she is talking the Diné way), which can be glossed as *Diné* (Navajo) + *-k'eh* (according to) + *-jí* (way, direction of) and *yáł-* (he/she) + *-ti'* (talk), reminds us that some Navajos consider living the Navajo way to also be speaking Navajo (see Chapter 6).³

The weeping was a kind of stylized weeping and is used by Navajo women as a metasignal of sincerity and tradition (see Hill 1990 on metasignaling; see also Urban 1991). It is marked by an ingressive airstream, sobbing, creaky voice, and falsetto vowels (see Urban 1991:156).⁴ Like the weeping described by Jane Hill (1990) for Mexicano personal narratives and the ritual wailing described by Urban (1991) for South America, this weeping is also connected with gender. Both Navajo men and women weep publicly though not identically. For example, Navajo men also wept when they talked about language loss. However, it differs from the polyphonic wailing and weeping described by Urban (1991), Feld (1990) for the Kaluli of Papau New Guinea, and Charles Briggs (1993) for the Warao of Venezuela, in that such weeping is often done individually among Navajo women. This stylized weeping can be seen at other highly charged public events. For example, at the end of Jeff Spitz and Bennie Klain's documentary film *The Return of Navajo Boy*, Elsie May Cly Begay embraces and weeps when her younger brother John Wayne Cly returns to the family after having been removed by missionaries when he was a small boy (he is now in his forties). Her weeping signals sincerity about his return and positions her as a traditional Navajo elder woman. As Keith Basso (1990:97), citing Navajo Priscilla Mowrer, notes about Navajos returning after absences of longer than six months, "when the returnee is male, the female greeter may embrace him and cry." This is public weeping. Likewise, during the 2005 dedication of the Bosque Redondo Memorial, Nicole Walker, a Navajo woman, interrupted Senator Pete Domenici's speech and wailed (see Denetdale 2007a:311). Bosque Redondo is where many Navajos were incarcerated by the federal government from 1864–68 (see Denetdale 2007b). At least one Navajo, writing in the *Navajo Times*, noted the iconicity of that weeping to Navajo ancestors. Navajo Chester C. Clah wrote that, "Nicole Walker made her entrance wailing like our grandmothers did back then" (cited in Denetdale 2007a:311). When Navajo elder women wept at community meetings concerning Proposition 203, they were signaling their sincerity and linking the language and themselves with their elders. It is a powerful rhetorical device for Navajo women.

All of that said, Navajos also speak English, Navajo English, and *Navlish* (a code-mixed form; see Chapter 3) and they use those languages to express important feelingful identities as well. Stylized weeping, for example, can be done when the speaker is speaking English, Navajo, or some combination of both. If we do not focus on what Navajos are actually doing with languages, we miss a great deal of what it means to be a contemporary Navajo.

Navajo Poetry: A Brief History

In 1933 a short eight-line poem was published in *Indians at Work*, a United States government publication (Hirschfelder and Singer 1992).[5] The poem was composed by a collection of Navajo students at Tohatchi School, New Mexico. This poem, "If I Were a Pony," is one of the first published poems by Navajos. It was written in English, with no use of bilingual Navajo. Other poetry in English followed. In the late 1960s and early 1970s, Blackhorse Mitchell (1968, 1969, 1972a, 1972b, 1972c), among others, published a number of poems in English about things Navajo, about the future, about the past, about grandparents, and about herding sheep. During the early 1970s, Gloria Emerson (1971, 1972) was writing politically engaged poetry that was being published in San Franciso in *The Indian Historian*. During the 1970s more and more Navajos began to write poetry. In 1977, Nia Francisco published a poem in Navajo in the journal *College English* (1977b). In the 1980s and 1990s even more poetry was published by Navajos; the poetry appeared in major literary journals as well as in university presses. By the mid-1980s individually authored books of Navajo poetry were appearing. Poetry was published in Navajo and English and combinations of the two as distinct codes. However, poetry that intermixes Navajo grammatical forms with English forms—that is, code-mixed forms—is almost nonexistent.

As the 1933 example suggests, much of the early Navajo poetry was supported by the U.S. government. The Bureau of Indian Affairs (BIA) promoted the teaching of creative writing and poetry at BIA schools in the late 1960s and 1970s. A crucial feature in the poetry of Navajo poets in the 1960s and 1970s was their ability to display a command of English. Later this changed. Navajo poets wrote in Navajo to display a command of Navajo (see Webster 2006c). A suggestion of the importance of the use of poetry as a display of English language proficiency can be found in a brief editor's note in the *Navajo Times*. The note comes from a short-lived feature during 1962 titled "Poet's Corner":

> The following short poems were written by Eugene Claw, a Navajo Junior at Manuelito Hall and display a fine grasp of the English language as well as imagination and good poetic syntax (May 16, 1962, 14).

As an example of "a fine grasp" of English, there were no examples of bilingual Navajo in Claw's poetry. Other examples could be cited from government publications, but this example should suffice to give a sense of the importance of poetry as an exemplar of English language command. More recently, Diné College has published collections of poetry written in Navajo by students in the Navajo creative writing courses at Diné College (Casaus 1996; Begay 1998). Likewise, during the short-lived run of the "Navajo Page" in the *Navajo Times*, a number of poems were published in Navajo to highlight Navajo language literacy. In both cases, however, poetry was seen as an exemplar of language command (notably reckoned in terms of literacy).

Navajo poets, however, write poetry not *just* as an exemplar of language command or literacy; rather, they write for a multitude of personal and social reasons. As, I might add, I believe Eugene Claw did. We need to understand to what uses Navajo poetry in any code may or may not be put. Indeed, some poets who write in Navajo do so to create a corpus of literary materials in Navajo. Others write in Navajo for purely—or at least primarily—aesthetic reasons. They simply believe certain things sound better in Navajo. Concerning this distinction, Rex Lee Jim writes:

> I write to make sense out of who's Navajo and who's Diné. I write to make sense out of this writing. I think—am I feeling it?—the bottom line is that I write to communicate with myself. That's why

> I write mostly in Navajo. I only wish I could have written this in Navajo. (2000:243)

Again, because literacy in Navajo is still relatively uncommon, many Navajos write in English because they cannot write in Navajo. Tohe, for example, was taking courses in Navajo literacy while I was doing fieldwork in 2000–2001. While she was fluent in Navajo, she did not write Navajo as well as she would have wanted. Most of her poems in her 1999 book of poetry were in English with some code-switching into Navajo. However, her more recent 2005 book of poetry is in both Navajo and English. There are poems written entirely in Navajo. Luci Tapahonso had this to say in a 1995 interview:

> I think because I learned how to write in English I, um, couldn't associate written poetry with Navajo, although I think the process of writing poetry begins in Navajo for me because it seems to me my basic thought processes and basic, um, expression occurs in Navajo but, because I learned how to write in English, then my writing of poetry almost has to be in English, I don't associate written Navajo or I can't write written; I have a real hard time writing in Navajo, the written process has to be in English. ("LINEbreak," October 12, 1995, interview; transcription by Webster)

I think we need to take seriously what Tapahonso says above about her poetry being influenced by Navajo. Many of the poets I have interviewed stated that their written poetry was influenced by the Navajo language and by the "oral tradition."

Much of contemporary Navajo poetry is in English and it is often through English that Navajo poets assert a Navajo identity. By writing in English, these poems are more accessible to the larger non-Navajo, English-speaking society, but—and this is in no way trivial—they are also more accessible to many young Navajo readers who are not literate in Navajo. Indeed, for many Navajos who are not literate in Navajo, poetry composed in Navajo is still largely accessed as an oral phenomenon. Navajo poets who write in Navajo can be heard performing their poems on KTNN. They also perform at public venues before largely Navajo audiences (at fairs, concerts, individual homes, at Diné College, at the Navajo Nation Museum, coffee shops, and the like; see Appendix B). Such performances are also announced on KTNN and reported in the *Navajo Times*.

Navajo Poetic Devices

CHANTWAYS

One of the key focuses in Navajo studies has concerned language and specifically a general view by many Navajo and non-Navajo researchers of the importance of language and Navajo language in particular. For example, Harry Hoijer (1971), Clyde Kluckhohn (1960), and Gary Witherspoon (1977) have all discussed the importance of categorization within Navajo semantics. However, the importance of language to Navajos was described and discussed as early as the work by Washington Matthews in the 1880s and 1890s (see Matthews 1994, 1995, and 1997). Matthews (1994) was one of the first authors to call Navajos "poets." He was speaking of oral poets, but he was also clear to note that he believed that the Navajo language had the capacity to reproduce all the formal English poetic devices and possibly more (Matthews 1994:25; see also Faris 1994:189–191). Among the devices described by Matthews (1994:28) concerning the various religious chantways and poetry was "repetition." Matthews was clearly talking about the various forms of parallelism found within Navajo chantways (see Walton 1930; Reichard 1944; McAllester 1954, 1980a; Witherspoon 1977; Frisbie 1980; Faris 1990; Field and Blackhorse Jr. 2002). Parallelism has also been described for Navajo written poetry (Webster 2004).

It is important to note, that when Matthews was discussing "Navajo poetry," he was most often discussing the *hataal* (chants) and *sin* (songs) of the Navajo. Here is an example of parallelism in a Navajo chant and a Navajo written poem.

(2) *Shikee biyá níchʼi doo,*
Shijáád biyá níchʼi doo,
Sitsʼíís biyá níchʼi doo,

Shíni' biyá níchʼi doo,
Shinééʼ biyá níchʼi doo

Wind will be beneath my feet,
Wind will be beneath my legs,
Wind will be beneath my body,
Wind will be beneath my mind,
Wind will be beneath my voice
(Field and Blackhorse 2002:224)

(3) Sąʼah naagháí bikʼeh hózhóón nishłįįgo naasháa doo
Sąʼah naagháí bikʼeh hózhóón nishłįįgo naasháa doo
. . .
Tádídíín ashkii nishłįįgo naasháa doo
Aniłtʼánii atʼééd nishłǫǫ naasháa doo
. . .
Níłtsą bikąʼ tʼáá shee naałtingo naasháa doo
Níłtsą biʼáád tʼáá shee naałtingo naasháa doo

Hózhǫǫgo naasháa doo
Hózhǫǫgo naasháa doo
Hózhǫǫ naasháa doo
Hózhǫǫ naasháa doo
(Jim 2000:236)

May I be Everlasting and Beautiful Living, walking
May I be Everlasting and Beautiful Living, walking
. . .
May I be Pollen Boy, walking
May I be Ripener Girl, walking
. . .
May Male Rain continue to shower me, walking
May Female Rain continue to shower me, walking

May I be Everlasting Beauty, walking
May I be Everlasting Beauty, walking

May I be Everlasting Beauty, walking
May I be Everlasting Beauty, walking
(Jim 2000:236-237)

Jim's poem is self-consciously connected to chantways both through the use of parallelism and the conclusion of the repetition of *Hózhǫ́ǫgo naasháa doo* and *Hózhǫ́ǫ naasháa doo*, both forms Jim poetically translates as "May I be Everlasting Beauty, walking." Matthews (1995:302) presented the form as *hozógo nasádo* and translated the form as "In beauty may I walk." This form occurs in a number of chantways. *Hózhǫ́ǫgo* (In beauty), where *-go* is a subordinating enclitic marking "in," is quite common in a number of chantways on its own.

INITIAL FRAMING DEVICES

There is a distinction between chantways and poetry because Navajo orthographic poetry is often spoken of by Navajos as *hane'* (story, narrative).⁶ As I pointed out in the introduction, when I discussed such issues with Navajo poets and Navajos more generally the most common Navajo term was *hane'* while the most common English term was "poetry." Like Navajo narratives, Navajo poetry can incorporate songs into the narrative. Luci Tapahonso, for example, often breaks into song in many of her poems. Indeed, some of the songs take on features of Navajo lullabies. But, as a general descriptive term, *hane'* seems to be the most common form. As such, I want to now outline some features of Navajo narrative poetics. I will focus primarily on initial framing devices, but other poetic devices will be discussed as well (on other studies of framing devices see Hofling 1987; Scollon 1976). Framing devices in narratives tend to be relatively salient to native speaker awareness and are therefore logical points to investigate the transference or lack of transference both across mediums and across languages.

Many traditional Navajo narratives (Coyote stories, emergence stories) begin with a number of framing devices. For example, *jó 'akódaa jiníłei* (that's what they would say) and *'ałk'idą́ą́' jiní* (a long time ago they said) are both used at the beginning of many traditional Navajo narratives.⁷ The use of these devices places the narrative in the past, connects it to the "voice of tradition," and acts as an epistemic distancing device. It allows Navajos to recognize that what follows will be set in a world that differs from the current world. In example 4 below, I show *'ałk'idą́ą́'* used in the opening of a Coyote narrative told by John Watchman to Edward Sapir.

Another initial framing device concerns Navajo narratives that are about *Mą'ii* (Coyote). Coyote is a trickster figure among the Navajo and while the narratives are often humorous to various degrees, they are also important in a number of curing ways and have deeper meanings than non-Navajos often assume (see Toelken 1971, 1987, 2002). Here the framing device is the use of the narrative initial conjunction *'áádoo* (and then), sometimes in combination with a verb of motion *-dlosh* (to trot) (often in the progressive aspect)[8] or sometimes in conjunction with the dubitative enclitic *–shį́į́*. The use of a temporal conjunction as a discourse marker frames a narrative as a part of a larger series of narratives. In Navajo this series of narratives is often known as *Mą'ii jooldloshí hane'* (stories about the trotting Coyote). *-dlosh*, on the other hand, can sometimes act alone to mark a Coyote narrative and, indeed, Coyote can remain nameless in the opening frame. The naming of Coyote as *Mą'ii* or one of its many orthographic variants can also frame a poem as a Navajo "Coyote poem" (see Webster 2004). Such devices are both framing devices and genre signatures (Shaul 2002). What we do not find in Navajo poetry is the repeated and regular use of discourse markers such as *'áádóó, ńt'éé* (then) and *'áko* (and) that we find in Navajo narratives. In Navajo narratives these discourse markers are a part of the poetic structuring of the narrative. Their repeated and regular use in narratives does not seem to transfer to Navajo written poetry.

Below I present the openings of several Coyote stories to show various opening formats. I then present the openings of two Coyote poems to show how they connect with the oral formats. The translations are adaptations that I have done in consultation with Blackhorse Mitchell. Primarily, I have translated *jiní* as "it is said" following Mitchell when he did translate this form, and I have consistently translated it (Morgan left it untranslated). I have also consistently translated *jooldlosh* as "trotting along."

(4) 'ałk'idą́ą́' ma'ii jooldlosh, jiní
(Sapir and Hoijer 1942:20)

long ago coyote trotting along it is said

(5) Łah jį́įgo Mą'ii jooldlosh jiní
(Morgan 1949:5)

once day -in coyote trotting along it is said

(6) Łah jį́įgo Mą'ii jooldlosh jiní
(Morgan 1949:10)

once day -in coyote trotting along it is said

(7) Łah jį́įgo Mą'ii jooldlosh jiní
(Morgan 1949:13)

once day -in coyote trotting along it is said

(8) Łah jį́įgo Mą'ii jooldlosh ńt'éé
(Morgan 1949:16)

once day -in coyote trotting along it was

(9) Łah jį́įgo Mą'ii jooldlosh
(Morgan 1949:21)

once day -in coyote trotting along

(10) Aadóó nináánáádááh   jiní
(Haile 1984:100)

and (then) he was running around again it is said

(11) Aadóó -shį́į́   dah   náádiidzá jiní
(Haile 1984:101)

and (then) DUBITATIVE ENCLITIC start off again set out it is said

(12) Aadóó   -shı̨́ı̨́   (dah)   ... jiní
(Haile 1984:95, 97, 99, 103)

and (then) DUBITATIVE ENCLITIC (start off) ... it is said

(13) One day Coyote was trotting.
(Jim 2004:324)

He was trotting, trotting.

(14) And Coyote struts down East 14th
(Belin 1999:3)

Harry Hoijer once told Keith Basso in 1973 that, "even the most minute occurrences are described by Navajos in close conjunction with their physical settings, suggesting that unless narrated events are spatially anchored their significance is somehow reduced and cannot be properly assessed" (in Basso 1996:45). Within Coyote stories and other traditional Navajo narratives place names act as a framing device (Webster 2004). For example, many Coyote narratives begin at specific named locales within the Navajo homeland. The narratives then have Coyote move along a series of named and knowable locations. Likewise, many narratives concern events that occurred at the various named sacred mountains of the Navajo (see Jett 1995). Klara Kelley and Harris Francis (2005) have described Navajo myths as laying out "maps" of Navajoland and thus as aids in "wayfinding" (see also Newcomb and Reichard 1937:69–74 on the "symbolism of locality" in the Shootingway). I suggest that the use of named locales in Navajo Coyote narratives is both an expression of Navajo ethnogeographical knowledge and a way to indexically ground the narrative as Navajo. Below, I present two examples of the beginning of narratives with place names. The first example is from a Coyote narrative and the second is from the opening line of a version of the "Origin of the Night Chant." Note that both examples use the form *jiní* clause final.

(15) Ńléí dibé ntsaa bee nástł'ahdę́ę́' tséyaa hatso hoolyéédę́ę́' náshjaa' hastiin jideeshzhee' lá jiní.

Somewhere in a draw of La Plata Range [Big Sheep],
   along a place
called Big Rock Cave, Old Man Owl had started on a hunt
   [it is said].
(Haile 1984:Navajo 115, translation 53; adapted by Webster)

(16) Jó kojí 'abąąhílghozh hoolghe [wolyé], jiní

Well, on this side, is a place called They Stand Up Sharply
   in a Row
Along the Edge, it is said.
(Sapir and Hoijer 1942:Navajo 137, translation 136; adapted by Webster)

I will also return to the use of place names in orthographic poetry later in this chapter when I discuss the rhetorical use of four and the sacred mountains. Place names occur in a number of orthographic poems. Some poets write the place names in Navajo and then give their English equivalent (often not a translation, but the English name for the place). Other poets write them in Navajo and do not give an English equivalent. Some give the place names only in English. In the following poem, Chee describes a place in the Chuska Mountains. She names the place only in what should be understood as an English gloss of the Navajo source.

(17) It smelled like sweaty horses, and
      salted fat wrapped in a cold tortilla.
      From these rides, my father says,
      they named the last hill,
      before it was a power station, Where Coyote Sits.
      He tells of memories that happened
      before the highway
      when rides into town had the heart of storytelling.
      (Chee 2001:38)

THE QUOTATIVE *JINÍ*

Another device that is used to varying degrees by different narrators is the quotative *jiní* (they say, one says). This form is the combination of the fourth person pronominal *ji-* (one) and the verb of speaking *-ní* (to say). The fourth person is used mainly for people who are considered socially distant (the dead, for example) (see Uyechi 1990). The form acts as a quotative device that indicates the speaker does not have firsthand knowledge of the events being described. As such, it seems a logical device for many narratives. In many traditional Navajo narratives *jiní* occurs at the conclusion of every clause. Barre Toelken and Tacheeni Scott (1981) and Webster (2004) argue that the form is a crucial ethnopoetic organizing device for Navajo Coyote narratives. Charlotte Frisbie (1980:376) has pointed out that the form occurs in other Navajo mythic narratives as well (see also Faris 1994:188). Most of the above examples show the form *jiní*. The form is often reduced to a single syllable *jn* or *jiin* in actual performances and in the published poetry.⁹ Blackhorse Mitchell has suggested that *jiní* should only be used at the beginning and ending of Coyote narratives. In those instances, it acts as an opening and closing framing device. In William Morgan's (1949) collection of Coyote narratives, *jiní* is used sparingly at the beginnings of those narratives. The use of *jiní* in written poetry resembles the more restricted use of the form in oral narratives. Here are three examples from written poetry.

(18) Na'ízhdíłkidgo t'éí hoł ééhózin
Áko ą́ą, háádóó ma'ii haaldloozh jiní
Shįįgo doo baa hane' da
(Jim 1998:69)

Ask and you will know,
And so, surely, from where does coyote start trotting, it is said?
During summertime those stories are not told.

(19) 'inda mą'ii nachxǫǫgo tłóódi nagha jiin'

they said the coyote walked around outside that night pouting.
(Tapahonso 1987:31)

(20) Jiní
It has been said

> Dinétah was once ocean
> so it is not strange that I married a sheepherder who
> (Belin 2002a:58)

In example 20, Belin uses *jiní* as an evidential that hedges scientific knowledge about water covering parts of the Southwest. Her use is ironic here. It places Western knowledge in the same genre as traditional narratives. Neither is privileged as more or less accurate. It should also be noted that there is native speaker awareness of the form *jiní* (see Murray 1989; see also Silverstein 1981). For example, Mitchell explicitly explained to me when, where, and how often the form should be used at the beginning of Coyote narratives. Tohe (2005) has written about the form *jiní*. Here is how she describes and exemplifies its use. Note, also, that in her example she begins the citations of stories with the use of a place name in Navajo.

> Jiní, *they say*. We accept jiní as part of our stories on simple faith. It's not important who said it, but that it was said. The stories become part of our collective memory. Our stories begin and end with jiní. At Ya'dziilzihii is the place named after a contest where young men shot flocks of arrows toward the clouds to see who could shoot the farthest, jiní. At Séí Delehí, lover's tryst took place on the wide sandy bed near the tamarisks, jiní. (Tohe 2005:11)

It is important to note that *jiní* is still a salient feature for many Navajo, used now in both storytelling and in poetry (also a kind of narrative). I will return to this topic in Chapter 5.

SOUND SYMBOLISM

Another poetic device found in both narratives and chants is the use of sound symbolism (see McAllester 1980a; Frisbie 1980). Rex Lee Jim provides an example where a poem is based on the onomatopoeia *tłig* (click). Note also the parallelism used in this poem. Here is the opening of the poem.

(21) Tłig
Niyol nee ní'į́'
Tłig
Nibeedí nee ní'į́'
Tłig
Tséghájooghałii nee ní'į́'
Tłig
Nikeéyah nee ní'į́'
Tłig
Nidiyin nee ní'į́'
Tłig

Click
I stole your breathing
Click
I stole your survival tools
Click
I stole your living goods
Click
I stole your land
Click
I stole your gods
Click
(Jim 1998:8)

In Chapter 2, I discuss another example of onomatopoeia (*ts'ǫǫs* [suck]) in a poem written in Navajo by Rex Lee Jim (see also Webster 2006c, 2008b). There I note that Jim has pointed out that one cannot "really translate" the onomatopoetic words into English. This, then, raises the question of translating sound symbolic words across widely disparate languages. For as Nuckolls (2000:235) has pointed out, sound symbolic forms "communicate not by referring but by *simulating* the most salient perceptual qualities of an action, event, process or activity" (emphasis in original) (see also Anderson 2005). Can one transfer the "simulation" of sound across languages? Can one translate onomatopoeia? The written poetry in English by Navajo poets suggests that is not now being done.

I will return to the use of onomatopoeia and ideophones in the next chapter.

QUOTED SPEECH

Another poetic device that we can list is the repeated and regular use of quoted speech in many traditional Navajo narratives (Collins 1987). In traditional narratives, quoted speech is relatively common, while quoted thought is not common. Indirect reported speech is not used in Navajo. All reported speech must be in the form of quotation. The reluctance to quote others' thoughts has to do with a general Navajo ethos against imposing an interpretation on another individual (i.e., by asserting what someone else is thinking; see Lamphere 1977). It supports Navajo notions of individual autonomy. Quoting thought in Navajo poetry is also relatively rare as well. Narratives and poetry are often built up on quoted speech. Tohe's (1999:16–17) poem "Sometimes Those Pueblo Men Can Sure Be Coyotes" is a case in point. Below I provide the relevant passage that shows that this poem is built on quoted speech and, in fact, quoted speech in Navajo.

(22) we had just pulled onto Central
 when one of us said
  Éí hastiin ayóo baa dzólní this man is very handsome
  Éí laa' I agree
 then we were making all kinds of comments about him in Diné
 our enthusiasm running away with us
 saying those things adolescent girls say

And later in the poem:

(23) we did this
 all the way back to the Indian School
 not ever thinking he might understand us
 until we got back
  A'héhee' at'ééke he said thank you, girls
 (Tohe 1999:16–17)

In the oral performances of this poem that I have recorded, Tohe will raise her voice pitch when quoting the girls talking about the "Coyote" Pueblo man. She will lower the pitch of her voice slightly when quoting the final response by the Pueblo man. These stylistic features aid in the humor of this poem. Such sonic displays are lost in the written version.

RHETORICAL FOUR AND SACRED MOUNTAINS

Another important device is the use of the number four and the repetition of actions, actors, and objects around the number four (Reichard 1944; Kluckhohn 1960). Things tend to happen four times. The fourth time draws the event to a conclusion. There are four sacred mountains that must be ordered correctly. There are four sacred directions, and so on. I think it worth noting here that the four sacred mountains are often cited in Navajo in English-dominant poems. Here is an example:

(24) Sis naajiní rising to the east,
Tsoodził rising to the south,
Dook'o'osłííd rising to the west,
Dibé Nítsaa rising to the north
(Tohe 2002:100)

Another example where place names are retained in Navajo, can be found in Tapahonso's poem "This is how they were placed for us." Here is the first relevant passage:

(25) By Sisnaajiní, we set our standards for living.
Bik'ehgo da'iiná
(Tapahonso 1997:39)

The poem concerns the origins, emergence, and traditions of Navajo people. *Sisnaajiní* glosses as roughly "black belt crossway." It is often associated with Blanca Peak in the Sangre de Cristo mountains. It is the Navajo sacred mountain of the east. In Navajo cosmology there are at least four sacred mountains, each identified with a particular direction and color. The next line glosses as roughly "in accordance with life." The place name, as Basso (1996) and others working with Athapaskan place names have pointed out, is quite descriptive; it presents a mental image. The image is of a white mountain with a black streak running across it. Such placenaming practices, using the Navajo word, argue for a prior placement, one that subverts the U.S. ability to inscribe its will on Navajo sacred sites.[10]

Throughout the rest of the poem Tapahonso calls forth each of the four sacred mountains; she uses the Navajo term for each. *Tsoodził* glosses as "cone-shaped mountain" and is often associated with Mount Taylor near present day Grants, New Mexico. This mountain is particularly important to many Navajo. Not only is it the sacred mountain of the south and associated with the symbolically important color turquoise, but—as the story goes—it was the mountain Navajos returning from their four year imprisonment at *Hwéeldi* first saw and recognized, realizing they were close to *Dinétah*.

Moving in a prescribed manner in this poem, Tapahonso next singles out the sacred mountain of the west. Here is how she begins:

(26) This is how they were placed for us
E'e'aahjigo, Dook'o'oosłííd sida.
(Tapahonso 1997:40)

The Navajo phrase glosses as roughly "to the west *Dook'o'oosłííd* sits." *Dook'o'oosłííd* is often associated with the San Francisco Peaks just outside Flagstaff, Arizona, and can be glossed as "it never melted and ran off the summit." *Sida* is a neuter perfective verb, with *si-* as third person and *-da* as the neuter perfective form of "to sit, to have position." As Hoijer (1951) pointed out a number of years ago, in Navajo there is a distinction between verbs of movement (active)—by far the more populous—and verbs of stasis (neuter)—fewer in number. Neuter verbs have one paradigm, whereas active verbs have a multiplicity of paradigms including such aspectual categories as progressive, imperfective, perfective, iterative, and optative. Furthermore, again as Hoijer (1951) pointed out, the neuter perfective forms seem to have the semantic connotation of the "withdrawal" of motion, something has come to rest. This implication—because it is based on a verbal distinction within Navajo—is hard to capture in English completely.

Finally, Tapahonso describes the sacred mountain of the north. *Dibé nitsaa*, often associated with Hesperus Peak and glossed as "Sheep It-Is-Large." Notice that Tapahonso begins with the sacred mountain of the east, moves south, then west and ends—where things must end—in the north. This is the correct way to recite the sacred mountains. One must begin in the east, where all things begin, and end in the north. This poem is an example of proper speech. She has not chosen the order of these mountains willy-nilly, rather they reflect back on an ideology concerned with proper speech and also aid in perpetuating a form of proper speech as an exemplar of that speech. I should add further that, like clan names, some Navajo are of the opinion that because they are sacred mountains and because the place names are the quoted words of the ancestors, you cannot translate them into English. Let me add, however, that I do not mean to imply that there is only one place name per mountain. That is not the case. Many of the sacred mountains have multiple names. The sacred mountains and their attendant place names are efficacious precisely because they are Navajo. The English place names and translations lack that "sacredness."

As I pointed out, not all Navajo poets use the Navajo place names; instead they sometimes use the English place names for Navajo places. In this next example, Maggie Bahe, a senior at Wingate High School in 1971, reflects upon the Vietnam War through the four sacred mountains. Note that they are again ordered from east to north, but in this example they are all in English. Bahe also expresses a number of symbols associated with each particular mountain and direction. Also, and this point was raised by Barre Toelken in reviewing a previous version of this chapter, note the attendant motion involved with the four directions. Bahe appeals to all four directions both vocally and physically.

(27) I raise corn pollen to the East
Where Mt. Blanco is setting.
I ask the White Stone to help my brother,
To give him courage to live again this day.
Again I turn to the South
And let my tears go,
Looking up to see the blue sky

Where some of my brothers are looking down
To see if I pray for my brother as I prayed for them.
Smiling with pride that I did my duty for my brothers,
I ask Mt. Taylor to protect my brother for the day.
West, looking at San Francisco Peaks,
I rise to my feet
And let go of some of the corn pollen,
Asking the Holy Shell to protect my brother
From being hit.
I want his body to be as hard as the Abalone Shell
That nothing shall pass through.
I kneel again to the North,
Mt. Hespersus.
This time asking for peace for the whole world
(Bahe 1971:5–6)

The use of fours (and twos) recurs throughout many of the poems as well as the oral narratives. An example of the use of four in an oral narrative concerns Coyote. In this example, again from Morgan (1949), we find quoted speech being used to create changes in the world. Coyote requests something four times and the world changes. This example comes from the beginning of a familiar Coyote narrative variously known as "Coyote and Skunk" or "Coyote Makes Rain" (see Hill and Hill 1945). Hamill (1983), in discussing a version of this narrative, cites this as an example of a "Navajo syllogism." Following Hymes (2003), I call this a "providential world." The world provides when implored in an appropriate manner. Requests, ideally, should not be turned down if asked four times.

(28) 'Áádóó Mą'ii 'ání,
    "Tó shikee' bik'i doolkǫǫh.
    Tó shikee' bik'i doolkǫǫh.
    Tó shikee' bik'i doolkǫǫh.
    Tó shikee' bik'i doolkǫǫh."
    Tó bikee' diilkǫ' jiní.

    Then Coyote said,

"Rain cover my feet!
Rain cover my feet!
Rain cover my feet!
Rain cover my feet!"
The rain covered his feet, it is said.
(Morgan 1949:22)

METANARRATIVE EXHORTATION HÁÁHGÓÓSHĮĮ́

A final device that should be highlighted is the use of *hááhgóóshįį*. Toelken and Scott (1981:109) comment on the use of *hááhgóóshįį*, which they gloss as "!!!." This device is used in a number of Coyote narratives and seems to mark crucial sections of the narratives. In this respect, the device seems to call into relief key moments of the narrative and as such it functions much like a metanarrative exhortation (Nuckolls 1992:74). However, when I asked Blackhorse Mitchell to translate a narrative with this form in it, Mitchell left the form untranslated. I have not, as of yet, found this device used in written poetry. Below I present an example from Berard Haile (1984:92) as told by Curly Tó Aheedlíinii. The translation is by Mitchell. I have edited that translation by including "it is said" each time it occurs (Mitchell largely left that form untranslated) and putting parentheses around Mitchell's insertion of "Coyote" when the form does not occur in the Navajo version. The change in tense from "it is said" to the final "it was said" reflects Mitchell's only translation of that form in the following section. Following Toelken and Scott (1981), I translate *hááhgóóshįį* as !!!. I have chosen this translation over such forms as "really, really" or "pay attention," which were variously offered by others, because I want to highlight the nonreferential quality of this utterance. Note also, this segment of the narrative is from the crucial moment when Coyote, having feigned death to trick the prairie dogs, jumps up and begins killing them after Skunk "Gólízhii" does what his name suggests he does—*go-* (one) *-lízh-* (urinate) *-ii* (the).

(29) Ákohgo shį́į́ hááhgóóshį́į́ nikídazhdiiljool jiní
Náhidiitah jiní
Mą'ii yéeni'
Tsahaałééni' yił haalwod jiní

Hááhgóóshįį hata' nikidiiłhaal jiní
Ła' hadádadziswod jiní
(Haile 1984:92)

It made each !!! dancer kneel to clear their eyes, it is said.
When (Coyote) got up, it is said.
The Coyote
Took out his club, it is said.
!!! Then started clubbing down the dancers, it is said.
Eventually some got away, it was said.

AN EXTENDED EXAMPLE OF THE INTERPLAY OF POETIC DEVICES
I think it important to observe that almost all of the above poetic devices that I have described for oral narratives and chantways can be found in orthographic poetry. Parallelism, the use of *jiní*, the use of place names, onomatopoeia, the use of temporal conjunctions as openings, the use of four as a recurrent trope, and the breakthrough into song all occur in various orthographic Navajo poems written by a variety of Navajo poets. They occur in both English and Navajo language poems. Place names, character names (such as *Mą'ii*), and *jiní* are often code-switched into Navajo in English language dominant poems. In other cases, the English conjunction "and" does the work of the Navajo form '*áádoo*. Yet the repeated and regular recurrence of such discourse markers does not transfer from Navajo narratives into written poetry. The very organizing structure of narratives is not transferred across codes, nor is it transferred across mediums.

I want to now give an example of the interplay of various poetic devices within a single narrative-like poem. I want to show how the use of the initial formulaic framing device can be used in Navajo orthographic poetry and how parallelism can also be used. The example is from a poem by Tohe (2002:100–104), "In Dinétah" (we should not be surprised to find a place name in Navajo). Here is how the poem begins:

(30) Ałkidą́ą́' adajiní nít'ę́ę́'
      (Tohe 2002:100)

Here is a rough gloss of the opening phrase:

Long ago according to them it used to be

As I noted above this formulaic device is found at the beginning of many traditional Navajo narratives. The use of the device at the beginning of this poem locates this poem within a framework of traditional Navajo narratives. That is, following Erving Goffman (1974) and Webb Keane (1997), it allows Navajo readers and listeners to recognize this poem within a meaningful framework of prior discursive expectations. When I have seen Tohe perform this poem at public venues she always uses the formulaic opening frame in Navajo. Such formulaic phrases as *ałkidą́ą́' adajiní nít'ę́ę́'* and *jó 'akódaa jiníłei* can inspire thought and reflection. Here is how Luci Tapahonso describes *jó 'akódaa jiníłei* and the process of poetry composition:

> My poems always begin first in Navajo. So whatever form, they begin in Navajo. This might be a certain phrase, like today, for some reason, I was thinking a lot about this phrase, which would be "Jó 'akódaa jiníłei." It seems like I would think of something, and in the end I would just somehow put at the end of that: "Jó 'akódaa jiníłei" (That's what they would say), I guess that's the way you would translate this. And I began to realize that as the phrase came into my mind more and more, that somehow that was the beginning of a poem. That line was going to be significant. And when I put it down in English, "Jó 'akódaa jiníłei, Jó 'akódaa jiníłei, Jó 'akódaa jiníłei," the way that that would finally appear in English might be, "That's what they would say," "*That's* what they would say," or it might be something else, like "A long time ago, they would say that a lot." So the English version would be different. However it finally ends up in English, the original part of it, the original thought, the spark of it, started in Navajo. (Tapahonso in Binder and Breinig 1995:115–116)

Here, it should be noted, we see an explicit link between orthographic poetry and oral poetic traditions. Tapahonso connects the two explicitly by evoking the formulaic framing device *jó 'akódaa jiníłei*. Like the use of *jiní* in a number of poems about Coyote, *jó 'akódaa jinítei* and *ałkidą́ą́' adajiní nít'ę́ę́'* are direct links between the oral tradition and the emergent orthographic tradition. They are also direct links in Navajo.

I want to move to the end of Tohe's poem "In Dinétah" and show another use of Navajo oral poetic devices within orthographic poetry. Here is how Tohe concludes her poem:

(31)   In Beauty it was begun.
            In Beauty it continues.
                In Beauty,

                    In Beauty,

                        In Beauty,

                            In Beauty.
                            (Tohe 2002:104)

The ending of this poem replicates the ending of a number of Navajo chantways (see Matthews 1995, 1997). "In Beauty" is likely a translation of the Navajo form *hózhǫ́ǫ́go*. This form is based on the key Navajo concept *hózhǫ́* (see Witherspoon 1977; Farella 1984). The form *hózhǫ́ǫ́go* can be found at the end of numerous Navajo chantways and is often glossed as "beauty, harmony, peaceful." When it occurs at the end of chantways it normally occurs four times, as we see in the above example. As Field and Blackhorse Jr. (2002) have suggested, the use of four repetitions gives a sense of "surrounding" because of a metonymic linkage with the idea of the four sacred directions. The title of the poem is "In Dinétah" and here *Dinétah* is understood as the land within the four sacred mountains. The use of the chant-like conclusion in this poem thus suggests surrounding and completion.[11]

I will return to this poem in Chapter 5, but for purposes here, there are two things that I find particularly noteworthy about it. First, the poem begins in Navajo with a formulaic narrative framing device. Second, the poem ends in English as a chant. Thus Tohe puts two genres (narrative and chantways) into dialogue by using formal devices such as the formulaic opening of a narrative and the formulaic closing of a chantway (see Bakhtin 1986; see also Bauman 2004). She also puts Navajo and English into dialogue within this poem. While I will discuss this poem in greater detail in a later chapter, I want to note that there is often a common view of language as an index (if not an icon) of identity. Navajos speak Navajo. Again, this was a view that was often expressed to me by Navajos (including Navajos who did not speak Navajo). It is often performed when Navajo poets who do not speak Navajo fluently still introduce themselves in Navajo. The use of Navajo can and does index Navajoness. However, as this poem indicates, Navajoness can be indexed by traditional poetic devices that have been transferred into English. Navajos can and do use English to index Navajoness. Elsewhere in this poem Tohe intertextually links to Billie Holiday when she invokes "strange fruit." She is connecting Navajo oppression and captivity with other historical examples of oppression. Likewise, when Tohe invokes the terms "Cat" or "Stomp" in one of her poems, she is using English to connect with a generation of Navajos who attended boarding schools. I had to ask Tohe about the meanings of Cat and Stomp because those terms fell outside my stock of knowledge. While it may seem obvious, I want to point out that using English does not always or irretrievably index "colonizing ways of speaking." Navajos—and this point is more general, I believe—have not simply been forced to speak English and passively accepted it. Rather, Navajos have engaged English and actively adapted it, whether by the use of traditional poetic devices transferred into English or by the use and literary use of Navajo English.

Conclusions

In this chapter I have suggested ways written Navajo poetry has been influenced by Navajo verbal art. Thus, I have been concerned with the use of various poetic devices (*jiní*, for example) in both written and oral Navajo traditions. This was done for two reasons. First, Navajo poets themselves speak of the oral tradition influencing their poetry. If we are to take Navajo poetry seriously, we must actively engage the discussions about Navajo poetry by Navajo poets. Second, many Navajos with whom I have worked speak of poetry in Navajo as *hane'* (story, narrative). Thus, it seems useful to understand the comparison between poetry and storytelling. One way to do this is to understand the narrative devices that they share. How is a Navajo poem *hane'*? A number of ways have been suggested here. Another way that Navajo poetry is like storytelling is that, like stories, Navajo poems are, by-and-large, meant to be shared. As Laura Tohe once explained to me, "poetry is performance." Other ways will be the focus of a number of the remaining chapters in this book.

Of course, there are examples of Navajo poetry where the visual nature of the poetry is more important than any oral performative component. For example, Esther Belin's poem "Check One" (1999:12):

(32) ☐ Diné
      ☐ Other

This poem seems a clear case of a poem that relies on the visual aesthetic at the expense of the performability of the poem (i.e., the oral aesthetic). I have never seen Belin perform this poem before an audience. Obviously, the visual nature of writing lends itself to certain aesthetics that are lacking in the auditory realm (and vice versa). This poem is an intertextual reference to census questionnaires and other regimenting bureaucratic devices. As such it plays with a literacy reference.

A second goal of this chapter has been to compare poetic devices in Navajo with their realization in written orthographic poems. That is, did the lexico-grammatical code necessarily change or was there a transfer of discourse routines across languages? Thus, following Field (2001), I wanted to know what was retained across the shift from Navajo to English. A number of examples were given. One obvious example concerned the use of repetition, parallelism, and the rhetorical force of four. Here also we see the use of "and" by Esther Belin and "one day" by Rex Lee Jim in the openings of their "Coyote poems." These connected with the use of 'áádóó (and [then]) and łah (once) in a number of Coyote narratives. Likewise, several Coyote poems begin in a similar manner as Coyote stories with Coyote on the move (Webster 2004).

Not all the poetic devices outlined here did survive the transfer. *Hááhgóóshį́į́* (!!!) does not appear in any of the written Navajo poems I have investigated. As a metanarrative exhortation it may be quite difficult to transfer across languages. The repeated and regular uses of discourse markers as poetic structuring devices, either across mediums or across languages, also did not appear in the poems I investigated. In isolation, as a framing device, initial particles were transferred, but as a recurrent feature of the poetic structuring of a poem, such devices have not been transferred. Likewise, even *jiní* (it is said) has not been transferred consistently across codes. As Mitchell explained to me, the form can be cumbersome and, indeed, in English language translations it is often not translated at all. Other features of Navajo, such as sound symbolism would also be likely to be lost in English translations. In the next chapter, I discuss the play of sounds in a poem by Rex Lee Jim about *na'asts'ǫǫsí* (mouse). That layering of sounds is lost in a translation to English. Indeed, the naming of animals seems a fruitful place to investigate such moments of incommensurability (see Landar 1961; O'Neill 2008; Webster 2006c; Zolbrod 2004). Likewise, the indexical framing devices such as *Ałkidą́ą́' adajiní nít'ę́ę́'* do not appear to be transferable either. They work because they are Navajo. Likewise, the use of *Mą'ii* (or one of its many variants) grounds a poem or narrative in Navajo traditions and not a pan-Indian "Coyote tradition" (see Bright 1993). The use of *Mą'ii* localizes the poem.

One way to explain the lexical and syntactic objectification of Navajo poetic devices (see Moore 1988), that I have been calling code-switching, is to see it as the playing out of tensions between what can be transferred across languages and what cannot. Here, I think it is important to recall House's (2002) critique of Slate (1993), when she argued that not all Navajos would agree on what was meant to be "saved." Looking at what Navajo poets leave in Navajo and what they can or will transfer into English allows us to understand what Navajo poets feel are incommensurate between English and Navajo. That some poets consistently present the sacred mountains in Navajo while other Navajos do not tells us that individual Navajos vary with respect to the incommensurability between codes. Poetry, then, becomes an avenue to understanding what some Navajos feel are important features of Navajo and what forms can be transferred across languages. Four as a rhetorical device can be partly transferred. Triadic directives can be transferred. Metanarrative exhortations may not transfer across languages as well, and we can appreciate this by seeing that Navajo poets do not attempt such transfers. It may even resist transference from an oral medium to a written medium.

In paying attention to what Navajo poets try to transfer across codes, it also allows us to gauge what the felt connections to languages are. Many poems are explicitly about language and the importance of language, the importance of Navajo. One cannot read Tohe's poem "Our Tongues Slapped into Silence" (Tohe 1999:2–3) without sensing the oppressive implications of English and the felt connections to Navajo, a language actively being repressed. However, it is written in English. Nor can one read Tohe's poem "The Names" regarding the corruption of Navajo names in English, with its lesson on Navajo lexical semantics, without sensing the felt connections to language:

(33) Tohe, from T'óhii means Towards Water.
Tsosie. Ts'ósí means Slender.
And Yazzie, from Yázhí, means Beloved Little One/Son.
(Tohe 1999:5)

And yet, we cannot deny the felt connections to language and identity that many poems written in English by Navajo poets have had and continue to have. It is the felt connections to language that matter. What I am trying to suggest is that we need to also investigate the ways that Englishes are being used by Navajos to assert and circulate frameworks of meaning that we might term Navajoness.

Finally, Navajo language is a threatened language, in the sense that new speakers are not learning the language at a rate that will ensure the continued persistence of the language. The literature reviewed above speaks to the macrolevel processes that are occurring. That is, it examines how education, government programs, economic factors, and the like all conspired in ways to impede the retention and perpetuation of Navajo speakers. Languages are, however, only clusters of individual speakers. With this in mind, the work by Dick (1998) suggests the importance of understanding the lingual autobiographies of Navajo speakers and readers. Likewise, the work by Field (2001) looks at the specifics of triadic directives (in Navajo, English, or in combination) among

Navajos. Recently, Friedrich (2006) has argued for the centrality of ethnopoetics in language and culture studies. One of the hallmarks of ethnopoetics has been the investigation of the individual speaking subject. Another hallmark has been the careful attention to linguistic details in verbal art. One way to approach the understanding of language shift and language death may be to use ethnopoetics, as this chapter has attempted, to understand the felt connections that speakers have toward their languages. An examination of the poetic practices of a people may reveal what features of language they believe are and are not commensurate. That is, what features of a language are maximally salient and meant to be kept. As the above examples suggest, however, we should not expect agreement on what features can and cannot be transferred across languages. Macrolevel investigations that neglect ethnopoetics and more microlevel research may miss the larger felt connections between speakers and their languages.

TWO

Poetics and Politics of Navajo Ideophony

However much we may be disposed on general principles to assign a fundamental importance in the languages of primitive peoples to the imitation of natural sounds, the actual fact of the matter is that these languages show no particular preferences for imitative words. Among the most primitive peoples of aboriginal America, the Athabaskan tribes of the Mackenzie River speak languages in which such words seem to be nearly or entirely absent, while they are used freely enough in languages as sophisticated as English and German.

Edward Sapir, *Language*

Introduction

In *Language*, Edward Sapir (1921:8) suggests that the Northern Athabaskan speaking peoples of the Mackenzie River region (Canada) did not use many onomatopoetic or "imitative" forms in their language. Sapir's point was to challenge the belief that non-European languages, the languages of so-called primitives, had more sound symbolic forms than did European languages. While attempting to discount a certain bias toward Native American languages, Sapir may have been understating the importance of sound symbolism in Athabaskan languages. For example, among the Slavey (Northern Athabaskan), who live along the Mackenzie River, they use the evocative onomatopoeia *sah, sah, sah* for "the sound of a bear walking unseen not far from camp" (O'Grady et al. 2005:137). Melissa Axelrod (1993:79–81) describes the onomatopoetic (ONO) as one of the aspectual categories of the Northern Athabaskan language Koyukon. As Axelrod (1993:79–80) explains, "seventy-four roots (12 percent of the corpus) allow (or have exclusively) onomatopoetic derivatives." Sapir also may have missed something of the differences that people assign to the use of ideophones. This is, not, however, to say that Sapir was unconcerned with sound symbolism.

His work on Nootka ways of speaking and the evoking of social types (often derogatory, sometimes affectionate) through sound symbolism is an ample and noteworthy example (Sapir 1985:179–196; see also Hymes 1979; Woodbury 1987).

In this chapter I focus on the uses of sound symbolism, onomatopoeia, and ideophony in a variety of Navajo verbal and written genres. In particular, I am concerned with the use of "sound imitative" expressions (Hinton, Nichols, and Ohala 1994:3). This class of sound symbolism attempts to "simulate" some nonlinguistic activity or image in a linguistic form (Nuckolls 2000:235). They are feelingfully iconic. Following the terminology of Clement Doke (1935), these are "ideophones." Doke (1935:118) defines ideophones as follows:

> A vivid representation of an idea in sound. A word, often onomatopoeic, which describes a predicate, qualificative or adverb in respect to manner, colour, sound, smell, action, state or intensity.

Ideophones are then a kind of sound symbolism that can be composed of onomatopoetic forms. They are affective-imagistic uses of language (following Kita 1997).

Ideophony in Perspective

There has been much recent work on the use of ideophones among African languages, much of it building off of earlier and foundational work (see Samarin 1970, 1971, 1991; Moshi 1993; Childs 1996; Hunter and Oumarou 1998; see also Doke 1935). Ideophones have long been an established topic of inquiry among Africanists. As Dennis Tedlock (1999:118) notes, "the study of ideophones has become a part of the Africanist subtradition in linguistics." William Samarin (1991:59–60) has discussed the "delight" that Gbeya speakers take in their expressions of ideophones. Ideophones can then be considered a kind of pleasurable form of expression. Linda Hunter and Chaibou Oumarou (1998) show that many Hausa metalinguistic terms are often in the form of ideophones. Ideophones are also "among the most magical expressions in African languages" (160). Philip Noss (2001) has reported on the use of ideophones in written

Gbaya poetry. He identifies two types of uses of ideophones in Gbaya poetry. The first type concerns written poetry where ideophones intermingle with nonideophones and intertextually link the poem to other aesthetic genres (folktales). The second type finds entire poems written in ideophones. G. Tucker Childs (1996:99) notes that, among urban Zulu speakers he has worked with, ideophones are a likely indicator of "language vitality." Thus the decline of ideophones may suggest the relative peril a language is in. Lupenga Mphande (1992) has argued that Western educational policies and Western inscriptive practices have led to a disinclination for African authors to use ideophony in contemporary written African literature.

Janis Nuckolls (1992, 1995, 1996, 2000, and 2006) has provided some of the most interesting work on ideophones, poetics, and narrative involvement, working among the Runa (Pastaza Quechua) of lowland Ecuador (see also Kohn 2005). She has specifically shown how ideophones can be used in narratives to create a sense of "sound symbolic involvement" (Nuckolls 2000). As Nuckolls (2006:41) writes, "ideophonic performances are distinctive from what is typically understood as performance, however. They exist as fleeting moments of performance within discourse which may itself be minimally or maximally performative." They are performances on top of performances. As Nuckolls (47) argues concerning Runa beliefs and academic discourse,

> Yet, articulating this mood [emotionally riveting and objectively factual] is critical for understanding why ideophones have suffered such neglect within linguistic anthropology, an issue that is related to their severe restrictedness in Standard Average European cultures, and related as well, to their fragility in situations of language contact.
>
> I have argued that underlying the use of ideophones by Runa is a disposition to perform by means of linguistic sound, a sentiment of animacy that is common to humans and nonhumans . . . By "animacy" I mean a quality of aliveness that is evident through movement, change over time, or through responsiveness or reaction to surroundings.

A lack of focus on ideophones may be a result of a lack of seriousness that "Standard Average European cultures" bring to their use. As Hymes (1960:111) notes, concerning linguists and their discussions of sound symbolism, "the minor role of onomatopoeia is stressed, its dependence on the pattern of particular languages noted, and classrooms encouraged to titter at 'bow-wow' theories of language origin" (see also Durbin 1973 for a detailed discussion of this matter).

Samuels (2004a:299) argues that one modernist version of language sees it as "a tool for clear and transparent communication." That is, language is about reference or semantics, or "naturalizing semantic content as the overwhelmingly central definition of language" (316). Doowop or punning, in the case that Samuels describes, or ideophony here, challenges such reference-centric views of language, forefronting iconicity (and the felt attachments that adhere to such forms). Samuels (299) links such "nonsense" forms—forms that challenge the dominant reference-centric view of language—with "marginalized social and linguistic groups." Doowop or ideophony can then be understood as, in Scott's (1990) terms, "acts of resistance."

Nuckolls's suggestion that ideophones are connected to conceptions of animacy, especially as they relate to movement, resonates with the work of Witherspoon (1977) on Navajo conceptions of "animacy," "agency," and "movement." Many of Witherspoon's examples come from the relationship between movement, classificatory verbs, and the Subject Object Inversion (see also Hale 1973). As Witherspoon (1977:140) argues, "The Navajo world is a world of motion . . . a world of things in motion and things at rest, but one in which even things at rest are defined by the withdrawal of motion and are classified according to their ability or potential to be moved." The emphasis on movement in Navajo linguistic forms was also noted early on by Hoijer (1951). Following Nuckolls, if Witherspoon and Hoijer are correct, then, Navajo seems a likely place to examine the use of ideophones.

Indeed, Nuckolls (1999:227) highlights the work of Witherspoon and Gladys Reichard (1950) as early examples of sensitive research on Native conceptions of language and the creative power of language. What Reichard (1944:51) calls for Navajos, "sound power." This is the compulsive power of language, that proper language use can change the world

(Reichard 1944; see also Witherspoon 1977; McAllester 1980a). However, following Field and Blackhorse (2002), we should also note that for language to be efficacious it must also be aesthetically pleasing. One way that language becomes aesthetically pleasing is through the use of sound symbolism (see Reichard 1950:256-262).

Native North American languages have received far less systematic research concerning ideophones (but see DeLisle 1980; Mithun 1982; Aoki 1994; Samuels 2004a:314-316; see also Durbin 1973 and Hofling 2000:535-539 on Mayan). Childs (2001:70), in an otherwise stimulating chapter, calls for comparative studies of ideophones and, while he singles out Chinese, Japanese, African, Meso-American, and Australian languages, he makes no mention of Native North American languages. Tedlock (1999:119) provides a few Zuni examples of ideophones in his short paper on ideophones in *Journal of Linguistic Anthropology*. In an earlier work, Tedlock (1983:44) notes that in Zuni, ideophones "are used more frequently in narrative than in everyday speech." In what follows, I will suggest that Navajo ideophones can be found in a variety of verbal genres beyond narratives. He also argues that such forms lend "immediacy" to the narrative (69). This is also certainly true of Navajo ideophones and of ideophones more generally (see Nuckolls 1992). Tedlock (1999:119-120) concludes his brief description of ideophony with a discussion of the use of ideophones in written poetry. Tedlock was not discussing Native American written poetry in that piece, though I will turn to examples of ideophony in contemporary Navajo poetry in what follows. As Sherzer (2002:17) argues, "sound symbolism is a potential in language, which is actualized in discourse, especially verbally artistic discourse." It is to those potentials in Navajo that I now turn.

Ideophones and Onomatopoeia in Navajo

The ethnographic literature on the Navajo has a number of suggestive discussions of onomatopoeia and their use. Reichard (1950:282) comments that, "Navaho ritual contains many onomatopoeic elements, which may exist independently without 'word content' or may be stems, parts of words depending upon grammatical forms."[1] Here we see the use of ideophones in ritual, but also the way that they can be integrated into Navajo grammar (as verbs). According to Reichard (1950) the use of onomatopoeias and sound symbolism aids in making chants more aesthetically pleasing and hence more efficacious. Clyde Kluckhohn and Dorothea Leighton (1946:249–250) noted that, "an automobile is called by one of two terms (*chidí* or *chuggi*) which imitate the sound of a car." Here we see an onomatopoeia being used as a noun. *Chidí* is still the term for "automobile" and has now been productively extended to airplanes as well (*chidí naat'a'í* [the chidí that flies about]).[2] However, as Benally and Viri (2005:91) note, the Navajo word *chidíłtsooí* (*chidiltsxoo'i*), "school bus" or "the yellow chidí" is being replaced by young Navajos with the English lexical item "bus." Here is a case where the productivity of the onomatopoeia is being curtailed by the current language shift.

Let me add, however, that the second form—*chuggi*—has fallen out of use (in fact, one reliable elder Navajo consultant had never heard of the form). One Navajo consultant did explain to me that *chuggi* had been used for slower automobiles and that *chidí* was used for faster automobiles. This perspective was then confirmed by other Navajo consultants when I suggested it as a possible explanation for why *chuggi* had fallen out of use. It is not surprising to see a front vowel /i/ associated with speed or rapidity and a back vowel /u/ used for slowness. This follows a general pattern of synesthetic sound symbolism, whereby front vowels tend to be associated with smallness and rapidity and back vowels tend to be associated with largeness and slowness (see Hinton, Nichols, and Ohala 1994:4).

Navajos that I know will sometimes use the term *hodiits'a'* (there is a sound) to talk about onomatopoeia in Navajo (see also Austin-Garrison 1991:48). *Hodiits'a'* can be used to describe both onomatopoeia and echoes. Robert Young and William Morgan (1987:432–433) provide 65 onomatopoeic forms in their massive Navajo dictionary and grammar. These forms cover a wide range of actions and activities. Navajo ideophones are, in general, monosyllabic in structure (though see *chidí*). Some are phonotactically interesting, such as *zghǫz* (swishing sound, like a whip). The initial consonant cluster of /zgh/ (where a voiced alveolar fricative is followed by a voiced velar fricative) is not a regular phonological combination in Navajo (it appears, then, to violate Navajo phonotactics). Here is a brief sampling of Navajo ideophones:

(1) *zghǫz* for the swishing sound, like a whip
   biib for the beeping of a car
   wąą for the growling of a dog
   ts'os or *ts'ǫǫs* kissing and sucking
   zǫǫz for the sound of a bumblebee in flight
   tłiizh for the sound of a tree crashing
   woł for the gurgling of a brook or creek
   chxosh for the sound of splashing or the "fizzing" of soda
   k'ol also for the sound of gurgling water
   ch'izh for the rustling of dry leaves

Many of these onomatopoeic forms can be used as a noun or as a verb stem; for example, *-ts'ǫǫs* (to suck) or *-woł* (to gurgle). (I will return to the productivity of these two forms below.) Onomatopoeias can be nominalized through the use of the nominalizing enclitic *-ii*; as in *gáaii* or *gáagii* (crow) (*gáa* "the cawing of a crow" + *-ii* NOMINALIZING ENCLITIC) (see Landar 1985:489) (for comparative purposes *gai'hí* "crow" [Lipan]; *gáagee* "crow" [Jicarilla]; *gaagé* "crow" [Western Apache]; *gaaye* "crow" [Mescalero]; *ghaal* "crow" [Plains Apache]). Another nominalized example, as Laura Tohe first brought to my attention, concerns a word for "soda" in Navajo: *tó dilchxoshí* (*tó* "water" *di-* thematic prefix relating to sound *-lchxosh* "it is splashing, fizzing" *-í* "the one"). Navajo ideophones seem most closely aligned with verbs, but they are also related or relatable to other word classes such as nouns (see Axelrod 1993).

Herbert Landar (1985:489) notes that Navajo ideophones (he calls them "interjections") often occur in "reduplicative pairs." In many of the examples that follow, ideophones do appear in either reduplicative pairs or in pairs of reduplicative pairs. Landar also notes that some ideophones have a phonological similarity to verbs. In such cases, there appear to be two patterns. The first concerns those ideophones that are phonologically similar and have similar "meanings" (i.e., *dlaad* "ripping" and *-dlaad* "to rip"). Sometimes these forms evoke the sound symbolism in expressions like *dilch'il* (it pops) (*di-* thematic prefix relating to sound + *-l* classifier + *-ch'il* "to pop, crack"). These forms are reminiscent of the onomatopoeic aspectual category described for Koyukon by Axelrod (1993:79–81) (i.e., *delkk'ekk* "it is making a choking sound" *de-* thematic + *le-* classifier +

-kk'ekk "choke" ONO). The second involves those that are phonologically similar but with different "meanings" (i.e., *dog* "thump" versus -*dog* "fill [bag] till it bulges"). The first pattern is, again, reminiscent of the discussion by Childs (1996) concerning certain Zulu ideophones. Landar, however, does not give examples of the discursive use of ideophones or their full range of expressive potential, intermingling in multiple poetic genres as they do. I will turn to examples of Navajo ideophony in a variety of verbal and written genres below.

In Navajo, often after an ideophone there is the form *yits'a'go* or *yiists'ą́ą́'*, which glosses as "it sounded, it sounds" (see also Young and Morgan 1987:359; Yazzie and Speas 2007:375). This device indicates that an ideophone has just been produced. It functions very much as a verb of sounding (a quasi-*verba dicendi*?), indicating that what has preceded it was an ideophone (see Voeltz and Kilian-Hatz 2001 for cross-linguistic comparative purposes). It is, however, as examples below will attest, not an obligatory device. Below I present three examples that show the form that ideophones take with *yits'a'go* that I elicited from a Navajo consultant. Examples from narratives and poetry will be presented later. I have capitalized all the glosses (provided by the consultant) of the ideophones in the following examples.

(2) k'az k'az yits'a'go
SHEAR SHEAR it sounded

(3) dil dil yits'a'go
HEAVY FOOT STEPS HEAVY FOOT STEPS it sounded

(4) woł woł yits'a'go
GURGLE GURGLE it sounded

According to Young and Morgan, -*ts'ą́ą́'* is a verb stem that "describes the production, existence and hearing of sound" (Young, Morgan, and Midgette 1992:625). This verb stem also forms the base for the Navajo verbal phrase for onomatopoeia *hodiits'a'* (there is a sound) (*ho-* is a locative; *dii-* inceptive; and–*ts'a'* is a verb stem related to perceiving sound). Another example offered by a Navajo consultant was:

(5) 'ashkii abingo alizh nit'éé,' **chaazh chaazh** yits'a'go sizį́
boy in-the-morning one-urinates then CHAAZH CHAAZH
it-sounds one-is-standing-up

In the morning the boy went to the "bathroom" and he went **chaazh chaazh** standing up.

Here *chaazh chaazh* evokes the sound of a boy (*'ashkii*) urinating (*alizh*). The use of the classificatory verb stem –*zį́* "one person is standing" adds to the sense that the person urinating is a male (*si*- si perfective neuter prefix + -*zį́* "one living actor is standing"). According to my consultant this is the kind of thing Navajos often say or, as he said, "in the use of Navajo language conversational wise, a lot of times we speakers use the actual sound to describe the sound of the objects." Another Navajo consultant made a similar comment about the regular use of Navajo sound symbolism. He gave an example that code-switched from English to Navajo for the ideophone, describing a car with something metal hanging from it, he said, "That car is going *k'azh, k'azh, k'azh* all the way down the street." Here *k'azh, k'azh, k'azh* evokes the sound of metal scraping against the road. Here also "going" replaces *yits'a'go* and precedes the reduplicated form. Both consultants suggested that younger Navajos were less likely to use such forms today.

More recently, Evangeline Parsons Yazzie and Margaret Speas (2007:375-376) have included a brief section in their Navajo language textbook about Navajo "sound effects." Here they are discussing Navajo ideophony. They provide eighteen sample sentences that use ideophones in Navajo. Yazzie and Speas (375) go on to note that "sound effects also add humor to a conversation," and this echoes the delight that many Navajos have expressed to me about the use of Navajo ideophones. They also note that the ideophone is followed by either *yiists'ą́ą'ii'* (the sound that was made) or *yiits'a'go*, which they gloss as "as it is making that sound" (375). Below are two examples from Yazzie and Speas (375-376). The glossing is mine and I have again bolded the ideophones in the example sentence.

(6) Shizeedí, "**Gǫǫzh, gǫǫzh, gǫǫzh,**" yiits'a'go bááh bisgą' yi'aał.
my-cousin GǪǪZH GǪǪZH GǪǪZH it- sounds bread dry
3S-to-chew

My cousin makes the sound "**Gǫǫzh, gǫǫzh, gǫǫzh**" as he chews dried bread

(7) 'Ashiiké **mal, mal, mal, mal,** yiits'a'go tsį́į́łgo 'íiyą́ą́.'
boy MAL MAL MAL MAL it-sounds quickly he-ate

The boy makes the sound **mal, mal, mal, mal,** as he quickly eats.

Yazzie and Speas (2007:375–376) gloss *mal* as a sound that simulates either speaking that is not understood or "eating hurriedly" and *gǫǫzh* as a sound that simulates "a crunching sound." In the above examples we see the use of ideophones in a fourfold set or in a triplet. This pattern will also be found in the examples below. Ideophones appear in reduplicated sets, pairs of reduplicated sets (fourfold), or in triplets. Let me add that the form *mal* has also been extended to various nominalized nouns as well. For example, Latter Day Saints are known as *Gáamalii*, which uses the ideophone *mal*, suggesting "speaking that is not understood." *Gáamalii bikéyah* (the land of Gáamalii) is one name for Utah.[3] Finally, when Yazzie and Speas (375) refer to ideophones as "sound effects" they echo the comments made by my Navajo consultants about the function of ideophones as being like "movie sound effects." It should also be noted that in 2008 the textbook was adopted by the state of New Mexico as the official textbook for teaching Navajo language in public schools. Also note that in the popular textbook also published by Salina Bookshelf in Flagstaff, Arizona, on the Navajo language by non-Navajo scholar Irvy Goossen (1996) there is no significant discussion of such "sound effects."

Navajo is a verb-based language (Young 2000; Neundorf 2006). A single verb can be an entire sentence. One compelling argument is that Navajo is a pronominal argument language and as such nouns are adjuncts (optional) to the clause (Willie and Jelinek 2000). The verb can take a series of prefixes that include mode, subject prefix, and object prefix. It has been widely remarked that the Navajo language is "precise" (see

Kluckhohn 1960:81). This precision has often been expressed in terms of referential content of verbs. However, as Kluckhohn (1960:81) states:

> The Navaho are interested in words insofar as they categorize events with some precision. They are not interested in words just as expression of belief. The words of a chant myth must be just right because they prescribe a course of behavior that must be followed with minute exactness.

As one of my Navajo consultants humorously explained, "By now you should understand that Navajo language is very descriptive! It's not like using whiteman language. Single word may have many different meaning in Navajo." The precision of Navajo comes not from "referential" content, but rather from felt pragmatic iconicity. A word "fits" the moment and is made understandable in relationship to that moment. Words become iconic, in that they are felt to bear a natural fit or resemblance with the event being evoked.[4] Ideophones are one such example of the pragmatic or feelingful iconic precision of Navajo. As that Navajo consultant went on to explain concerning onomatopoeia, "the storyteller is making or trying to make a sound . . . to give an imagination to the listeners." And earlier in our discussion, "it's a descriptive word that shows a lot of imagination." Onomatopoeia can, then, be used to "give an imagination." They are a poetic and aesthetic device that involves the listener in the narrative; what Nuckolls (1992) has termed "sound symbolic involvement." The ability for narratives or poetry to evoke an "image" was one feature that Navajos often gave in their aesthetic evaluation of a story or poem.

The comments above had come in a discussion of the use of onomatopoeia in a Navajo Coyote narrative. Coyote stories, also known as *Mą'ii jooldloshí hane'* (stories of the trotting Coyote), are a well known genre of oral literature on the Navajo Nation (see Toelken and Scott 1981). From a comparison of the collections of Coyote stories transcribed by Edward Sapir from John Watchman (Sapir and Hoijer 1942) and by Father Berard Haile from Curly Tó Aheedlíinii (Haile 1984), it seems that Curly Tó Aheedlíinii used ideophones more often than did Watchman (both used ideophones). This may be due to different individual styles for telling these stories.

I should also add that Coyote's Navajo name *mą'ii* is phonologically distinctive. Nouns that begin with the phoneme /m/ are relatively rare in Navajo. This phonological distinctiveness calls attention to Coyote when he is explicitly named. Here we see phonotactics (the distribution of phonemes) increasing the saliency of Coyote's name. Many narrators also use a nasalized voice when quoting Coyote (Toelken and Scott 1981:83). Thus Coyote is recognizable through the sounds of his words and the distinctive sound of his name. Such phonic devices, while not ideophonic, work to increase the sound involvement of listeners; that is, they engage the listener in the narrative moment.

Ideophony in Navajo Place Names

I want to turn now to a variety of examples of ideophony in Navajo discourse. My first example of the use of ideophones comes from Navajo place names. A number of writers have noted that Athabaskan place names are highly descriptive (see Basso 1996; Jett 2001). Hoijer (1953:557), for example, noted that the Chiricahua Apache named their ethnogeographical environment with "care and precision." Basso (1996:89) has described the ways that Western Apache place names allow Apaches "to picture a site from its name." However, beyond picturing places through place names, in Navajo the sounds of the place can sometimes be evoked as well. For example, in Navajo, one place name for Taos, New Mexico, is *Tówoł*. Here *tó-* (water) is attached to the ideophone *-woł* (gurgling). In this example, *-woł* has been productively adapted as a verb stem (Young, Morgan, and Midgette 1992:659). Another example of the use of a place name with an ideophone is *Tséé'dóhdoon* (Rumbling Rock) (see Wilson 1995:62). Both *dóh* (rumbling) and *doon* (booming) are listed as separate ideophones in Young and Morgan (1987:432). In this place name the ideophones are combined into a reduplicative set (where the ideophones reverberate off the sounds of each other). Another place name that shows an evocative use of ideophony is *Tóniil'aha'nii* (sound of something moving in water out of sight) (Linford 2000:274). Here the ideophone *niil* (hoofbeats) (see Young and Morgan 1987:433) suggests the kind of animal that is moving—out of sight—through water. This is a hoofed animal, not a human being or, for that matter, a small animal. Such place names use ideophones for poetic purposes. Take as a final example, one place name used for Albuquerque, New Mexico, *Bee'eldíildahsinil* (*bee'eldíil-* [a ringing sound is made] *dah* [up] *si-* perfective–*nil* [plural objects sit]. Embedded within this place name is the ideophone *diil* [ringing]). The Navajo name for Albuquerque draws attention to the ringing of bells that were used on the Rio Grande to signal boats transporting people across the river (see Wilson 1995:2). The place names do not just describe the place rather they evoke the sounds of the place in the description (compare with Feld 1996:108). This is, again, the precision of iconicity.

Compare, on the other hand, a place I was taken to during fieldwork in 2007. This place is called *Tsé doon* (popping rock). However, in this case, the place name does not evoke the sounds of the place, but rather acts as a description of what will happen if the rocks are fired. According to a Navajo consultant the rocks at *Tsé doon* will explode if fired.

Ideophony in Navajo Narratives

I want to look now at examples of the use of ideophones in Navajo narratives. Here are two examples from narratives documented by Pliny Goddard and Sapir. In the examples below, the ideophones have been bolded and no effort at "translating" them has been made.

(8)   Kodεyε "**xawu,' xawu,' xawu,' xawu'**" ists'ą djin
      Then, "**xawu,' xawu,' xawu,' xawu'**" it sounds, they say.
      (Goddard 1933:60–61)

(9)   "**Dil, dil, dil**," yiists'ą́ą́.'
      "**Dil, dil, dil**," was heard.
      (Sapir and Hoijer 1942:42, 45)

Dil, dil, dil is here triplicated and meant to simulate the sound of several people walking. *Xawu,' xawu,' xawu,' xawu'* appears to be a sound associated with one of the Holy People (see Reichard 1950; Frisbie 1980). *Djin* is Goddard's way of writing *jin*, which is a phonologically reduced form of *jiní* (they say).

In the next example, Porcupine has climbed inside of Elk and Elk is taking Porcupine across a river. This narrative, titled by Berard Haile as "Porcupine, Elk, and Coyote," was told by Curly Tó Aheedlíinii. Porcupine is attempting to make sure that Elk has crossed the river completely. After Porcupine is sure that Elk has crossed the river completely, Porcupine extends his quills and pierces Elk's heart. It is only when Elk makes the *dil, dil* sound that Porcupine is convinced. Here the ideophones act as an evidential, proving that Elk is now on solid ground (the translation is adapted from a translation done in consultation with Blackhorse Mitchell).

(10) Nikináázdeestał, ńt'éé' **dil, dil**, yiists'ą́ą́' jiní.
T'áadoo tó diists'ą́ą́' da jiní.
(Haile 1984:104)

When he stamped his feet again, there was the sound **dil, dil**, they say.
There was no sound of the river, they say.

Here is another example, from a Coyote narrative also told by Curly Tó Aheedlíinii, where *yits'a'go* follows the ideophonic expression. Also in example 11, we see the use of the metanarrative exhortation *hááhgóóshį́į́*, which Toelken and Scott (1981:109) gloss as "!!!." The following example comes from the narrative "Coyote and Skunk." The passage is after Skunk has climbed into a tree with a number of well-cooked prairie dogs and is throwing down meatless bones to Coyote. I have bolded the ideophones in the examples.

(11) "Díí shoókę́zíłę́ń," jiní.
Hááhgóóshį́į́, **jįįz jįįz** yiits'a'go
(Haile 1984:94)

"This is for me," they say.
!!! Listen to that **jįįz jįįz** sound!

Young and Morgan (1987:432) describe *jįįz*(h) as a "crushing-crumbling sound."

In another version of "Coyote and Skunk," told by John Watchman to Edward Sapir, Watchman uses the ideophone *ts'os* (suck, kiss). In example 12, Coyote has feigned death and various animals are celebrating his death. At one point *hazéíts'ósii* (chipmunk) (or sometimes glossed as "little chatterbox")[5] leaps up on Coyote's body. I have reorganized the text to reveal something of the line structure, the ethnopoetic structuring, of Watchman's narrative (on Watchman's poetics see Webster forthcoming a).

(12)   'Áadi 'índa Hazéists'ósii,
       "Nishą́?
          'Ákǫ́ǫ́ náádílgheed!
             T'áádaats'í 'aaní.
                Daaztsǫ́," ho'doon'iid, jiní.
'Áádóó 'ákǫ́ǫ́ náájílghod.
    Ńt'éé,' "t'áá'aaníl ma'iiyę́ę daaztsą́lá!"
Yikáá' haasghodii' dahnahacha.'
    "ts'os, ts'os,
        ts'os, ts'os," nóo dahnahacha.'
           (Sapir and Hoijer 1942:22; edited by A. K. Webster)

And only then Chipmunk,
    "What about you?
        You also run over there!
           It may really be true.
                He is dead," It was said to him, they say.
And then he also ran over there.
    Then, "It is true that Ma'ii is indeed dead!"
He got on top of his body and skipped around.
    "ts'os, ts'os,
        ts'os, ts'os," he said as he skipped around.

The image here, as it was described to me, is of Chipmunk dancing on top of Coyote kissing the air or a "high pitched chuckle." Or as my Navajo consultant suggested, "like the way Snoopy dances." I should note, that in the Curly Tó Aheedlíinii version, Prairie Dogs break into song when they hear that Coyote is dead (see Haile 1984:92; see also Webster 2004). Thus in one version there is a breakthrough into song and in another version there is the use of ideophones. Both examples, however, call attention to the moment and are, I suggest, heightened affective expressions (performances on top of performances). Navajo ideophony, like the stylistic use of reduplication by Southern Paiute narrators documented by Pamela Bunte (2002), is a poetic option. Navajo ideophony is an exceptional ethnopoetic device.

In the following example, told by Charlie Mitchell to Edward Sapir in 1929 at Crystal, New Mexico, we find the use of aspiration, a nonphonemic sound in Navajo, in the ideophonic expression (Sapir and Hoijer 1942:300). Reichard (1948:15), however, did suggest that aspiration in Navajo was a way to "indicate an augmentative." I would, following Woodbury (1987), term this use of aspiration a meaningful phonological process. Thus a meaningful phonological process creates "special expressive or other pragmatic meaning" (Woodbury 1987:686), in this case "augmentative." Likewise, Navajo does not have a phonemic /p/. Both the aspiration and the use of [p] mark this form as distinct. The example comes from an "ethnological narrative" that has been titled "Naming in the War-dance and the End of the Dance" (Sapir and Hoijer 1942:297). In example 13, I have updated the orthography and included the superscript [h] to indicate aspiration.

(13) Nda'áahgo, "bída'dosooł," niih.
T'áá'áko "pʰáa, pʰáa, pʰáa, pʰáa," dajiníigo.
When he has finished the song, "Blow at (the enemy)!" he says.
At once, "pʰáa, pʰáa, pʰáa, pʰáa," they say.
(Sapir and Hoijer 1942:300–301)

Hoijer, in the notes to the Navajo texts, writes this about the sound: "A heavily aspirated p plus vowel to simulate blowing" (Sapir and Hoijer 1942:470). This then is an ideophone for "blowing." This form does not occur in the list of onomatopoeia given by Young and Morgan (1987). In its rhythmic repetition it seems reminiscent of the ideophones described for Runa speakers by Nuckolls (1992). Again, through aspiration and repetition, this form attempts to simulate the sound of blowing.

Ideophony in Navajo Song

In Matthews's (1994:27) collection of Navajo "legends," he provides the following "translation" of a "Dove Song," which is a gambling song (I have slightly altered the orthography of the ideophone and the glossing here). Matthews, I want to note, was an Army doctor who documented Navajo language and culture in the 1880s. He was critical of those who would dismiss Navajo verbal art as "a succession of grunts" (see Matthews, 1994:23). Speaking of poetic devices, Matthews (25) claims, "if the language were reduced to a standard spelling, we should find that the Navaho poets have as many figures of these classes as the English poets have, and perhaps more." One such poetic device was the use of onomatopoeia.

(14) **Wosh wosh** picks them up
      Wosh wosh picks them up
      Glossy Locks picks them up
      Red Moccasin picks them up
      Wosh wosh picks them up

According to Matthews (1994:27) the *wosh wosh* of the song, "is an onomatope for the dove, equivalent to our 'coo coo'; but it is used as a noun." Here we see an ideophone being used as a noun. The sound imitative form evokes the dove without explicitly referencing the dove by name (*hásbídí*). Note that Matthews does not attempt a translation into English within the song text.

In another example provided by Matthews (1894:191), he presents the following song:

(15) The corn grows up.
      The waters of the dark clouds **ol, ol.**
      The rain descends.

> The waters from the corn leaves **ol, ol**.
> The rain descends.
> The waters from the plants **ol, ol**.
> The corn grows up.
> The waters of the dark mists **ol, ol**.

In Matthews (1894), he translates *ol, ol* into "drop, drop." I have reorganized the line structure here and replaced Matthews's "drop, drop" for the onomatopoetic form *ol, ol*, which he cites (this is likely *k'ol* [plop], described by Landar 1985). The reorganization of line structure is here a heuristic device to highlight the forms of parallelism. Not only does this song describe the rain, it also evokes the sounds of the rain through the repeated use of the ideophone *ol, ol*.

Finally, David McAllester (1980a:20) notes that in the Dawn Songs (songs associated with the Shootingway) onomatopoeia *ya'ó*, "is prolonged by the singer, on the high notes, to sound like a coyote." Here again we see an onomatopoeia used in song (for comparative purposes see Briggs 1996:208–211). Ideophones in songs are often mentioned by Navajo consultants as particularly delightful. As Frisbie (1980:355) writes, "amidst the overwhelming symbolism in Navajo ceremonialism is that based on sound," as discussed above, these include onomatopoeias. Sound symbolism is pervasive in Navajo songs (see again Frisbie 1980; Reichard 1950; McAllester 1980a).

Ideophony in Contemporary Navajo Written Poetry

I want to turn now to examples of the uses of ideophones in contemporary Navajo written poetry. The first example is from a poem that was written by Navajo poet Rex Lee Jim. Other examples from Jim on the use of onomatopoeia could be given (see Chapter 1), but this poem uses a number of devices that have been discussed above for oral genres and thus suggests something of the active continuity of poetic forms across mediums. Below I present the poem in Navajo and then an English glossing that I did in consultation with Rex Lee Jim. I have again bolded the ideophones.

(16) na'asts'ǫǫsí
 ts'ǫǫs, ts'ǫǫs
 yiits'a'go
 íits'ǫ́ǫ́z
 (Jim 1995:37)

 mouse
 suck, suck
 sounding
 kiss
 (Webster 2006b:39)

The word for "mouse" in Navajo can be morphologically analyzed as something akin to "the one who goes about sucking." It is built up of an onomatopoeia that has productively become a verb -*ts'ǫǫs* (to suck) and has then been nominalized by the use of a nominalizing enclitic -*í* (the one). Jim then uses that play-on-ideophone-turned-noun in line two where the onomatopoetic word *ts'ǫǫs* is in a reduplicated form. *Ts'ǫǫs* has at least two interlinking evocations: one is the sound of sucking through a straw and the other is the sound of a kiss. This is particularly interesting because a number of Navajos I discussed this poem with stated that *na'asts'ǫǫsí* could not be analyzed into its constituent morphology. For them *na'asts'ǫǫsí* meant only "mouse" and not "the one who goes about sucking." The third line is again the standard way to acknowledge that what has just been said is onomatopoetic. That line—I should add—is also implicated in the alliteration that tumbles through the poem /ts'/. One gloss for this line suggested was "that's how it sounds," however Rex Lee Jim in discussing the glossing suggested "sounding." I follow his suggestion. The fourth line means something akin to "it kissed," "it sucked," or "to perform a sucking rite." There is a certain amount of semantic ambiguity here that Jim is attempting to evoke.

Notice that Jim is playing with the meaning of *ts'ǫǫs* and the sound /ts'/, and in doing so he is drawing on the various connotations and the semantic relations those connotations may evoke within the poem. He is making ambiguity of meaning, through the highlighting of sounds, maximally salient. Here we see the way that -*ts'ǫǫs* as verb stem, nominalized noun, and onomatopoeia is "interwoven" into the poetics and aesthetics of Navajo expressive culture (see Woodbury 1998:244 on "interwoven"). The precision of meaning comes through its pragmatic and feelingful iconicity and not solely through its referential or semantic content. It is the ideophone that links meaning and creates connections. When I discussed this poem with Jim, he told me that one of the goals of his poetry was to make people think about language, "most of my poems are written to stimulate thoughts and that involves thinking about semantics and etymology." Jim went on to state that one cannot "really translate" such forms from Navajo into English. Jim uses ideophony in this poem to stimulate thoughts. Indeed, some Navajos that I have spoken with about Jim's poetry have pointed to the semantic ambiguity that he evokes through his poetry as a positive aesthetic achievement. Rather than forcing a singular interpretation, they say, Jim opens up a number of competing senses that one can reflect upon. This, I might add—the not forcing of a singular interpretation—resonates with a general Navajo ethos that I have heard, *t'áá bee bóholníih* or, in English, "it's up to him/her to decide" (see Lamphere 1977 for a useful discussion of this ethos). People should be allowed to make their own decisions and their own interpretations. In general, Navajos that I spoke with were reluctant to speculate on what a poet meant by a poem. Instead, many Navajos explained to me the images or associations that a poem evoked.

At a live performance of this poem by Rex Lee Jim to an audience composed of primarily Navajos, on July 18, 2001, in Window Rock, Arizona, several Navajos in attendance smiled and laughed during this poem. One Navajo woman told me upon hearing this poem that it evoked the image of a little mouse going about kissing. When I asked another Navajo in attendance what she enjoyed about the poem, she told me she enjoyed the "way the sounds go together." Here we see the delight that comes from the use of ideophones.

Let me add that *ts'ǫǫsí* can also be used as a nickname. One Navajo consultant explained to me that he had a nephew that was known as *Ts'ǫǫsí*. This was a shortened form of *na'asts'ǫǫsí* (mouse). When his nephew was a baby the family had taken to calling him *na'asts'ǫǫsí* because of a bathing incident, but this form had been shortened to *Ts'ǫǫsí*, which was clearly recognized by the family as being both the sound of sucking or kissing as well as a shortened form of *na'asts'ǫǫsí*. Here again we see the productivity and interwovenness of ideophones in Navajo verbal expressions.

Here is another example of the use of an ideophone in Navajo poetry. The poem is by Gloria Emerson (2003:33) and is titled "Table Mesa, N.M." Here is the relevant excerpt from the poem (I have again bolded the ideophone):

(17) of songprints
of **w'u, w'u,**
déłi biyiin,
of first things, first
(Emerson 2003:33)

In a footnote after the poem, Emerson (2003:35) describes the sound as follows, "approximated sound of an approaching deity." The next line glosses as *déłi'* (crane) *biyiin* (its song) or (songs of cranes) (Emerson 2003:35). As Emerson explained to me, this poem was meant as an attempt to "deify gravity" and the use of *w'u, w'u* was meant to be evocative of both the sound of Navajo deities and the sound of a crane taking flight over water. The use of the *w'u, w'u* in a reduplicative pair resonates with the earlier discussion of the form of Navajo ideophones. Also, the use of an ideophone to connect with a deity connects with the discussion by Frisbie (1980) concerning one of the functions of Navajo sound symbols (where deities are associated with various sounds or calls). Here Emerson connects the use of ideophones to Navajo ceremonialism. Likewise we again see a continuity of use between oral genres and contemporary written poetry, especially in the use of intertextuality. Emerson's use of *w'u, w'u* also intertextually links beyond the internal coherence of the poem to a broader set of Navajo aesthetic practices (ceremonialism, songs, narratives, and place names). The use of ideophony is not a seamless carryover from Navajo oral tradition. Rather, it is an actively selected poetic option.

One Navajo educator shared with me a number of unpublished poems that her students had written that use ideophones. One example that she read to me used *k'az, k'az* for the sound of shearing sheep. This reduplicated form was then followed by *yits'a'go*. This poem then used an ideophone in a reduplicative set and it was followed by the form *yits'a'go*. This poem was written for a Navajo language class at Diné College. Its use was seen, by the teacher that shared this with me, as a display of language command (Navajo) and of creativity and of evocation. As she said about this poem, "you can really hear it when you read it."

In an article by Bernice Casaus (1996:5) concerning the poetry being written in Navajo literacy classes, she presents a poem by Minnie Bidtah. Here is the poem and a translation (done in consultation with Blackhorse Mitchell). I have again bolded the ideophones.

18) Nídii'nééh
Minnie Bidtah áyiilaa

Na'ahóóhai ání yitis'a.'
Háadi shı́ı́ łééchąą'í nahał'in yitis'a.'
Béésh bii' ko'í bii' ních'ih tsiih yitis'a.'
Didooljéé' yists'ą́ą́.'
Ch'ił, ch'ił dóó **hwoosh, hwoosh** yitis'a.'
Nizhónígo, hazhóó'ígo honiidoi.
Nił hóyée'go sínítínée, ts'éénídzíı́d.
Tł'óo'di dibé biyo' **díng, díng, díng,** yitis'a.'
Dibé yázhí dóó tł'ízí yázhí ádaaní yitis'a.'
Me'é'ęę, me'é'ęę, dibé yázhí
bimá bich'į' ádaaní yitis'a.'
Dibé ch'énil yits'ą́ą́.'
"Nídii'nééh! Níláahgóó dibé ch'ínı́jéé,'" jiní yits'ą́ą́.'
Ts'iii, ts'iii, ghaaz, ghaaz
Nímasii yit'ees yitis'a.'
Tł'ish, tł'ish, tł'ish
ájílééh yitis'a'
"Nídiidáahgo. íyą́ą́ dóó díbé bikéé' dílyeed."
"T'óó iłhoshgo nigod dóó nikétsíín gónaa dich'íizh doo.
Nitsii' dah dichxosh dóó yaasts'ílí bee disxos doo.
Gház, gház, gház yiits'a'go ádích'idgo naninaa doo."
Na'ahóóhai ánii yitis'a.' Dibé biyo' diits'a.'
"Nídoo'nééh," jin"i yiitis'a.' Nímasii yit'ees yiits'a.'

"Haalá nit'įįgo, ánít'į.
T'óó la' ajiłhosh.
Níłch'i halne'é haagééś.
Áłt'ąą la' hanáá' ąą'ájiilaa."

Get Up!
Made by Minnie Bidtah

I hear the rooster calling
Somewhere I hear a dog barking
I hear a sound of someone adjusting fire in the stove
I hear the light of the fire
I hear **ch'il, ch'il** and **hwoosh, hwoosh**
Slowly, pleasantly it got warm
Although lying being lazy, wake up
I hear the bells of sheep **díng, díng, díng** outside
I hear the calls of lambs and goats
I hear the lambs calling to their mother, **me'é'ęę, me'é'ęę**
I hear the sheep exiting
I hear the sheep out at the corral, "Get up!" I heard.
I hear the **ts'iii, ts'iii, ghaaz, ghaaz** of potatoes frying
I hear the **tł'ish, tł'ish, tł'ish** sound of someone
"Get up, eat and then go after the sheep."
"If you just sleep, your knees and ankles will become chaps.
Your hair will be bushy with glitters of nits.
You will be **gház, gház, gház** yourself walking around."
I hear the rooster crowing, I hear the sheep bells jingling
I hear someone say, "Get Up!" I hear the potatoes frying.
"What's wrong, why?
Gosh you still asleep.
Turn on the radio.
About time you've opened your eyes."

Bidtah uses "*ch'ił, ch'ił dóó hwoosh, hwoosh*" (*dóó* glosses as "and") for the sounds of the crackling and popping of a fire. Later she writes of the sound of sheep bells, "*tł'óódi dibé biyo' díng, díng, díng yitis'a*" (outside sheep bells sound ding, ding, ding). The whole poem is a series of ideophones that evokes the sounds of Navajo life. Another line concerns the "baa" of a little sheep, *me'é'ęę, me'é'ęę, dibé yázhí* (me'é'ęę, me'é'ęę, little sheep). Still another evokes the sounds of potatoes frying, *ts'ii, ts'ii ghaaz, ghaaz nímasii yit'ees yitis'a'* (potatoes cooking sounding *ts'ii, ts'ii, ghaaz, ghaaz*). Here the ideophones simulate the sound of grease crackling. Later Bidtah presents the *tł'ish, tł'ish, tł'ish* of someone walking about. Blackhorse Mitchell described this sound image as, "like walking in the mess of a very soft mushy kind of clay." Compare, for example, these lines of poetry by Barbara Sorensen (1996:A-7) from a poem published in the *Navajo Times* on the coming rain on the Navajo Nation, which also uses *tł'ish, tł'ish, tł'ish* to evoke the sounds of walking in mud. During the mid-1990s the *Navajo Times* published a Navajo Language page that meant to highlight contemporary Navajo literacy efforts. The publication of poetry written in Navajo was one common element of that effort. Note also the use of the ideophone again in a triplet form.

19) Tł'ish, tł'ish, tł'ish yits'a'go,
    Nihikee' t'áágééd hashtł'ish bii' nináánéi'né.

   With the sounds of **tł'ish, tł'ish, tł'ish,**
   We played in the mud without our shoes.

Finally, Bidtah uses the ideophone *gház, gház, gház* for the sound of someone scratching. Note that the ideophones are followed by the use of *yitis'a* (it sounds). Throughout the poem we see patterns of reduplicated ideophones (e.g., *ch'ił, ch'ił*) or triplets of ideophones (e.g., *gház, gház, gház*). Casaus (1996) presents this poem, with its use of ideophony, as a positive example of contemporary Navajo poetry. At least one Navajo consultant, upon seeing this poem, remarked that it made him hungry imagining the sound of potatoes frying.

In a collection of poetry published by the Diné Teacher Education Program out of Diné College, Tsaile, Arizona (Begay 1998:3), Marilyn Hubbard writes a poem titled *Pé'sii Laanaa* (I want Pepsi) (where *laanaa* is an optative particle), which uses *k'ol, k'ol yiits'a'go* to evoke the sound of drinking *tódílchxoshí* (soda pop), which Blackhorse Mitchell poetically translated for me as "popping water." The pun here between "soda pop" and "popping water" is not, I believe, incidental. Both Sapir (1932) and W. W. Hill (1943) noted a Navajo propensity for punning in the early parts of the 20th century. Hill (18), for example, describes how a Navajo man transformed "Studebaker" into the Navajo phrase *hastoi bibía* (old man's stomach) based on the feeling that they sound alike. Another, contemporary example, involves the Bashas grocery stores, which dot the Navajo Nation. Some Navajos are fond of calling them *béézhaazh* (scraped away) because of the similarity in sounds or phonological iconicity between Bashas and *béézhaazh*. One Navajo I knew enjoyed punning "God" with the Navajo word *gad* (juniper trees) and asking, rhetorically, why Christians were so interested in trees. Take, also, the example of *kǫǫ́ stłé* (give me your socks) for "cornflakes," which still amuses some Navajos today. Or take the relationship between urinating donkeys and television. According to the joke, older Navajos first misheard "television" as *télii alizhgo* (donkey is urinating) (Wilson 1970:44). My own attempts at Navajo were sometimes opened up to interlingual punning as well. One time when I was sitting at the kitchen table of a Navajo friend's house with Rex Lee Jim, we were talking about the nature of poetry, and he described poetry as *hane'* (story, narrative). I repeated the form accidentally as *hánii*. Jim then pointed out that we were not dating and I did not have to call him "honey." My friend, who was at the stove, and I laughed, and I became more cautious about saying *hane'*. Such cross-language puns can frequently be found in Navajo verbal art and contemporary poetry.[6]

Martha Austin-Garrison (1991) has written about the five senses method of teaching Navajo creative writing.[7] One of the senses that Austin-Garrison discusses is sound and she provides a list of 85 Navajo ideophones (Austin-Garrison 1991:48). She points out that there are many such sound words (*hodiits'a'* [there is a sound]) in Navajo and that they can aid in the aesthetics of Navajo poetry. Austin-Garrison's (1991) article and Casaus's (1996) article are both written entirely in Navajo and were aimed at a literate Navajo audience (a relatively small group): an audience composed of educators. Both articles were also published in the *Journal of Navajo Education*, which was also aimed at an audience composed of Navajo educators. Likewise, the inclusion of Navajo "sound effects" in the recent Navajo textbook by Navajo educator Evangeline Parsons Yazzie and linguist Margaret Speas again suggests a positive view of the use of Navajo ideophones. These discussions mostly focus on the delight that such ideophonic displays evoke. The use of *hodiits'a'* is something that is encouraged by these Navajo educators.

Finally, here is an example from Tohe (2005:9). In a poem (rumination) on *Tséyi'* titled "Deep in the Rock," Tohe writes the following:

(20) Deep in the rock, crows make echoes, **gáagii gáagii**. Their
 name is pure
 onomatopoeia.
 (Tohe 2005:9)

Here Tohe uses the Navajo term for crow as an ideophone. She is building on the onomatopoetic form within the noun *gáagii* and using the very name for crow as an ideophone. Note that she reduplicates the form as well, thus the second form echoes the first. She is highlighting the onomatopoetic structure of the Navajo noun. She is calling attention to its sound. Her poem is a meta-ideophonic rumination, highlighting the onomatopoetic form within the noun *gáagii*. She is thus, like Jim, drawing out the saliency of the onomatopoetic form in Navajo. Like much verbal art, she is placing the linguistic form on display for contemplation, calling the form into metalinguistic awareness. Tapahonso (2008:73) also uses *gáagii* onomatopoetically in a recent collection of poetry (the form is reduplicated in the poem).

The use of ideophones can be found in contemporary Navajo poetry, both poetry written for Navajo literacy classes and poetry written by more well-known poets such as Rex Lee Jim and Gloria Emerson. Indeed, ideophones are a part of the five senses approach to creative writing. However, not all Navajo educators that I have spoken with felt ideophones were appropriate in written poetry. One Navajo consultant (an educator) said that such sound symbolic and ideophonic forms should not be encouraged in Navajo writing (poetry or otherwise). This consultant evaluated ideophones negatively because they were not "like English literature." By this, the consultant then suggested that English literature, as that consultant had been taught it, "really describes." Here my Navajo consultant echoed the view discussed by Samuels (2004a) above, which sees language as primarily reference or semantics. Ideophony, here then, evokes connections and thus fails to "describe." This consultant appears to have internalized the educational bias against ideophony that is also on display in the *Arrow* publications. That is, this consultant had internalized the negative views of sound symbolism that appear to have accompanied English language instruction and transferred them to Navajo as well. Here we see the potential fragility of Navajo ideophones when they are evaluated by outside aesthetic standards. This is the very negative evaluation of Native languages that Sapir (1921) was arguing against when he suggested that Mackenzie River Athabaskans did not use many sound imitative forms in their language. However, Navajo poets like Rex Lee Jim are clearly challenging that evaluation and highlighting the importance of ideophony in Navajo.

Conclusions

Following Childs (2001:70), I argue that Navajo ideophones, "are quintessentially social, the mark of local identity" and, I would add, intimacy. Much like, for example, Nia Francisco's (1988:25) use of "Naabeeho," evoking a regional Navajo pronunciation of "Navajo," in her poem about being a "Naabeeho Woman Poet," also acts as an index of local identity and intimacy. I was once corrected by a Navajo poet on the "proper" (i.e., Navajo) way to say Navajo. As he pointed out, "in Naabeeho, we have no *v*" (Navajo does not have a phonemic /v/). According to him, if I wanted to sound like I knew what I was doing—and he thought I should—I should say, "Naabeeho."

In the examples above, the use of ideophony in Navajo place names and in Navajo poetry about home life evokes that sense of locality. The use of Navajo ideophones, because they can be negatively evaluated by non-Navajos and some Navajo educators, can also be seen as an index of intimacy. Likewise, the decision to use ideophony in contemporary Navajo poetry places it in opposition to a more prevalent Western linguistic ideology. Finding examples of ideophony in narratives collected by early anthropological linguists like Sapir and Goddard and by missionaries such as Haile in the early 20th century is important, especially when such forms were often considered extra-linguistic or pre-linguistic (Silverstein 1994:40). As Mphande (1992:119) notes for African ideophones, "ideophones are visibly absent from the African folk narrative texts translated under the influence of missionaries and missionary-trained scholars who were the pioneer researchers in the field of African language study." Mphande (119) goes so far as to describe the erasure of ideophony from the written records of early linguists and missionaries as "textual genocide." Likewise, the very visibility of Navajo ideophony in contemporary Navajo poetry is also noteworthy. Richard Watson (2000:401) points out that, "even a highly acclaimed African writer like Ngũgĩ wa Thiong'o uses few, if any, ideophones because of a European based education." There certainly were no examples of Navajo ideophony in the Bureau of Indian Affairs publication *Arrow*, which meant to highlight Native writers writing English language poetry. But this was English language poetry that lacked the use of sound symbolism. Now many Navajo educators actively promote the use of "sound effects" in the creative writing of Navajo students.

For some Navajo poets, the use of ideophony stands in opposition to a Euro-American linguistic ideology that devalues such sound symbolic forms and uses (see Nuckolls 2006; see also Samuels 2004a). It has often been argued that the use of ideophony appears "fragile" in language contact situations (Nuckolls 2006:47; see also Childs 1996). Certainly the examples described for urban Zulu (Childs 1996) and for Runa speakers (Nuckolls 2006) attest to the potential fragility of ideophones. One Navajo consultant was quite pessimistic about the continued use of such forms among younger Navajos. It was a potential loss that they were not pleased about. On the other hand, the active use of ideophony in a variety of poems, including poetry written in Navajo language writing classes, suggests an active resistance to that Western linguistic ideology. We might then, see the use of ideophony in Navajo poetry as an act of resistance, or an "art" of resistance (Scott 1990).

Lest it be thought that Navajo poets are not concerned with resisting what some perceive as Western (Anglo) literary traditions, let me provide another brief example. One afternoon I was sitting in the home of a Navajo poet friend and he showed me a recent poem he had written and typed up. When I commented that I liked the new poem and found it interesting, he asked me if I had noticed anything about the form of the poem. Nothing leapt out at me. He then pointed out that unlike all his other poems, this poem had been centered on the page. He then told me that he had intentionally centered the poem as a way to break with the literary practices he had been taught in school decades earlier. This poet had attended BIA schools and he had been taught there that "everything had to line up on the left side." His centering of the poem on the page was an act of resistance against what he perceived as Western literary practices as articulated by BIA schooling.

The final chapter of Sapir's (1921:221) *Language* is titled "Language and Literature," and here Sapir reminds us of the importance of literature and aesthetics to the study of linguistics and the cultural. Sapir also reminds us that, "every language is itself a collective art of expression. There is concealed in it a particular set of esthetic factors—phonetic, rhythmic, symbolic, morphological—that it does not completely share with any other language" (Sapir 1921:225). All of that is true. However, the concealing of ideophony, as Mphande has argued, was not due to a lack of familiarity by scholars with a language, but rather an active concealing of a poetic device that was not considered to be part of language. The use of Navajo ideophony in contemporary poetry brings new meaning to the old trope in anthropology about "poetics and politics." Language—poetic language—is multifunctional (Jakobson 1960). The ideophony found in contemporary Navajo poetry can certainly be considered both poetic and political. If Euro-American poetry, as understood by Navajo poets, neglects or avoids the use of sound symbolic forms like ideophony, some Navajo poets, in contrast, actively select to incorporate the poetics of ideophony into their poetry. In this way, Navajo poets index that their poetry is not Euro-American poetry and, in so doing, ideophony becomes iconic of Navajo poetics. Since it can be linked back to a variety of verbal genres it gains feelingful iconicity as a sign of continuity. Its use is also aesthetically pleasing and thus delights as well.

THREE

Language, Language Ideology, and Navajo Poetry

Language—like the living concrete environment in which consciousness of the verbal artist lives—is never unitary.

M. M. Bakhtin, *The Dialogic Imagination*

Introduction

In this chapter I focus on what is *not* represented in much of the use of the Navajo language in contemporary Navajo-written published poetry. Instead, I suggest that the Navajo used serves as an icon of proper Navajo usage. It presents a "purist" view of the Navajo language and largely obscures communicative practices of younger Navajos. This is especially true in how it excludes, almost completely, what Charlotte Schaengold (2003, 2006) has termed "bilingual Navajo" and what some of my Navajo consultants termed *Navlish*. The use of Navajo in Navajo-written published poetry (that is poetry written by Navajos) aids in producing a purist linguistic ideology (see Hill 1985; Kroskrity 1992a, 1992b; see also Silverstein 2003b). This ideology emphasizes the separation between Navajo and English. That is, the use of the Navajo language in these poems tends to replicate "standard" Navajo as a language minimally influenced by outside languages (see Young 1989). As Mikhail Bakhtin (1981:294) notes, "certain dialects may be legitimized in literature and thus to a certain extent be appropriated by literary language." In investigating this issue, I will also discuss briefly the contemporary sociolinguistic scene on the Navajo Nation as well as Navajo linguistic ideologies.

Schaengold's (2003) discussion of bilingual Navajo was not published until after I had returned from fieldwork in 2001 (though I was familiar with Canfield's 1980 discussion of Navajo/English code-mixing). After reading her article, I was struck by the fact that examples of bilingual Navajo were almost completely absent in the poetry that I had documented during fieldwork. In fact, it was an example of bilingual Navajo by Esther Belin, published after my initial fieldwork (in 2002), that inspired me to go back to the published Navajo poetry and make a more systematic survey. Finding examples was nearly impossible (I was only able to find four more examples).

That was surprising because during both my initial fieldwork and more recent fieldwork, I commonly heard bilingual Navajo on the Navajo Nation, where Navajo clitics and affixes were often attached to English language nouns, and examples of bilingual Navajo on billboards and signs was also common. I heard bilingual Navajo at Navajo fairs, in conversations at restaurants, at the mutton stands on the side of the road, at the trading post in Lukachukai, Arizona, at the tire shop in Chinle, in schools in Tohatchi, New Mexico, as well as on long drives listening to KTNN. Because it involved both Navajo and English, it was some of the first "Navajo" that I was able to comprehend. I have not attempted a detailed sociolinguistic survey of the uses of bilingual Navajo on the Navajo Nation. It is, however, from my experiences and field notes, impressionistic as they may be, as well as the data cited by Schaengold (2003, 2004, 2006), Kip Canfield (1980), McLaughlin (1992), and others, a relatively common communicative practice. Certainly, when I asked Navajos about it in 2007 they easily recognized the practice and were able to provide examples. In fact, some of my Navajo consultants offered the metalinguistic term Navlish to describe the code-mixed style (some consultants use Navglish as well).

Language Ideology and Linguistic Purism

Robert Moore (1988) has discussed the ways that the Wasco language has come to be thought of as a set of "words." Here words then become objects of display, objects that can be "brought out" (Moore 1988:467). A language becomes an object, or object-like. Such an analysis links with the work of Michael Silverstein (1979, 2003b) concerning language ideologies (see also Rumsey 1990; Kroskrity 2004). "Language ideologies," as Paul Kroskrity (2004:498) writes, "are beliefs, or feelings, about languages in their social world." Or as Kathryn Woolard (1998:3) notes:

> Ideologies of language are not about language alone. Rather, they envision and enact ties to identity, to aesthetics, to morality, and to epistemology. Through such linkages, they underpin not only linguistic form and use but also the very notion of the person and the social group, as well as . . . fundamental social institutions.

Silverstein's (2003b:542) discussion concerning the Worora language of Australia, presented by Rev. Mr. Love, for example, shows the ways that "outright bad morphology and syntax in the translated texts were taken to be the authoritative Christian Word in Worora." Here a particular form of Worora, based on the historical contingencies of Rev. Mr. Love's linguistic abilities and translation practices, has become valorized as an exemplar of "high register value" Worora (Silverstein 2003b:542). Again linguistic practices become an object of contemplation and discussion, and thus a "language" is created through discursive practices. "Languages" are then an imaginable set of metasemiotic stereotypes (see Silverstein 1998; Agha 1998). They are nameable objects: "Worora" as different from "Wasco" as different from "Navajo" as different from "English."

By metasemiotic stereotypes, I follow Asif Agha (1998) and understand them as stereotypes of the uses, forms, and functions—including notions of the discreteness and abstractness of "languages"—of semiotic practices. As Agha (1998:151–152) writes:

> Metapragmatic stereotypes about identity mediate between two pragmatic orders: the pragmatic phenomena that they construe, and the pragmatic phenomena that they enable. The fact that such stereotypes are consciously grasped makes them culturally preeminent in certain ways: They become reportable, discussable, open to dispute; they can be invoked as social standards, or institutionalized as such; they allow (and sometimes require) conscious strategies of self-presentation; they serve as models for some individuals, counter-models for others.

When such stereotypes are tied to a whole clustering of semiotic practices, we can speak of metasemiotic stereotypes. Semiotic practices become indexes and icons of and for metasemiotic stereotypes of "languages," "dialects," "styles" and the like. As Silverstein (2000:121) writes, "standardization, in turn, is the imagination and explicit, institutionalized maintenance of a 'standard' register—a way of employing words and expressions for reference and predication based on institutionalized prescriptions and proscriptions of various sorts—such that purportedly the best speakers and writers in the population index their adherence to all of them."

Such nameable languages, then, are often "objectified" at the expense of, or in opposition to, internal sociolinguistic diversity (see Gal and Irvine 1995). One such metasemiotic stereotype, influenced by our linguistic awareness (see Silverstein 1981; Hill 1985), concerns language or linguistic purism. Jane Hill (1985) insightfully showed how the rhetoric of linguistic purism can be deployed as an assertion of power in spite of any command of a "pure" code. Discussing Mexicano (Nahuatl)-speaking people's sociolinguistic practices in the Malinche Volcano region of Mexico, she shows the ways that Mexicano and Spanish have been mixed in the speech of many Mexicanos. Such mixing concerns the lexicon, morphology, syntax, and phonology. However, as Hill (1985) notes, the linguistic consciousness of such forms differ. The purist discourse focuses on the saliency of the town name San Miguel Canoa, while less salient features of morphology and phonology are ignored. Lexical items become a focus for purists' discourse. And such purist discourses are ways for Mexicanos to assert a degree of authority over other Mexicanos, regardless of one's linguistic abilities.

Consider also the recent discussions of "syncretic Rapa Nui" and "purist Rapa Nui" on Easter Island, as described by Miki Makihara (2007). Syncretic Rapa Nui, which combines both Spanish and Rapa Nui, is widely used there, and there are "positive attitudes toward linguistic syncretism" (Makihara 2007:62). As Makihara goes on to state, "the use of purist Rapa Nui registers has largely remained restricted to interethnic and public settings where the association between linguistic codes and ethnic identity remains highly salient." According to Makihara (63), this positive valuation of syncretic Rapa Nui is due in no small part to a linguistic ideology that promotes "syncretism." This contrasts with a Navajo linguistic ideology that does not value "linguistic syncretism."

Kroskrity (1992a, 1992b) has described the linguistic ideology among the Arizona Tewa. According to Kroskrity (1992a, 1992b) there are four interrelated notions about Arizona Tewa language. These "pervasive principles" (Kroskrity 1992a:113) are: (1) "regulation by convention" (a tendency to use fixed forms in such genres as song and prayer); (2) "strict compartmentalization" (the use of language within specific contexts); (3) "linguistic indexing of the speaking self" (the use of language choice to index social personas); and (4) "linguistic purism" (a disinclination to mix languages or styles or registers). Thus, within the kiva (a ritually important place) foreign words are not to be used, and outside the kiva code-mixing is condemned (Kroskrity 1992a:113). However, within narratives the use of English, Tewa, or Hopi can be used to index social identities (Kroskrity 1992a:114).

There is much within Kroskrity's description of Arizona Tewa that resonates with Navajo linguistic ideology. There is a thorough-going literature that describes a general Navajo principle of regulation by convention (see Reichard 1944; Witherspoon 1977). This is most clearly manifest in the ideal that Navajo chantways should be verbatim replications—given the contingencies of the world (see Faris 1994)—of previous chantways (Reichard 1944; Kluckhohn 1960; Witherspoon 1977). It can also be found in the formulaic introductions of clan relations that Navajo poets often give at the beginning of public performances. Likewise, strict compartmentalization—the use of Navajo in certain contexts—can also be found. Among some Navajos that I have spoken with about such matters, for example, Navajo is still the preferred language of curing ways and ceremonials (both for the practitioner and for those in attendance). Indeed, this aspect of Navajo linguistic ideology has found expression in Navajo poetry (as I will discuss below).

Given, as Henry Shonerd (1990:193) put it, the nearly "400-year history of attempts to suppress" Navajo—which continues today through passage of an English-only proposition in Arizona and with Navajo language discrimination on-the-job lawsuits in Page, Arizona (see Zachary 2005)—it probably should not be surprising to find that for many Navajos there is an oppositional linguistic ideology that sees *Bilagáana bizaad* "English" (whiteman's language) and *Diné bizaad* "Navajo" as wholly distinct codes that reveal telling attributes about their respective speakers. Here

Navajos seem to concur with Raymond Williams (1977:21) that "a definition of language is always, implicitly or explicitly, a definition of human beings in the world." Navajos have explained to me that "Navajo is verb based and English is noun based" (i.e., Navajos are concerned with process, and Anglos with things); "Navajo is more powerful spiritually, English is more powerful in the secular world" (i.e., Navajo is the language of ritual; English is the language of external power); "Navajo pronouns are connected like Navajos, English pronouns are isolated like Anglos" (i.e., since Navajo pronouns are bound morphemes this is similar to the ways Navajos are connected via clan relations; English has free morphemes and reflects the relative disconnectedness of Anglos); and "Navajo is more poetic than English" (i.e., Navajos are born poets; English is a "flat" language). In each case, Navajo is positively valorized and contrasted with a negatively viewed English. Let me add that, when Navajos claim that Navajos are "born poets" (as a number of Navajos did so claim), they are tapping into and linking with a wider discursive field that aestheticized and aestheticizes Navajos (see Bsumek 2008).

Many Navajos, though not all, see the ability to speak Navajo as essentially linked to being Navajo (see House 2002). The speaking of Navajo indexes Navajoness; but is also iconic of being Navajo. Language—or discursive choices of semiotically salient forms—become an icon of being Navajo (see Gal and Irvine 1995). That is, speaking Navajo becomes naturalized as "what Navajos do." Here one is reminded of the use of *Dinék'ehjí yałti'* (he/she talks in the Diné way). It is certainly naturalized as "what elder Navajos do." Such a belief, however, is now in tension with the perception that a number of younger Navajos do not speak Navajo or speak bilingual Navajo. This tension can be seen in contemporary Navajo poetry as well.

From Sapir (1921:196), through the work of Hoijer (1939) and Nicholas Mirkowich (1941), to more recent work by Young (1989), it has long been noted that Athabaskan languages and the Navajo language in particular are "highly resistant" to linguistic borrowing. As Young (1989:304) notes, "Spanish and English loanwords integrated into the language [Navajo] historically aggregate little more than fifty terms, all of them nouns." Navajo linguist Alyse Neundorf (1982) provides a brief primer on the ways to develop new words in Navajo, based on Navajo noun morphology. Many Navajos that I have spoken with are aware of the lack of lexical borrowing from English or Spanish into Navajo and consider this a point of linguistic pride. As it was explained to me on numerous occasions, Navajos can make their own words and such Navajo words will be more "descriptive" than, in most cases now, English. More recently, however, one Navajo performer I know has begun to incorporate a comedic skit into his performances highlighting "all the Spanish words" in Navajo. He singles out, for example, *'alóós* Sp. *arroz* (rice), *siláo* Sp. *soldado* (policeman), and *béeso* Sp. *peso* (money). He does not, however, include a discussion of the possible influence of English on the emergence of the grammaticization of tense in Navajo using the temporal adverb *ńt'éé* (then) (see Chee et al. 2004). Indeed, one Navajo consultant described the temporal adverb as a "past tense marker." It is possible, given that many Navajos have learned English language grammatical rules in schools, that "past tense" has been internalized as a feature of all languages. Be that as it may, lexical items are salient markers of language influence; grammaticization of tense to align more with English tense is less salient (see also Kroskrity 1993). It is, however, still the case that Navajos often valorize the Navajo language for its lack of lexical borrowing.

Navajo Language in Navajo Poetry

Luci Tapahonso is easily the most famous Navajo poet on the Navajo Nation. While I was doing fieldwork, Navajos often asked me what I was doing on the Navajo Nation. I would reply that I was studying Navajo poetry. Invariably, they would then recommend the work of Luci Tapahonso. This was true not just of Navajo educators, but of Navajos in general. One story can stand for many here. Once, while driving from Lukachukai to Flagstaff, Arizona, my car broke down. I was able to get a tow truck to tow me the two-and-a-half hours to Gallup, New Mexico, for repairs. During the drive, the tow-truck driver and I talked about a number of things. He explained, for example, some of the differences between how young Navajos speak Navajo compared to elders. We also talked about the rodeo and how he had competed in it and about traveling with it. When he asked me what I was doing on the Navajo Nation, I explained that I was studying Navajo poetry. He then recommended the poetry of Luci Tapahonso and the poem about her uncle. That poem is "Hills Brothers Coffee," and it is to that poem I wish to now turn.

Below I present five short excerpts from "Hills Brothers Coffee." The first is from Tapahonso's 1987 book of poetry *A Breeze Swept Through*. The second example is from Tapahonso's 1993 book of poetry *Sáanii Dahataał: The Women are Singing* (note the use of Navajo in the title). The third example is from Tapahonso's 1997 book of poetry *Blue Horses Rush In*. The fourth example is from a performance that Tapahonso gave in 1995 on "LINEbreak," a radio program produced in Buffalo, New York, that interviews various authors about their works. The fifth and final example is from a public performance I recorded in 2001 at Window Rock, Arizona, on the Navajo Nation before a largely Navajo audience (this event is described in more detail in the next chapter).

(1) My uncle is a small man
in Navajo we call him little father
my mother's brother.
(Tapahonso 1987:8)

(2) My uncle is a small man.
In Navajo, we call him, "shidá'í,"
my mother's brother.
(Tapahonso 1993:27)

(3) My uncle is a small man.
In Navajo, we call him "shidá'í,"
my mother's brother.
(Tapahonso 1997:97)

During her radio interview on LINEbreak, mentioned above, Tapahonso said, "So essentially what I did was keep the syntax the same. The sentence structure in Navajo is almost the complete opposite of English, so I'll read it. It's called 'Hills Brothers Coffee'":

(4) My uncle is a small man
In Navajo we call him shidá'í

> My mother's brother
> He doesn't know English
> But his name
> In the white way
> Is Tom Jim
> (LINEbreak, October 12, 1995, transcription by Webster)

At the Window Rock performance, Tapahonso prefaced her reading by saying, "I'm going read, uhm, a number of some poems that you've probably heard before, and that I've learned over the years, that I have to read or somebody's gonna sco:ld me [laughter]. So I'll start with 'Hills Brothers Coffee' because, uh, I think we could all use a cup of coffee now [laughter]. We'll just have to think about it. Uhm, 'Hills Brothers Coffee'":

(5) My uncle is a small ma:n
In Navajo we call him shidá'í yáázh
My mother's brother
He doesn't know English
But his na:me in the white way
Is
Tom
Jim
(Window Rock, July 18, 2001)

When Navajo poet Hershman John reflected on a Navajo poetry style, he commented that the use of Navajo words was an obvious feature of that style. That observation is certainly true today. It has not always been true. As I discussed in Chapter 1, the first poetry written by Navajos (that I have been able to locate), dates back to around 1933. That poetry was written entirely in English. In the late 1960s and early 1970s the Bureau of Indian Affairs published a literary journal of Native writers called *Arrow* as part of a larger effort by the BIA to use poetry as a means to teach English. As such, Navajos seldom used Navajo words in the poetry published by this journal. This changed. Nia Francisco published poetry in Navajo in 1977 in the journal *College English* (at the suggestion of David

McAllester) (1977b). But writing in Navajo and code-switching between English and Navajo in Navajo poetry really only took hold in the 1990s.

We can actually track that development in the work of Luci Tapahonso. In the 1987 version of "Hills Brothers Coffee," the Navajo kinship term *shidá'í* (my + maternal uncle) is not used. Instead there is an English gloss for the Navajo term. In the later versions the metalinguistic commentary includes that Navajo form and the English gloss has been dropped. Indeed, the later examples seem to implicitly posit a degree of incommensurability between Navajo and English. Tapahonso was at the vanguard of the use of Navajo words in Navajo poetry. This poem tracks the change rather accurately. It would be a mistake, then, to think that the use of Navajo words in Navajo poetry is in any way a given. There is a natural history to this poem and to the way that it has changed over time. Poetic traditions such as contemporary Navajo poetry do not appear de novo, rather they have histories, they are implicated in other genres, and they change over time.

"Hills Brothers Coffee" is also one of Tapahonso's signature poems. The example above of the young tow-truck driver speaks to that. As do, I might add, Tapahonso's comments at Window Rock in example 5. "Hills Brothers Coffee" is a fan favorite and for many in the audience it is an expected poem that she will perform. As she says, if she does not perform certain poems she will be "scolded." I should also add that in the Window Rock example she actually expands the Navajo that she uses. She says not just *shidá'í* (my maternal uncle), but *shidá'í yáázh* (my maternal uncle + little "my little maternal uncle"). The use of the affective *yáázh* (little) adds poignancy to the moment. The audience at Window Rock was largely Navajo, and it was pushing ten o'clock at night by the time she finally performed her poetry and this poem (the first poem she performed that night). There is a touch of the feelingful pragmatic iconicity to the use of the affective form. I am reminded of the comments an older Navajo woman once made to me, that her favorite expression in Navajo was when she called her infant grandchild *shiyázhí* (my little one). Note also that the form used in 2001 comes very close to capturing something of the English gloss from 1987. Part of Tapahonso's style, a style that Navajos commented on, concerned this poem and her use of Navajo and Navajo English (especially the use of rhetorical repetition).

Notice that Navajo syntax (canonically subject/object/verb [SOV]) is said to influence English here. This resonates with the statements a number of Navajo poets made about their poetry being composed first in Navajo and then partially transferred into English. As ethnomusicologist David McAllester (1980b:17) once pointed out, "word order is one of the linguistic clues to Navajo thinking." Tapahonso echoes that sentiment here.

Here is an "iconic" poem by Navajo poet Luci Tapahonso, a poem that many people (both Navajos and non-Navajos) associate with "the" Navajo poetry style and certainly Tapahonso's style. A part of this style is recognized as Tapahonso's use of Navajo English (as she describes in example 4 above) and with her use of Navajo words. But the Navajo word is not in the first published poem. It enters the poem in 1993, is then tweaked in 1995, and is then relatively codified by 1997. The result of this codification can be seen in the 1995 oral performance and in the expandability of Navajo in the 2001 oral performance. My point here is only to show that a poem that many consider an example of the dialogue of English and Navajo did not begin that way. In fact, when we look at it over time we see how Tapahonso has calibrated her own individual style.

With this natural history of *shidá'í yáázh* in Tapahonso's poem in mind, we can turn to recent scholarly work on the use of Navajo in Navajo poetry that is written predominately in English. Susan Brill (1997:135), for example, argues that, "the Navajo language is used in many of their stories to move their reader-listeners into the Navajo worlds of those stories, even when those stories are predominantly in English. The use of the Navajo language firmly roots the stories within a Navajo world—be that the world of the mythic, the everyday, or, in many cases, both." Further on, Brill (1997:138) argues, concerning the use of Navajo in the poetry of Navajo poet Luci Tapahonso, "when Luci Tapahonso shifts to the Navajo language in her writing, she does so as a means of inviting her listener-readers into the worlds of her stories and poems." Robin Riley Fast (2007:190), in critiquing Brill's view, argues, instead, that "Tapahonso's use of the language functions in part to remind non-Navajos that there are limits to our access and our welcome."

Given a number of conversations with a variety of Navajo poets and non-poets alike, I argue that Fast's perspective is more in alignment with a view espoused by Navajos that I know, that Navajo and English are at certain crucial and feelingful times incommensurate. A part of what the switch from Navajo to English suggests then, is the relative incommensurability between Navajo and English. This is made explicit in the following example from Luci Tapahonso's "They are Silent and Quick," which presents a portrait of constructed dialogue between older mother and middle-aged daughter:

(6) "What is it?" She asks. "What's wrong?"
There are no English words to describe this feeling.
"T'áá 'iighisíí biniina shil hóyéé," I say.
Because of it, I am overshadowed by aching
It is heaviness that surrounds me completely.
"Áko ayóó shił hóyéé.'" We are silent.
(Tapahonso 1993:14)

The poem is meant as a slice of contemporary Navajo life (they are speaking on the phone). The use of Navajo here suggests intimacy between mother and daughter. But note that it also comments directly on the relationship between English and Navajo. Here Tapahonso explicitly posits (a form of metasemantic commentary) that English is deficient in respect to the expression of emotions. The Navajo term *hóyéé*, which we can gloss as "terrible, tragic" is not "translated" by Tapahonso. The English glossings are, by implication, incomplete renditions of the Navajo expression.

In discussions with Navajos about the nature of translation between Navajo and English, some Navajos have explained to me that Navajo place names cannot be translated into English because the Navajo forms are the original forms and are connected to the ancestors. In replicating and reinforcing this linguistic ideology we find that a number of Navajo poets do not translate Navajo place names into English-dominant language poems. Here is an example from Tohe's "In Dinétah." Note that the title also contains the Navajo term for the traditional Navajo homeland.

(7) Sis naajiní rising to the east,
Tsoodził rising to the south,

> Dook'o'osłííd rising to the west,
> Dibé Nítsaa rising to the north
> (Tohe 2002:100)

The representation of sacred mountains in an east to north trajectory also reproduces ideals of proper speech and is a recurrent feature in much Navajo poetry. As we saw in the first chapter, the use of Navajo place names in English language poetry is also a recurrent feature of Navajo poetry. It aids in a metasemiotic stereotype articulated most explicitly by Tohe when she told an audience in Illinois that, "we'll always use our own names for the places on our homeland." It also matches with the account of Navajo linguistic practices given by Mirkowich (1941). Mirkowich (1941:314) describes how Navajos will use Navajo place names— such as Be-il-dil-da-si-nil (in the current orthography Bee'eldííldahsinil, bee'eldííl- [a ringing sound is made] dah [up] si- perfective -nil [plural objects sit])—in place of English town names—such as Albuquerque— that Navajos consider to be within traditional Navajo territory. However, in everyday practice and in Navajo poetry, Navajos do use English language place names for places within the traditional Navajo homeland. Note that the Navajo name for Albuquerque as discussed in Chapter 2 draws attention to the ringing of bells that were used on the Rio Grande to signal boats transporting people across the river (see Wilson 1995:2). Embedded within this place name is the ideophone dííl (ringing).

A number of Navajo poets use some version of the phrase 'ałk'idą́ą́' jiní (long ago, they say) in the openings of their poetry. This form is a genre framing device that indexes that a certain kind of hane' (narrative) is about to take place. In discussing 'ałk'idą́ą́' jiní, Denetdale (2007:43) notes, "this way of beginning a story gives an indication of how old the story is, for it has passed through many generations since time immemorial. The phrase reflects an important measure of responsibility that the listener takes on to see that the story continues to be relayed." Here are two examples, one from "In Dinétah" by Tohe (2002:100), which recounts a Navajo-centric history of the Navajo, and one from "The Dark World" by Hershman John (2007:47), which recounts certain events from the origin of the Navajos:

(8) Ałkidą́ą́' adajiní nít'ę́ę́'
    They say long ago in time immemorial:
    the stories say we emerged...
    (Tohe 2002:100)

(9) Ałk'idídą́ą́' jiní
    Listen and remember...
    (John 2007:47)

When I asked Hershman John about the use of the Navajo form, he told me it was "necessary." It was necessary in the sense that this is how Navajo stories of long ago need to begin. It was also how his grandmother always began such stories. Such uses indexically link the Navajo poem with Navajo narrative traditions and here with a specific narrator, creating an intertextual linkage between poetry and oral genres. They also reinforce ideas about proper ways of speaking, creating a metapragmatic example of the proper way to begin stories of long ago: Navajo stories of long ago begin with *'ałk'idą́ą́' jiní*.

Contemporary conversations in Navajo also use *'ałk'idą́ą́'* (or its phonological variants) to index traditional genres of "long ago." For example, Field (2007:641) provides the following example of a stretch of conversation between two 40-year-old Navajo men discussing high school. Field labels the two men E and T, and we pick up the conversation at line 6 with E speaking. I have simplified Field's transcription system. Glossings are given below the line in Navajo and italicized. *Eeei* is a discourse marker that indexes a playful stance by the speaker.

(10) E   eeei   6
         éí t'áá'aní   7
         it's true
         Asdzáníí łah shich'į́ dahighaa nt'éé.   8
         a woman was interested in me

     T   mm   9

     E   ahot'élá   10
         it is/was that way

T	nt'éé	11
	it was	
E	éí ałkidą́ą́	12
	long time ago	
	t'aadii highschoolyę́ędą́ą́	13
	still in high school back then	

In line 12, E casts his remarks into the distant past by invoking the formulaic form *ałkidą́ą́*. In the lines just preceding line 6, there had been much laughter. T and E are now in their forties and this device suggests, humorously I believe, the temporal distance between their lives today and their lives in high school. As Field notes, E is now in a wheelchair (Field 2007:641). The use of *ałkidą́ą́* here is ironic. However, that such formulaic forms are still used in contemporary discourse indicates the saliency of such poetic devices. Note also, in line 13, that E combines a Navajo suffix *-yę́ędą́ą́* (back then) with an English content noun—high school. This is an example of Navlish.

Another example of the use of poetry to articulate a metapragmatic ideal can be found in Norla Chee's (2001:24-25) "A Navajo Sing." Here is the relevant passage:

(11) Hataałii sings over the patient
Someone whispers, in English

"Diné bizaad bee yádaałti'"

This is an EnemyWay.
(Chee 2001:25)

Chee (2001:25) provides a glossing for the Navajo phrase in a footnote as "speak Navajo." The admonition expressed in this poem is reminiscent of Kroskrity's earlier discussion of the principle of strict compartmentalization. During an Enemyway ceremony one is to use Navajo and not English. This poem thus presents a metapragmatic ideal, which aides in reinforcing a metasemiotic stereotype.

There is another common metalinguistic commentary that again has been valorized as an icon of difference between not just Navajo and

English, but rather between Navajos and Euro-Americans. I was told more than once by Navajo consultants that Navajo does not have any "swear words" or "vulgarity." Tapahonso explains it this way to a popular regional magazine, "We believe that the wind comes in at the top of your head when your hair begins to grow, and every time you speak, it is the wind that speaks. So speech is sacred, and you are very careful about how you say things. The Navajo language has no cuss words and no profanity" (Baldinger 1992:35). Navajo storyteller and poet Sunny Dooley explained this linguistic ideology to anthropologist Maureen Schwarz:

> In Navajo, when you say it, it will happen. That's why they tell you, you shouldn't talk nonsense, you shouldn't just blah blah blah, you know. You just can't be talking any old way.... You can't be saying things any old way, meaning negatively, you know.... Like on television, you know, you hear people tell each other off, you know, and they don't think anything whatsoever about the power of their words. You know, and maybe English is not that powerful. I don't know. But it goes all the ways back to the fact that in Navajo, you can't swear. You can't say the "D" word, you can't say the "F" word, you can't say the "S" word. We don't have those words in my language.... We believe that when we say it, when it comes out of our mouths, it is like little, little bubbles, you know, that put into motion all kinds of events. And that's why it's vitally important in Navajo to be well spoken, to be speaking well all the time.
> (Schwarz 2003:10)

English, on the other hand, some Navajos pointed out is full of vulgarity. In fact, some Navajos that I knew made a point of switching into English to curse. This was another distinction between Navajo and English. English was vulgar and Navajo was not.

The use of vulgarity in Navajo poetry, in either English or Navajo, is relatively rare (but also somewhat poet dependent). Here is an example from a poem by Rex Lee Jim of English vulgarity in contemporary Navajo poetry. The poem is titled *Tó Háálį́* ("Spring") and here is the relevant passage:

(12) Tsodizin bee yádaati' yę́ęgóó
"Fuck you" t'éí dadiits'a'
Nahasdzáán shimá ha'níigo
Tóyisdzáán shimá ha'níigo
K'é bee yádaati' yę́ęgóó
"You want a good fuck?
Go see Sue or Mama,"
T'éí bee ak'ida ashchį́.
(Jim 1998:13)

Here is Rex Lee Jim's English version:

(13) Where prayers were offered
People scream "fuck you"
Where people prayed
"Earth, my mother,"
"Water woman, my mother"
Where people related to the place,
"You want a good fuck?
Go see Sue or Mama,"
Are scribbled onto metal barrels.
(Jim 1998:12)

According to Jim, in a conversation I had with him about this poem, the poem describes the actual conditions of the place *Tó Háálí* that Jim is discussing. *Tó Háálí* is a place name, and the poem describes the graffiti that has been scrawled near this place as well as the kinds of things one can hear there. Given that English is the predominant language of literacy among Navajos, it is not unlikely that the language of the graffiti would be in English.

The use of the English terms reflects a view that "white people" or *bilagáana* do not use proper speech. As Basso (1979) pointed out for Western Apache beliefs about the speech habits of white people, white people do not know how to speak properly. The English forms contrast with the Navajo prayers in the above example. The prayer in this poem shows the parallelism associated with prayers in Navajo (the glossing is mine and is meant to highlight the parallelism in the Navajo):

(14) Nahasdzáán shimá ha'níigo
    Tóyisdzáán shimá ha'níigo
    (Jim 1998:13)

Earth, my mother it is told about
Water woman, my mother it is told about

The shift between this formal parallel structured prayer and the vulgarity that both proceeds and follows it creates a heightened contrast between markedly different ways of speaking. The prayer structure is a model of proper speaking. The vulgarity in English is a model of improper ways of speaking. Juxtaposed as they are, the contrast is striking. The switch to English here is thus naturalized: English is the language of swearing and graffiti, and Navajo is the language of prayer. This recalls the comments a Navajo consultant made to me concerning the fact that English was more powerful in the secular domain and Navajo was more powerful in the sacred domain. In Jim's poem we see an expression of a view of Navajo as the language of prayer and English as a vulgar language. When Jim performs this poem before children or on KTNN he is reinforcing a view about both English and Navajo. It appears natural, for many Navajos, to switch to English to use vulgarity.

This poem reinforces a metasemiotic stereotype about the differences between languages and speakers. Recall Dooley's discussion of the lack of vulgarity in Navajo. There the lack of vulgarity is ascribed to the respect that Navajos have for proper ways of speaking and to the sacredness of speaking. Speaking is "powerful" and can cause things to happen and thus care must be taken in speaking. English and Navajo are again represented as oppositional.

Rather than see the use of Navajo as an invitation into a Navajo world (a la Brill 1997), I argue that such uses aid in reinforcing a linguistic ideology that many Navajos expressed to me in one form or another as the inherent incommensurability between English and Navajo. Poems by

Tapahonso, Tohe, and other Navajo poets are not just read by outsiders, they are also performed by the poets on the Navajo Nation before largely Navajo audiences. In such performances, then, attitudes about the form, function, and use of the Navajo language are circulated by Navajo poets to Navajo audiences. Encoded within many of these poems then are ideas about the importance of place names in Navajo, the inability of English to express certain ideas and emotions, and metapragmatic commentary on the contexts in which Navajo is not just appropriate but required. Such performances are often displays of proper ways of speaking.

Navajo poetry and the Navajo linguistic forms used, then, become both forms of traditionalization (Bauman 2004) and an affective register (Irvine 1990). Here Navajo acts as an affective code, indexing intimacy and locality. Through displays of the feelingful evocation of linguistic forms, such as *hóyéé* or ideophony, Navajo can act as an affective register, linking the use of Navajo with emotionally salient expressivity. Likewise, through the use of genre-signaling devices such as *'ałk'idą́ą́'*, they connect with a larger "traditional" stock of knowledge. Bauman (2004) has pointed to interesting ways of thinking about how narratives can take on the authority of tradition. Bauman (2004) describes the various poetic devices used in Icelandic narratives about magic poems and the ways they traditionalize a specific narrative. These poetic devices implicate stretches of discourse within the words of others, within tradition. Here I follow Jason Jackson (2005:279) and argue that "tradition is a symbol (a meaning, a feeling, a construction) that people form in the present about the nature of themselves and their beliefs in light of a particular understanding of a significant past." In this respect, tradition can be evoked through feelingful uses of language. That is, poetic language can create feelingful iconicity, where tradition transcends the moment-bound, real-time utterance and creates a sense of simultaneity with that tradition (Samuels 2004b). The past and the present are merged through poetic language. This is the positive valorization of an image of the Navajo language, a language that indexically links with tradition and with feelingfulness. For a language like Navajo that is threatened, this is a potentially empowering use of Navajo.

There is more, however: Navajo poets' use of Navajo language also creates specific views of the Navajo language from a particular vantage point. It creates an "imagined" Navajo language. As Bakhtin (1981:295) noted:

> The actively literary linguistic consciousness at all times and everywhere (that is, in all epochs of literature historically available to us) comes upon "language," and not language. Consciousness finds itself inevitably facing the necessity of *having to choose a language*. With each literary-verbal performance, consciousness must actively orient itself amidst heteroglossia, it must move in and occupy a position for itself within it, it chooses, in other words, a "language." [emphasis in original]

That is, Navajo poets, through their use of certain kinds of Navajo, aid in circulating a certain presentation of "the Navajo language." Far from being merely the use of Navajo in English-language-dominant poetry, such forms are implicated in the sociolinguistic dynamics of Navajo linguistic practices. Rather than merely connecting to some "Navajo framework," Navajo poets' use of Navajo also replicates a metasemiotic stereotype of the Navajo language. This image of the Navajo language is often contrasted with "the English language." As one Navajo once explained to me, "to say one word like in English language has a word for everything, but in Diné bizaad [Navajo language], that is why it's been said that Navajo language is very descriptive." The Navajo consultant was trying to explain to me the difference between English (which has a word for everything) and Navajo (which uses descriptive phrases that are often created on the spot to describe things). However, given a Navajo propensity for punning, even English words can have multiple meanings when reanalyzed into Navajo. The sociolinguistic situation, however, is more complicated than the image of the Navajo language often presented by Navajo poets. It is to that sociolinguistic complexity that I now turn.

Linguistic Diversity and Bilingual Navajo

Reichard (1945) wrote a short piece a number of years ago discussing some of the internal, dialectal divisions in Navajo. Muriel Saville-Troike (1974) also wrote of some of the phonological distinctions within and across

Southern Athabaskan languages (of which Navajo is a member). However, there has been an overarching trend in Navajo language research away from discussions of dialect diversity or sociolinguistic dynamics. Discussions of the relationship between Navajo and English or the diversity within Navajo have not been major focuses of Navajo language research. This is what Judith Irvine and Susan Gal (2000:38) describe as "erasure," which they define as, "the process in which ideology, in simplifying the sociolinguistic field, renders some persons or activities (or sociolinguistic phenomena) invisible." For example, according to Saville-Troike (1974:74), while it is often assumed that there is a general /t/->/k/ shift from Western Southern Athabaskan languages to Eastern Southern Athabaskan language, there is evidence for an internal dialectal /t/-/k/ variation in Navajo (thus *táá* and *káá* [three]). As Saville-Troike (1974:82) concludes, "one definite statement which *can* be made at this time is that no homogenous Navajo speech community has ever existed in the Southwestern United States" [emphasis in original].

Here I wish to suggest something of the uses of Navajo-English code-mixing in contemporary Navajo society as well as some of the forms of that code-mixing (see Schaengold 2004 for a fuller accounting). A number of years ago, Kip Canfield (1980) noted examples of what he called, "Navajo-English code-mixing." No less than Robert Young and William Morgan (1987:7) have this to say about the use of "mixing" Navajo and English:

> Bilingualism has grown as never before, and there is a distinct trend on the part of bilingual speakers to mix the languages. The Tribal Council has generally insisted upon linguistic purity, sometimes stopping speakers in the middle of their discourse to insist that they only speak one language at a time, but children and Navajo radio announcers, as well as bilingual speakers, generally tend to insert words and phrases from English into their Navajo language discourse.

I want to point out that Young and Morgan, the foremost Navajo lexicographers, echo the discussion concerning linguistic purity discussed above and they suggest something of the contexts in which this "mixing" of languages occurs. They, however, do not provide examples (it is also unclear if they are referring to "code-switching" or "code-mixing" or both). Susan Foster et al. (1989) describe examples of bilingual Navajo (code-mixing) used in spoken discourse among Navajo schoolchildren (they term it "lexically extended Navajo"). Foster et al. (15) go on to argue that, concerning bilingual Navajo, they have "significant evidence of its use by fluent bilingual speakers to convince us that this is a productive bilingual register." Here are examples from Kip Canfield (1980:219). Code-mixed forms have been bolded throughout. Unfortunately, Canfield provides little contextual information.

(15) **na'iish-crash** lá
1:pass out   EMPH
I'm about to pass out!

(16) shił **naweasy**
1:with   3:sick
I feel sick

(17) Swimming asht'į'
1:do/be
I'm swimming.

In example 10, we already saw an instance from a conversation between two 40-year-old Navajo men also documented by Field (2007:461). Example 18 below was documented by Field (2001:256) in a family setting. It is part of a larger triadic directive routine—a traditional Navajo way of making a directive—where a mother (M) is attempting to get her son (Ronald=R) to pick up toys. It is after the use of bilingual Navajo toward Ronald (the rest of the transcript is in English), that the mother engages a triadic directive for her daughter (Noreen) to aid Ronald (for a fuller discussion see Field 2001:256). The bilingual Navajo seems the last stop before the triadic directive (done in English). It is as if the mother switches stances when she uses the bilingual Navajo form. It is not just a triadic directive, but a change in footing from an English stance to a bilingual Navajo stance. She also repeats the bilingual Navajo phrase after Ronald requests clarification about the form just used. The mother repeats the bilingual Navajo form exactly. When the bilingual Navajo form fails to elicit a positive response from Ronald, the mother shifts again to English and turns her orientation to Noreen. We pick up the conversation at line 13 of Field's transcript (I have simplified the transcript).

(18) M: hurry up, pick up all those toys.   13
     R: no.   14
     M: box bii'naanijááh.   15
          put them back in the box   16
     R: huh?   17
     M: box bii'naanijááh.   18
     R: no.   19

I recorded example 19 at a poetry performance during field work in 2000–2001 (Webster 2006c:235). Let me add that the poet then performed poetry that code-switched from English into Navajo, but that there were no examples of bilingual Navajo in the actual poems performed. It is not the case that Navajo poets are unaware of bilingual Navajo (see also below), it is instead the case that the language they choose to use in their poetry is not bilingual Navajo.

(19)   I learned this from **my-nálí**
       paternal grandparent

Example 20 is from Navajo humorist Vincent Craig (such examples can be heard on KTNN [see Klain and Peterson 2001:126]) and it comes from a long ballad titled "Old Chi'zee" that was "recorded live at San Juan College," Farmington, New Mexico (Craig 1998). The lines below come after Old Chi'zee (a Navajo rapscallion) makes his entrance at the rodeo and has impressed "the ladies" (the transcription is mine):

(20)   And he tipped his hat
       he winked his eyes
       and the ladies said

"o:h **shi:ha:t**" [laughter]
1stPOSS heart
my heart

In looking at the linguistic features of these examples, we see that in example 15, the English lexical item "crash" has been integrated into Navajo with the use of a Navajo first person prefix and the emphatic particle *lá*. In example 16, the English form "queasy" has had the third person prefix affixed to it and it has been integrated into the clause. In both cases the English form has been inserted in place of a Navajo verb stem. In example 17, "an English verb is used in conjunction with a Navajo 'helping' verb" (Canfield 1980:219). Example 18 finds the English noun being used in a Navajo clause, and in example 19 the Navajo noun *-nálí* takes the English possessive "my" (in Navajo, kinship terms are part of a small set of nouns that are inalienable and thus require a constant possessor). In example 20, the Navajo possessive prefix is attached to the English noun. This example is quite well known; Craig has performed his comedy routines on the Navajo Nation since at least the 1970s and *shiheart* is a signature line for him. When Craig (as well as other Navajos) uses *shiheart*, it often takes on the nonliteral meaning of "my love." There is an intimacy, a playfulness, and a localizing quality to the uses of *shiheart* by Craig. Certainly the audience laughed after the use of *shiheart*. I used it as a prompt when discussing bilingual Navajo with Navajo consultants.

Schaengold (2003, 2006) has described some of the linguistic features of bilingual Navajo (such as examples 15–20). In all, Schaengold (2004:176–180) provides sixty examples of bilingual Navajo. Bilingual Navajo is based on the grammatical structures of Navajo and the content forms of Navajo English (a distinct dialect spoken by many Navajos; see Bartelt 1981; Leap 1993b) and English. It is a mixed code according to Schaengold (2003:250). I should add, however, that example 19 above has a Navajo content word and an English possessive pronoun and may fall outside Schaengold's definition of bilingual Navajo. Let me add that some of my consultants have spoken of bilingual Navajo as Navlish (sometimes also as Navglish). An older consultant who self-identifies as a bilingual speaker did use the term "talk bilingual" to describe what he does and would not use Navlish to describe it. The term Navlish, of course, is a productive pun based on Spanglish and echoed in Apaglish, an Apache-English code-mixing style found in San Carlos and Bylas, Arizona (see Samuels 2001:290). For comparative purposes, here is an example of Apache-English code-mixing from Apache linguist Britton Goode (b.1911–d.1981) concerning place names and presented by David Samuels (the bilingual form is bolded; *-gee* is a locative enclitic and this example is similar to examples of bilingual Navajo further on):

(21) Néé ałdó,' **San Carlosgee** Apache ndliinií ałdó' dát'éhé nohwi ni' lék'eh ni.'
We also the Apaches **at San Carlos** also had land all over at one time.
(Samuels 2001:286)

The example from Samuels suggests that the use of Southern Athabaskan morphology (here a clitic) on English-content words is not restricted to Navajos.

Schaengold (2003, 2004) provides a number of examples of bilingual Navajo, showing the uses of both nouns and verbs in bilingual Navajo. Here are two examples that will be relevant to the next section. Schaengold presents these examples, however, as largely decontextualized from their discursive contexts.

(22) **Town-góó** déyá
town-toward 1st.sing.go
I'm going **to town**.
(Schaengold 2003:244)

(23) **Bi-dlasses** ni-zhóní
3rd.poss. -glasses 3rd.sing. is pretty
Her glasses are pretty.
(Schaengold 2003:244)

In example 22, the enclitic *-góó* is attached to the English noun "town" giving it the sense of "to town" or "toward town." In example 23, the third person possessive prefix bi- is attached to the English noun "glasses" (modified to conform to Navajo phonotactics).

Schaengold (2003:248) also presents examples culled from Daniel McLaughlin's (1992) ethnography of Navajo literacy practices. These examples suggest that Navajos use bilingual Navajo in written utterances as well as in oral utterances. Here are the two examples that Schaengold cites from McLaughlin (1992: example 24 below is drawn from page 143 and example 25 appears on page 27). I have bolded the relevant forms again. The first example is from a personal note, and the second example is from a chapter announcement.

(24) Néínídzáago índída, hazhó'ó ni hodeeshniih. lady-to-lady **talkgo**. T'á'ash áko.
I'll tell you all the details, lady-to-lady, when you get back, OK?
(Schaengold 2003:248)

(25) Public Meeting deiil'aah k'ad **Thursdaygo**, naadiin táá'góó yoolkááł góne' . . .
We'll have a public meeting this coming Thursday the twenty-third at five o'clock . . .
(Schaengold 2003:248)

In both examples, the subordinating enclitic -*go* has been added to the English noun phrase. While there is not a great deal of contextual information here, the use of bilingual Navajo in example 24, seems to suggest a sense of intimacy.

Literate uses of bilingual Navajo are not uncommon. Walking through Diné College (Tsaile Campus) in autumn of 2007, I noticed several announcements and flyers with bilingual Navajo being used. For example, one flyer had *Learning Centerdi* (Learning Center-di [at]) written on it. Here we see a locative postpositional enclitic (-*di*) attached to "Learning Center." Note that -*di* (at) contrasts with another locative enclitic -*gi* (at). The -*di* form indicates that the Learning Center is physically more distant than it would be if it had been marked with -*gi*. Indeed, the Learning Center was housed in a different building than where the flyer was posted (one also suspects that since the flyer could go anywhere the distal locative enclitic was more appropriate).

During the fall of 2000, politically active Navajos had been posting signs along the roads of the Navajo Nation concerning the impending vote in Arizona on Proposition 203, "English for the Children." Such phrases as "Dooda prop 203" (no prop 203) or "Save Diné bizaad" (Save the Navajo language) appeared on a number of handmade signs. One sign had what I now take to be an example of bilingual Navajo, written on it: "Doo Prop 203 Da." In Navajo, negation can be done by circumfixing the affixes *doo-* and *-da* to the form that is to be negated. This sign was placed near the Tsaile Trading Post, which abuts Diné College. In its use, it highlights a feature of Navajo—negation through circumfixing—that is not readily available in English. Contrary to the other signs, this sign suggested the combining of English and Navajo, disrupting, however minimally, their discreteness.

Below is an example from a Navajo Christian hymn titled *Jesusgo Shí Doo* (I'd rather have Jesus). I have bolded the bilingual Navajo examples. Note that the bilingual Navajo form (Jesus-go [with Jesus]) is in the title of the hymn. The translation is mine.

(26) **Jesusgo** éí shí doo, óola dooda,
Jesusgo éí shí doo, yódí biláahgo,
Jesusgo éí shí doo, kéyah dooda
(Diglot Favorites n.d.:18)

I'd rather be **with Jesus**, than gold
I'd rather be **with Jesus**, than an excess of wealth
I'd rather be **with Jesus**, than land

The hymnal and the attendant tape with the hymns on it were purchased by me at the Gallup Flea Market (Gallup, New Mexico), in March of 2001, from a Navajo man who had a stand with a number of Navajo/English Christian hymnals and tapes for sale. David Samuels (2006) has noted that certain Christian denominations among the Western Apache are reluctant to "translate" some of the names of Biblical figures (including Jesus) into Apache. That seems to be the case here as well. Here Jesus has not been translated into Navajo, but rather a code-mixed form is used in this hymn. This pattern, of using the word Jesus, is used throughout the hymnal. There is a Navajo term for Jesus that I am familiar with—*Doodaatsaahii* (the one who does not die)—that was not used in the hymnal. As with the desire not to translate certain Navajo forms into English, this is an example of a resistance to translate English lexical items (proper nouns) into Navajo.

As an aside, at the Chinle, Arizona, Kingdom Hall (in the middle of the Navajo Nation), the Jehovah's Witnesses have a sign up that phonologically incorporates Jehovah into Navajo as *Jiihóvah*, but uses a bilingual Navajo form for possession on bi-Kingdom Hall (their Kingdom Hall): *Jiihóvah Yádahalne'í bi Kingdom Hall* (Jehovah Witness their Kingdom Hall). On their website they also have examples of bilingual Navajo: *Jiihóvah Yádahalne'í Bibee Bóhólníihii **biWeb Site*** (bi- 3rd person Possessive + Web Site [their website]; Jehovah Witness their duty [trust], their Web Site) (Watch Tower Website 2006). In this case, the Navajo form attaches to "new" technology. It is unlikely, however, that Navajos actually pronounce *Jiihóvah* the way the Jehovah's Witnesses write it. In English, while many words are spelled with an "h" at the end, this sound is not normally pronounced. The English phoneme /h/ does not occur word final. In Navajo, on the other hand, word final /h/ is pronounced, as in *gah* (rabbit).

In the summer and fall of 2007, I elicited examples of bilingual Navajo from three Navajo poets when discussing the topic of this chapter with them. I asked them if they knew of examples of bilingual Navajo, and suggested *shiheart* as an example. My use of "bilingual Navajo" was corrected to "Navlish" by these poets. One male Navajo poet immediately offered *shigirl* (my girl). Later when I discussed bilingual Navajo with two female poets, one offered *ship^{h}ant* (my pants) and then the other poet, with a nice poetic sense, added, *shihat* (my hat). The second form, *shihat*, echoes with the aspirated first form [p^h] and the word final voiceless alveolar stop /t/ while the vowel quality (nasal) is held constant. For these poets, knowledge of Navlish was readily accessible and potentially productive for punning. Yet it was not something that typically found its way into their poetry.

In the above examples we see the ways that Navajo and English can be intermingled morphologically and as a code-mixed Navajo/English or, as Schaengold terms it, bilingual Navajo, or, as some of my consultants called it, Navlish. Schaengold (2003) then goes on to describe some of the social contexts in which bilingual Navajo is used. She notes, for example, that younger Navajos may be fluent in Navajo, Navajo English, and bilingual Navajo. Younger Navajos tend not to use bilingual Navajo with older speakers, "for fear of being publicly corrected and shamed" (Schaengold 2003:249). As Schaengold (2003:249–250) further argues:

> In the Navajo community speaking this non-standard Navajo language is aptly called "talking bilingual," as understanding and speaking implies access to at least some English and some Navajo. Although there is probably a continuum of codes available in the mixed language, the speakers categorize them into a standard usage and a non-standard usage or vernacular code, and switch from Standard Navajo to Bilingual Navajo according to interlocutor and setting.

I should add that some elder Navajos will critique the "standard" Navajo of younger speakers as well. Finally, Schaengold (2006) argues against a strict purist view of language that would exclude recognition of the linguistic resources currently being used by young Navajos.

It is clear from the examples presented by Canfield that bilingual Navajo dates at least to the 1970s (which roughly coincides with the emergence of written poetry in Navajo). It seems likely, based on the examples presented by McLaughlin and the examples I encountered around the Navajo Nation, that bilingual Navajo is both an oral and a written practice. One can also hear bilingual Navajo regularly on KTNN (which broadcasts in both English and Navajo; see Klain and Peterson 2000). KTNN is the only radio station that has a signal strong enough to be heard throughout the Navajo Nation and, for many Navajos without access to television or the Internet, it provides crucial information concerning current events on the Navajo Nation. The use of bilingual Navajo on KTNN suggests the wide circulation that bilingual Navajo has; almost all Navajos that I have met listen to KTNN periodically throughout the day. Indeed, Navajos that I know who no longer live on the Navajo Nation listen to KTNN via the Internet (http://www.ktnnonline.com). One can also, then, find examples of bilingual Navajo on the Internet.

It seems clear from Schaengold's discussion of the social contexts of the use of bilingual Navajo that it is a devalued expressive option (see Schaengold 2003:251; see also Klain and Peterson 2000 on how this plays out concerning KTNN). I have also heard older Navajos critique the bilingual speech of younger Navajos, and I have heard stories about such criticisms from those who were criticized (see T. Lee 2007). Yet in my experiences on the Navajo Nation, bilingual Navajo appears relatively common both among younger Navajos and Navajos closer to their middle to late thirties. This tension may be behind the comments an older Navajo consultant made concerning the fact that Navajo was now very much influenced by both English and, as he said, *Naakaii* (Mexican), especially as it was spoken by younger people. This is in stark contrast to the situation on Easter Island as described by Makihara (2007). There the syncretic Rapa Nui is valued, and the purist Rapa Nui is restricted. Among Navajos, it is bilingual Navajo that is not highly valued, though like syncretic Rapa Nui, it is widely used in communicative practices (outside contemporary poetry). We can concur with Foster et al. (1989:15) that bilingual Navajo is a "productive bilingual register" among Navajos; it is just not a highly valued register.

Bilingual Navajo in Navajo Poetry

Given that bilingual Navajo is a part of the sociolinguistic scene on the Navajo Nation, and given its relative persistence and its use in writing, can we find examples of bilingual Navajo in the poetry of Navajo poets? The answer to this question raises interesting issues about the kind of language that Navajo poets are presenting through their poetry, the ways they legitimize certain linguistic forms and obscure other forms. The use of bilingual Navajo in written published Navajo poetry is practically nonexistent. For purposes here, I have focused on four venues of Navajo poetry. I have chosen them because they are public displays of Navajo language use and most of the books are well known and readily available.

I have looked at all the books of poetry authored by Navajos that I can locate.

1. *Arrow*, which was a creative writing journal produced by the Bureau of Indian Affairs from 1969–74 and edited by Terry Allen. This journal featured Native American creative writing, including Navajo authors. There are a few examples of Navajo lexical items found in this journal (see Webster 2006b for an example). Bilingual Navajo appears to be completely absent.

2. *The Navajo Times*. Bilingual Navajo was little used in the poetry published in the Navajo language page in the *Navajo Times* in the mid-1990s. In fact, in a survey I did of Navajo poetry published in it from 1962 until 2005, it was only in the Navajo language page that two examples of bilingual Navajo were found. Both examples consisted of the use of the subordinating enclitic *-go* (at) (see example 18). I looked at the *Navajo Times* because it circulates widely on the Navajo Nation and is, for many Navajos, the paper of record. Besides the Navajo language page, it also periodically publishes poems in the Letters section, the Education section, or the Entertainment section.

3. Books of poetry. I looked at 26 books of Navajo poetry published by well-known university presses and the like, as well as at small-scale publications and self-published books of poetry (see Appendix A for a list of the authors and the books surveyed). Twenty-two were either authored by or edited by a Navajo poet or poets. Here I have sought comprehensiveness. Three volumes (Allen, Evers, and Milton) were edited by non-Navajos but include poetry by Navajos in their collections. Terry Allen was an important figure in the *Arrow* series and taught creative writing to early and influential Navajo poet Blackhorse Mitchell (his poetry is in both the Allen and Milton collections). The Larry Evers collection is an important document in the emergence and recognition of Native American literature in the Southwest and includes work by Nia Francisco. Anna Lee Walters is Native American, but is not Navajo; however, she is married to a Navajo and lives on the Navajo Nation. Her edited volume

also contains the work of Navajo poets. The edited volumes provide a degree of time depth. Let me be clear here: in a survey of 26 books of Navajo poetry, by both established and less-established Navajo poets, there were only three examples of bilingual Navajo found in a total of three poems. Two of those poems were published in presses located outside the Navajo Nation (UCLA and Minnesota Historical Society), while the third was published by Cool Runnings (a music store and music production company on the Navajo Nation; Rutherford Ashley was a long time employee at Cool Runnings).

4. *TerraIncognita: An Alternative Dine' Zine*, a short-lived creative zine published by Rick Abasta in Window Rock, Arizona, during 2005, that featured poetry, short-fiction, and art work (in a number of vernacular orthographies the apostrophe after the vowel indicates high tone; see also example 31). There were no examples of bilingual Navajo in the zine. This was a locally controlled zine, and I had hoped it would yield examples of bilingual Navajo. It did not. Given the ability of bilingual Navajo to index intimacy, I had suspected that more locally controlled venues might have more examples. I was wrong.

To put this in perspective, let me discuss briefly a specific poet. Luci Tapahonso does not use a single example of bilingual Navajo in any of her published poetry that I have been able to locate. On the other hand, the three books of poetry published by Tapahonso listed in Appendix A all have multiple examples of code-switching from English-dominant poetry into Navajo (her code-switching is also the topic of Brill 1997 and Fast 2007). Code-switching into Navajo from English language poetry is quite common. Almost any book of Navajo poetry will include multiple examples. Navajos that I have interviewed recognize such code-switching as a part of Navajo poetry style. The same cannot be said for bilingual Navajo. Its lack of use stands in stark contrast to the much more common use of code-switching into Navajo from an English-dominant poem. In examples 5–9 and 11, there are ten lines that include some use of Navajo (which is a trifle of the total number of lines with Navajo in English-language dominant poetry). That doubles all the bilingual Navajo examples.

Or consider Rutherford (Ford) Ashley, who provides one of the three examples of bilingual Navajo in books of poetry authored by Navajos. Ashley has not taken formal classes in writing Navajo (see Webster 2006b). In his book, *Heart Vision 2000* (Ashley 2001), which came out while I was doing fieldwork, there are over twenty examples of code-switching into Navajo. Including, in his vernacular orthography, such quintessential Navajo phrases as *Sa'aghnaghai bi'ke'hozhogho* (long life and happiness) (Ashley 2001:291). In Ashley's book, there is one example of bilingual Navajo (see example 25).

Let me add that while vernacular orthographies, such as Ashley's, are often criticized by various Navajo educators I spoke with, Navajo poets continue to use these vernacular orthographies. Rex Lee Jim, for example, was often complimented by Navajo educators I spoke with for his writing in Navajo and then criticized for not writing Navajo "correctly." However, the use of vernacular orthographies persists because they both index the affective and feelingful relationship to language and reproduce an idealized Navajo that is wholly distinct from English. Written Navajo does not, in the hands of poets, yet produce a singular vision of the form of written Navajo.

It was only in 2001 that books of poetry written by Navajos included bilingual Navajo in their poetry (Ashley 2001; Chee 2001). Of the single-author books of Navajo poetry published since 2001 (there are five), there are no examples of bilingual Navajo. The Belin (2002b:8) example comes from an edited volume. One of the editors was Laura Tohe, who does not use bilingual Navajo in any of her poems, though she does code-switch into Navajo and she writes poems in Navajo. In Belin's (1999) earlier book, there are no examples of bilingual Navajo, though one could argue that the poem titled "On Telly Biliizh" (Belin 1999:61) is an example. As one Navajo consultant explained to me, and as mentioned in an earlier chapter, this is a well-known pun on the English word "television." That Navajo consultant read this poem and the attendant pun as a critique of contemporary television. When talking with Belin about this poem, she pointed out that "teli bilizh" was the term her mother had used for "beer" and, indeed, she had seen the poem as a critique of things done while drinking. She was certainly intrigued by the pun that my Navajo consultant had suggested. Such punning reminds us that meaning is contingent. And while not technically an example of code-mixing, it is an example of Navajos intermingling Navajo and English for expressive purposes. This playfulness can also be seen in Navajo-only examples as well. For example, one Navajo woman I know once told me about her cat who her family had named *gahsi*, which combined the Navajo word *gah* (rabbit) with the final syllable for the word *mosi* (cat). The cat apparently had a fluffy tail like a rabbit. She found the name to be quite amusing, and she laughed as she told me about it. This is the pleasure of language and speech play.

It is not just the raw numbers; where I found five poems that used bilingual Navajo, there were dozens of poems that code-switched into "standard" Navajo (and dozens more written in Navajo), but the sheer density of use marked them as hyper-salient. In each example presented below, there is one use of bilingual Navajo per poem. In most poems that switch from English to "standard" Navajo, there are multiple lines within the poem that switch as well (see examples 6, 7, 11, and 29).

Here I present all five examples I found where bilingual Navajo is used. The first two are from the *Navajo Times*. Of the next three, the only such poems found in the books of poetry listed in Appendix A, one is from the work of Esther Belin (who has taken classes in writing Navajo), herself a non-fluent Navajo speaker, the next is from Navajo poet Norla Chee, and the final example is from Ford Ashley.

(27) shí éí **Thanksgiving-go** shił nizhóní
(Holiday 1994:A-7)

my that **at Thanksgiving** with-me it is good

(28) ***Veterans Day-go***
(Woody 1994:A-7)

at Veterans Day

(29) With big teeth and smile Coyote asks, háágóóshą'?
Plaza'góó and before he can respond First Woman adds,
Shí k'ad dooleeł, hágoónee'
(Belin 2002b:8)

(30) Star Gazing
on a private night
in the anasazi desert

shí buddy and me beneath a juniper
Raven
sitting over There
waiting for the right time to fly into the story
(Chee 2001:6)

(31) Oh, **shi' love**, *mi amor, suave, suave*
Yes, my words are the lotion
the body lotion I rub between your toes
and along the underfoot
(Ashley 2001:350)

In example 27, by Marvin Holiday and published in the *Navajo Times*, we find a similar use of the subordinating enclitic *-go* attached to the English noun "Thanksgiving" that we find in the examples presented by McLaughlin (examples 24 and 25). This example comes from the "Navajo Language page" that was published sporadically in the mid-1990s and was often based on the creative writing of Navajo school children. Another poem (example 28), in the same December 1994 edition of the *Navajo Times*, includes a poem that uses the code-mixed form "*Veterans Day-go*." That poem is by Everrick Woody. The poems, given the month, were largely about recent and upcoming holidays (there is much writing about *tązhii* [turkey]). The example by Holiday is of interest because Navajo does have a term for Thanksgiving—*Késhmish yázhí* (little Christmas)—where Christmas has been phonologically incorporated into Navajo as *Késhmish*. Instead of using this form, Holiday uses the code-mixed form *Thanksgiving-go*. Other Navajo poets in the same edition of the *Navajo Times* used the non-code-mixed form *Késhmish yázhígo*. Holiday is highlighting the English origin of the holiday.

The Navajo Language page meant to showcase the use of Navajo literacy in schools; one key example of Navajo language literacy command has been poetry written in Navajo (and this has been primarily a purist

Navajo). Examples of bilingual Navajo are practically nonexistent on the Navajo Language page (save for the two examples discussed). It is suggestive, however, that Navajo students were being taught or at least allowed to use bilingual Navajo within school settings. Indeed, bilingual Navajo forms do turn up on flyers at Diné College where many Navajo language educators were educated. The *Navajo Times* examples are switches from predominantly Navajo language poems into bilingual Navajo. In both cases, the bilingual Navajo highlights the holidays as being incorporated into Navajo, like the English nouns being incorporated into Navajo morphology; so, too, Euro-American holidays have been incorporated by degrees into Navajo society.

The next three examples (examples 29–31) are switches from English-dominant poetry into bilingual Navajo. In example 29, Belin presents the English noun "plaza" with the Navajo enclitic *-góó* (much like we saw in example 21). The Navajo and bilingual Navajo forms appear to be the quoted dialogue of Coyote and First Woman. Coyote asks First Woman where she is going. It is intriguing that First Woman—important in Navajo sacred narratives—uses the bilingual code-mixed Navajo form in her response (toward the plaza). However, nowhere in this poem does Belin gloss the Navajo forms, nor does she provide footnotes concerning the Navajo forms. There is no attempt to explain the Navajo forms in English. Either one understands the Navajo forms or one does not. In fact, in talking with Belin about this poem she was unsure how many non-Navajos would even recognize that *plaza'góó* was a code-mixed form. Belin's use of bilingual Navajo puts Navajo and English into dialogue, through the code-mixed form. Belin, as I have noted elsewhere (Webster 2004:80), also uses Navajo English rhetorical forms in her poetry. Navajo English, that is, an English that has been influenced by the grammatical structures of Navajo, is used in Navajo poetry and is often highlighted by Navajo poets like Tapahonso (see example 4 above). The use of the bilingual Navajo form *plaza'góó* presents an image of the Navajo language and the English language not as exclusive to each other but, rather, as potentially intertwined, where there is an overt merging of Navajo and English. One might be tempted to think that the more purist Navajo may be associated with mythic events and traditional life and that bilingual Navajo may be associated with everyday events. It is certainly true that purist Navajo is often associated with traditional life (what one Navajo remarked about such poetry as "1930s Navajo") and mythic events. However, Belin here merges the mythic (Coyote and First Woman) with the contemporary in a manner evocative of the merging of Navajo and English with her use of bilingual Navajo. For Belin, the character of Coyote has been a useful way to interrogate contemporary life (see Webster 2004).

In example 30, Chee merges the mythic and the everyday in her poem. Chee's poem, titled "Shí Buddy" as well (the only poem with a bilingual Navajo title), is a complex set of images of the mythic Raven drinking "bootleg" under the stars, the "Ghost Roads" of "america" (Chee 1999:7), and ultimately the ideophony of Raven's laugh, "Caw, Caw, Caw," as he "flies out of the Night growing colder / a night for myths fallen on roadsides" (Chee 1999:7). Chee presents the Navajo first-person possessive pronoun in conjunction with the English noun "buddy," expressing something akin to "my buddy" (the reference here may be to the Earth itself). In example 31, Ashley uses *shi' love* (my love) along with *mi amor* (my love), linking the two forms with a sense of intimacy. Ashley's poem is a love poem. Ashley's example, like Belin's above, appears to be quoted speech. This is common in the use of the more idealized Navajo as well (see examples 6 and 11). Likewise, in both the Ashley and Chee examples, the use of the bilingual Navajo form seems to index a sense of intimacy between interlocutors. The use of *shi-* (my) on an English noun (buddy and love) aids in both the localizing of these lines of poetry and in their affective expressivity. Ashley and Chee's examples also resonate with Navajo humorist Vincent Craig's use of *shiheart* (my heart), as well as with signs such as the one on the road from Gallup, New Mexico, to the Navajo Nation that encourages Navajos to buckle up, using the phrase *shóó shí heart* (watch out my heart/love). The sign and the use of bilingual Navajo—intertextually linking to Craig and a common phrase on the Navajo Nation—have an informal quality.

Such examples of bilingual Navajo are relatively well known both in the speech practices of many younger Navajos and in literacy practices such as advertisements that litter the Navajo Nation and surrounding area. Bilingual Navajo is not, however, commonly represented in Navajo poetry. Instead, a specific "standardized" or "pure" linguistic form is presented, where Navajo and English mingle as discrete languages, but do not intermingle in the ways that bilingual Navajo does. To rephrase Brill's earlier discussion, given what we have seen of the uses of bilingual Navajo in poetry (or its almost complete lack of use): the use of an idealized Navajo language, which obscures sociolinguistic diversity, indexically grounds and iconically replicates these stories within an idealized and unitary Navajo linguistic world.

Linguistic purism—the expelling through erasure of certain untidy linguistic forms—can also be seen to be replicated in other scholarly literature. For example, in a recent insightful and thoughtful discussion of the history of the trope of Navajos as "borrowers" Erika Bsumek (2004) concludes with a discussion of the difference between the trope of Navajos as "cultural borrowers" and the lack of linguistic borrowing. Bsumek (2004:345) writes:

> Linguists claim that the Navajo language actively resists the integration of "loanwords." In fact, assertions of the Navajo disinclination to accept linguistic borrowings are scattered throughout literature even though no single author has explored the seeming incongruity between cultural borrowing and the lack of language borrowing.

While I agree with Bsumek's general point here—that the trope of Navajos as borrowers has been widely misused and selective (see Webster 2004)—I would add that the vision of Navajo linguistic practices has not been as clearcut as either Bsumek or some linguists would have one believe. For example, Navajos, after the 1950s, were increasingly bilingual in Navajo and (Navajo) English (see Spicer 1962:443), and James Kari and Bernard Spolsky (1974:57) noted a "marked increase in [English] loanwords in Navajo in the past 30 or 50 years." Bilingual Navajo dates at least to the 1970s (probably earlier). Navajo and English interlingual puns, as described in Chapter 2, date to at least the 1940s (see Hill 1943). These are day-to-day uses of languages. Bsumek's query only makes sense if we assume a degree of discreteness for both "language" and "culture," this view replicates certain assumptions that see language and culture as separate from each other (see Bauman and Briggs 2003).

Linguistic practices are cultural practices, and the "seeming incongruity" only arises within a specific set of assumptions about language and culture; assumptions that have often gone unquestioned (e.g., that Navajos speak *only* Navajo). What is needed, as Kroskrity (1992b:298) has shown concerning the notion of "linguistic conservatism," is to understand both the linguistic ideologies that inform such practices and the micro-details of those practices.

In general, there has been little research on sociolinguistic variations in Navajo (but see Reichard 1945; Saville-Troike 1974), instead variation has been largely erased as a unitary imaginary Navajo language has been constructed (see Gal and Irvine 1995 on this process; see also Silverstein 2000 and Irvine and Gal 2000). Such discourses assume that Navajo is somehow a bounded object and we are then focused on looking at lexical items "borrowed" into a language, instead of at the ways that languages and codes may intermix in speech practices. It is, of course, true that there is a tendency to coin new terms in Navajo instead of adopting outside terms. But as example 27 suggests concerning the bilingual Navajo *Thanksgiving-go* and *Késhmish yázhígo*, we should rather see these as options or potentials, not as absolutes.

Conclusions

To paraphrase Edward Sapir (1921), all languages leak. They are not self-contained units that show no influence from other languages. While it is generally true that Navajos have not borrowed lexical items into their language, it is not true that Navajo and English have not intermingled (both languages and people). Bilingual Navajo, a mixed code, is a clear contemporary example of the intermingling of Navajo and English. Bilingual Navajo can be found in everyday conversations, in schools, on KTNN, on the Internet, on billboards on and around the Navajo Nation, and on notes left for one another.

In contemporary written Navajo poetry there is a paucity of examples of code-mixing between Navajo and English (bilingual Navajo). Navajo written poetry then, tacitly at a minimum, presents a purist view of both Navajo and English. In contemporary written Navajo poetry both Navajo and English are imagined as discrete codes. While there is a great amount of Navajo language use in English-language dominant poetry, many of the uses of Navajo replicate metasemiotic stereotypes of Navajo as incommensurate with English and as compartmentalized within specific contexts. These uses of Navajo in contemporary poetry then feed into an idealized view of the Navajo language. This is an idealized view that connects the Navajo language with place names, kinship terms, clan names, ceremonial contexts, and stories of long ago. Both bilingual Navajo and "purist" Navajo can be used to create an affective register; however, bilingual Navajo does not intertextually link to forms of traditionalization. The uses of "purist" Navajo act as a form of traditionalization within these poems. That is, they pragmatically and intertextually link with aspects of the oral tradition and traditional practices. The Navajo used in these poems then comes to be recognized as exemplars of an ideal Navajo language community, icons of what are important cultural tropes among older Navajos. Here they serve a positive educational function. They also challenge the predominant homogenizing monolingual linguistic ideology in the United States (see Sherzer 2002:100; see also Silverstein 1996).

We should not expect Navajo poets to accurately document the complex dynamics of Navajo sociolinguistics. Rather, we should—as researchers interested in linguistic practices—be concerned with how Navajos represent the Navajo language and the English language and the relations between such codes (see also Meek and Messing 2007). As Bakhtin (1981) noted years ago, the representations of languages are never neutral or value free; they are, instead, fully implicated in the beliefs and values—the linguistic ideologies—about dialects, registers, codes, and styles, the very social pragmatics in which language use is always embedded. "Standard Navajo" becomes legitimized through the uses of Navajo in much contemporary written Navajo poetry, while bilingual Navajo or Navlish is largely erased (see Gal and Irvine 1995). While Susan Gal and Judith Irvine (1995) discuss colonial linguists in Africa and Macedonia who erased linguistic diversity through maps and other metasemiotic regimenting practices (see also Irvine and Gal 2000), the example I have been discussing here concerns Navajo poetry as a way to erase the contemporary sociolinguistic diversity on the Navajo Nation. The semiotic work done here then is, following Silverstein (2000:121), to create an "imagined (language) community." This, as Silverstein (2000) notes, reviewing Benedict Anderson (1991), is a part of the nationalist project of "imagined communities." This imagined language community then is a part of the larger process of Navajo nationalism (see Lee 2007; see also Denetdale 2006). Thus contemporary Navajo written poetry is linked with Navajo nationalism. One central feature of that Navajo nationalism, as Navajo scholar Lloyd Lee (2007:66) argues, is "the Diné language." Lee does not discuss what he means by "the Diné language." Is it a Diné language that will include bilingual Navajo? This is a question for Navajos to answer.

If, as I argued in Chapter 2, ideophony has been largely selected for use in the construction of a Navajo literary language as an icon in Navajo poetics, it seems clear that Navlish has largely *not* been selected as a part of the emerging Navajo literary language. The quite infrequent examples of bilingual Navajo in contemporary Navajo poetry can challenge the imagined language community view of Navajo and English as discrete codes. Bilingual Navajo challenges the imagined homogeneous language community, speaking discrete codes, indexing discrete identities. It suggests ways that Navajo and English can and are mixed (often with an English noun and either a Navajo enclitic or a Navajo possessive prefix). The uses of bilingual Navajo, limited as they are, then challenge the erasure in poetry of the sociolinguistic dynamics that can be found on the Navajo Nation. They are a counter discourse to the more naturalized literary and unitary presentation of Navajo (see Briggs 1992). They index, not to an idealized Navajo language community, but rather to the sociolinguistic complexities that exist today on the Navajo Nation. The potential for indexing intimacy through bilingual Navajo suggested by Chee and Ashley seems an empowering option as well. We need a more nuanced perspective on the uses of Navajo in contemporary Navajo poetry, one that recognizes both the ways it highlights the importance of the Navajo language and the ways it creates a particular image of the Navajo language. We also need to develop a more nuanced perspective on the uses of bilingual Navajo in contemporary Navajo society more generally.

Many scholars have approached the use of Navajo in contemporary written Navajo poetry as an unproblematic reflection of Navajo linguistic practice, as an invitation into an unproblematic Navajo world. In contrast, I suggest we need to understand the uses of Navajo as part of a discourse of linguistic purism that is tied to an oppositional linguistic ideology that sees Navajo and English as discrete and distinct "objects." Part of what Navajo poets are doing with their uses of the Navajo language and their nonuse of bilingual Navajo in their poetry is creating an object that can be understood as an index and an icon of the Navajo language. This is a Navajo that is relatively untouched by other languages. Navajo uses of the Navajo language in poetry aid, even tacitly, in the naturalization of this idealized Navajo language. It aids in the creation and circulation of metasemiotic stereotypes about both the appropriate uses of Navajo and the form of that code. This vision of the Navajo language shows little influence from English and thus replicates through practice a language ideology that posits Navajo and English as wholly distinct. While it valorizes an ideal vision of a "pure" Navajo language, it concomitantly obscures or erases other socially marginal linguistic codes. And in so doing, it closes off parts of Navajo sociolinguistic realities and in its stead creates an imagined Navajo language community.

FOUR

Performance, the Individual, and Feelingful Iconicity

Poetry is performance.

Laura Tohe, interview with author

Introduction

In the previous chapters, I have focused largely on poetic devices in Navajo and on the representation of language in such poetry. In this chapter, I turn to an analysis of how Navajo poets actually perform their poetry before audiences. I am concerned with how Laura Tohe, a Navajo poet, connects both to audiences and her own past through the feelingful attachments evoked through and by her performances. I am interested in understanding and analyzing the role of the individual and the individual articulation of a life story in Navajo poetry performances. In particular, I focus on three performances of the putatively same poem, "Cat or Stomp," by Tohe. One performance is the written orthographic poem. The other two are oral performances that I recorded. I argue that a focus on the individual performer and on multiple performances can provide insight into the relationship between linguistic and narrative constructions of self and identity within the constraints and opportunities particular mediums and contexts provide. I will also discuss the attachments that people (poets) bring to bear on aesthetic practices, what David Samuels (2004b:11) has insightfully termed, "feelingful iconicity."

Instead of focusing on a unified Navajo style, I want to engage the individual performers and performances and the ways such performances reverberate through Navajo ethnopoetics. It is in looking at individual performances that I believe we can better understand Navajo discursive practices, the locus of which is the individual (see Sapir 1927, 1938; Friedrich 1986, 2006; Johnstone 1996, 2000; Sherzer 1987).

Recently, Deborah House (2002) has attempted to examine "narratives of Navajoness." Yet her analysis of them is often superficial with respect to their poetic details. This chapter and later chapters, by contrast, take a discourse-centered approach to these performances (Sherzer 1987, Urban 1991). In so doing, I look at several key discursive features employed by Tohe in her performances of "Cat or Stomp." I pay particular attention to Tohe's shift from using "Diné" in the written version and "Navajo" in the oral versions. By focusing on such a narrow alternation and the framework in which it occurs, I hope to call into relief the relationship between the individual performer and the context of performance (Brenneis and Duranti 1986, Bauman 2004; Bauman and Briggs 1990). I show what careful attention to the poetics of these performances can and do suggest about the actual real-time production of "narratives of Navajoness." I intend to establish "narratives of Navajoness" not as abstractions but, rather, as on-the-ground discursive productions.

Following on the work of Sapir (1921), Hymes (1981), Friedrich (1986), Sherzer (1987), and Barbara Johnstone (1996), I also argue for understanding language and the performance of poetry as an aesthetic practice locatable within individuals. I look then at language as artistic and creative (see Johnstone 1996:180–181). Language is produced and circulated, creatively and artistically, by individuals, individuals who are often—but not always (see Silverstein 1981)—attuned to their language production. Navajo poets, as poets, are self-consciously aware of their poetic productions and of language as artistic and creative. In focusing then on the felt connections to language, the performances and contexts of the use of language through poetry to tell "a story," and on the individual artistry of the performer in the creation of that story, I hope to show how "narratives of Navajoness" are actually produced and circulated.

Feelingful Iconicity and Apachean Poetics

Focus on the individual has been a hallmark of some of the more sensitive research on Apachean poetics (Basso 1996; Samuels 2004b). Here I draw attention to the work of Basso (1996) on Western Apache place-naming practices and of Samuels (2004b) on Western Apache musical practices. Basso (1996) shows how Western Apaches can use place names to evoke and circulate a "moral landscape." The place names connect to specific narratives that allow Apaches to focus both on the words of the ancestors who named the location, but also the events that happened at places and the moral ramifications of those events on their own lives. Central to Basso is how an individual's life history is implicated in the use of such place names. Another feature is the feelingful evocation of language through place names.

More recently, Samuels (2004b) has shown how the contemporary production and circulation of music is keyed to individuals. Samuels examines the feelingful qualities of music, which, while superficially "Country" or some other genre, is actually deeply evocative of individual Western Apache life histories and experiences. Such a focus on individual experience and poetics blurs distinctions such as "Western music" versus "Apache music." Indeed, it is the importance of "feelingful iconicity" that is the focus of much of this chapter, as well as the rest of this book. Feelingful iconicity is, as I understand it, based on the "emotional attachment to aesthetic forms" (Samuels 2004b:11).

What I argue for here, by focusing on the performances of a single Navajo poet, is the blurring of some putative distinction between "Western poetry" and "Navajo poetry," for in the final analysis it is both and neither simultaneously. Moreover, it is feelingfully *Tohe's poetry* and, as an evocation of boarding school dynamics, it can be feelingful for specific audience members. I also want to argue that, as with Apaches singing in English, the feelingful attachment to poetics crosses languages. We need—as Samuels does—to respect the felt connections that Navajo poets have to English and the ways that English and Navajo can be comingled to produce differing feelingful connections.

While the poems are in English, they are clearly salient to other Navajos who attended boarding schools and who understand the categories of "cat" or "stomp" that were associated with the boarding schools. As such, Tohe's poem is an ethnographic account of the use of categorization by young Native Americans (particularly Navajos). However, more than that—I argue—it is a feelingful way for Tohe to connect with various audiences about a shared or potentially shared life experience. That the poem is in English may very well connect with the English-only policies in place at the Albuquerque Indian School. As such, the language of the poem may connect with both poet and audience about larger issues of domination. However, the poem is also a feelingful evocation of a part of Tohe's own biography. There is a tension in this poem, a tension that is stated explicitly when one audience member shouts out "AIM," between the nostalgia for childhood and the oppressive and controlling power of Indian boarding schools (see Iverson 1998). I will return to this point below.

The work by Basso and Samuels, as well as the work concerning Southern Athabaskan ethnopoetics (Toelken and Scott 1981; Basso and Tessay 1994; Webster 1999; Greenfeld 2001; Nevins and Nevins 2004), deals quite directly with the central aim of this work: namely, to focus on the individual poet and her performances. This work builds, then, on recent discussions concerning the place of the individual in language and culture studies. Again, Sapir (1985) presages much of these discussions. In Sapir's (1927) article concerning "speech" and "personality," he outlines a useful theoretical approach to the place of individual creativity in language studies. In order to understand the relationship between speech as an individual achievement and speech as a bio-sociocultural phenomenon, we first must demarcate which features of speech are purely biological, which are used by convention, and which are used by the individual for affect. In other words, we need to take what individuals do seriously and worthy of investigation, not merely as examples of "deviations" from some putative norm or thoughtless automatic responses, but rather as assertions of individual creativity.

The works of Friedrich (1979, 1986, and 2006), Hymes (1981, 2003), Sherzer (1987, 1990) and Alton Becker (1995) have focused ever more closely on the place of the individual in culture and language studies. These writers have located "language" within the individual, looking at individual creativity and suggesting that language may be overlapping individual systems (leaky systems at that). More recently, Johnstone (1996, 2000) has argued for forefronting the individual in discussing language. The focus, then, is on individual speakers and how they create, momentarily, language or discourse—by-products of Bakhtin's (1986) notion of language as speaking subjects. Talk then, individual talk, is where human beings display—consciously or unconsciously—their individuality (see Johnstone 2000).

Ethnopoetics, as a theory and a method, is meant to appreciate linguistic artistry as an individual accomplishment, predicated—no doubt—on the potentials and possibilities inherent in each language, but also on the individual artistic actualizations of those potentials and possibilities (Hymes 1981, Tedlock 1983, Sherzer 1990), the "poeticization of grammar" in Sherzer's terms (1990:18). Friedrich's (2006) recent review of ethnopoetics argues for a forefronting of ethnopoetics within linguistics and anthropology. Sherzer's (1987, 1990) call for a discourse-centered approach to language and culture is an obvious outgrowth of ethnopoetics, and once again looks to individual linguistic creativity as a central locus for understanding culture. As Friedrich (2006:219) writes, "culture is a part of language just as language is a part of culture and the two partly overlapping realities can intersect in many ways—for which process the term 'linguaculture' may serve." And the individual, the individual speaking subject—the poet—is inextricably bound up in and producing of linguaculture.

Likewise, I follow Bauman (1984, 1986) and Hymes (1981) and see performances as individual achievements within specific sociohistorical moments. It is important to understand, for example, the various demographics of the audiences that Tohe performs before. As Bauman (2004:2) argues:

> Social life [is] discursively constituted, produced and reproduced in situated acts of speaking and other signifying practices that are simultaneously anchored in their situational contexts of use and transcendent of them, linked by interdiscursive ties to other situations, other acts, other utterances.

Tohe's performances call forth images of the boarding school, where Native Americans were taken—often against their will—and forced to conform to some hyper-ideal view of "Western/Modern" U.S. society. In the performances to be discussed below, we will see how the audience, the contexts, of the performances situates and calibrates the use of "Navajo" or "Diné," for example. But what I want to also stress is how the creativity of an individual speaking subject can transcend those moments as well. This is, I believe, the key to understanding feelingful iconicity. Feelingful iconicity is not just the attachments to aesthetic forms, but also how they can transcend the situated real-time moment of performance; they are the felt connections that linger.

On Identity and Language

Sociolinguistics has often looked at the group to describe variation; they have neglected in some measure individuals as the locus of variation (this is made evident in the actuation question [see Johnstone 2000:409]). Another approach, the approach I take here, looks at individual speakers and the utterances they create. This is the approach that Hymes (1981) and Sherzer (1990) take: it looks at individual narrators and their creativity, their style, and how their narration is socially located. How do we understand Navajo poetry styles? This may be the wrong way to look at this question. A better question might be: What are the styles of individual Navajo poets? One option is the embedding of poetry in storytelling. Another option, to treat poems as isolated objects, also occurs with younger Navajo poets. These options—or perhaps constraints—are actualized for reasons; that is, individuals have agency, they invoke rhetoric and strategy. Tohe, for example, performs the three versions (one written, and two oral) for reasons. Each version is a specific utterance of a creative individual coproduced, certainly, by the audience. I am not interested in constructing some composite narrative of Navajoness; instead I want to look at specific individual articulations of narratives of Navajoness.

The question of identity is important and I want to add to what I said in the introduction. As I noted there, I follow Spicer (1975), and see identity as the ways people tell and re-tell, imagine and re-imagine their histories. Like Basso's (1996) discussion of Western Apache place names as being highly descriptive but from a particular vantage point (the structure of the place names reflect the orientation of the ancestors when they first saw the places), identity is also from a particular vantage point. This is a narrative view of identity (for other illustrations of this perspective see Erickson 2003; Denetdale 2007b; Van Vleet 2008).

Robert Le Page and Andre Tabouret-Keller (1985) have argued for the shifting nature of identity, to see identity as "acts" that can be managed through linguistic resources. In some ways, Silverstein's (2003b) discussion of "emblematic identity displays," where certain linguistic features can be put on display as emblems of identity also speaks to the contingent and socially constructed view of identity. Language, because it is often salient, often functions in various ways as identity markers, both as indexes of identity and at times icons of that identity. Both the works of Joseph Errington (1998) and Joel Kuipers (1998) focus on language and identity in Indonesia and on the shifting nature of identity in connection with the changes in local languages. Both look at situated moments of "talk," moments of code-switching, for example, as locations for identity work. Likewise, Kroskrity (1992, 1993) shows how Arizona Tewa have attached great ideological value to their language and certain domains of use for it (kiva speech). These approaches see language again as an emblematic display of identity. I certainly agree with this position in large measure and later in this chapter I will discuss the use of Navajo clan names as just such an emblematic identity display.

Recently, House (2002:43–55) has posited "narratives of Navajoness" based on her work on Navajo language shift at Diné College. My understanding of House's use of "narratives of Navajoness" is that they are discursive uses of stories to assert a "Navajo" identity. She summarizes and presents modest examples in English of how various Navajo educators talk about Navajoness and being Navajo. However, House lacks any significant detailed discussion and/or examples of language in use. We get composite narratives, narratives as abstractions, and not detailed analysis of specific narratives of Navajoness. That said, House's work, as well as the above work on language and identity, suggest that identity should not be understood as an immutable essentialized quality (see Kroskrity 2000a; see also Blot 2003) even, as House's (2002) research and my own fieldwork show, when some Navajos do describe language as an essential feature of being Navajo.

The difference between House's (2002) work and mine is that I look at specific instances of language—in this case English with some Navajo— in use. My work is discourse-centered in the microlevel sense (Sherzer 1987; Urban 1991). I believe, to understand "narratives of Navajoness," we must attend to the particulars of individual performances. By Navajoness I mean merely that a certain self, a certain identity, is constructed and understood as Navajo.

In Tohe's poetic tellings and re-tellings of her poem "Cat or Stomp," she is certainly using language as an emblematic identity display at times (her introduction in Navajo, to be discussed below, for example) and she is also, following Spicer (1975), using narrative—the tellings and re-tellings of her history from a particular perspective—as a way to assert and circulate her unique identity as a Navajo. This chapter is a part of the ability, as Bauman (2004) argues, of stretches of discourse to be decontextualized from one context (a performance at Window Rock) and recontextualized elsewhere (a chapter in this book). In so doing, it circulates Tohe's "history." They are Tohe's individual "narratives of Navajoness."

While the tellings and re-tellings of her history and the use of emblematic displays all work toward the shifting constructions of identities, I would like to pause and reflect again on the work of Sapir (1927) and its more recent articulation by Johnstone (1996). In Sapir's article on "Speech as a Personality Trait" (1927), Sapir seems to be arguing for a perduring sense of personality. As Sapir notes, we can affect certain pronunciations for social reasons (language as an act of identity), but is there not something also that is perduring? Can we not discern certain relatively perduring features of speech that may not be unique to the individual? This is what, I believe, Johnstone (1996) is trying to get at when she argues for the investigation of the "linguistic individual." If we look at the individual performances of Laura Tohe, will we not, at some point, begin to understand what is uniquely hers? To see language not just as the relative sharing of a lexical grammatical code, but also as the felt attachments that individual speakers have to the production and circulation of that language. What we might, following Sapir, term the creative speaker. By focusing on three performances of the putative same poem by Tohe, I want to understand the variations not just as responses to context (they are) but also as her unique responses to those changing contexts.

Performances of Poetry on the Navajo Nation

Many Navajo poets, as the example concerning Luci Tapahonso and the tow-truck driver suggests (Chapter 3), have achieved a level of recognition by other Navajos. Some poets, such as Luci Tapahonso, are often household names on the Navajo Nation. Navajo poets like Tapahonso, Tohe,

Belin, Nia Francisco, Norla Chee, Gloria Emerson, Rex Lee Jim, Sherwin Bitsui, Shonto Begay, and Blackhorse Mitchell have all been published by regional university and small presses. Some, like Jim, have been published internationally. Many of these poets also live on the Navajo Nation. Some, like Tapahonso and Tohe, teach at large southwestern universities and live off the reservation, but return frequently. There are also a number of younger and older Navajo poets who are less "famous." The motivations behind their writing poetry are complex. Three commonly repeated explanations for poetry were: (1) poetry is storytelling (Navajos often speak of poetry in Navajo as *hane'* [narrative, story]); (2) poetry is emotionally intense language use; and (3) poetry is shareable. In what follows, we can see the performance and circulation of this poem as an extended example of the above three features.

The primary language that Navajo poetry is written in is English. This is because Navajo literacy is still rather limited. While Navajo is still spoken by many residents on the Navajo Nation, literacy in Navajo is still not widespread. In writing in English, Tohe's poems are more accessible for the larger non-Navajo, English-speaking society, but—and this is in no way trivial—they are also more accessible to many young Navajo readers who are not literate in Navajo. Indeed, for many Navajos who are not literate in Navajo, poetry composed in Navajo is still largely accessed as an oral phenomenon. Navajo poets who write in Navajo often perform their poems on KTNN or at public venues.

In what follows, I will present the three versions of Laura Tohe's poem "Cat or Stomp." The orthographic version is from Tohe's 1999 book *No Parole Today*. The book focuses on Tohe's experiences in boarding school, and the title of the book works on two levels (one intentional and one discovered). The first sense of parole is that of a prisoner in jail who will not be released and reflects an attitude toward the boarding school as a prison. The second sense deals with the distinction Ferdinand de Saussure (1966) made between *langue* and *parole*, where *parole* represents speech. So in this sense the title reads "no speaking/speech today."[1] This was certainly true of speaking Navajo, as many of the poems indicate. The prohibition on speaking Navajo is most forcefully articulated in Tohe's poem and story "Our Tongues Slapped into Silence" (Tohe 1999:2–3).

The poem under consideration here, however, deals with which "group" a person belonged to during their time at boarding school. The nomenclatures for the groups were "cats"—who listened to Rock and Roll and wore bell-bottoms and the like—and "stomps"—who listened to Country music and wore wranglers and cowboy boots. The distinction between "cat" and "stomp" was widely known to a certain generation of boarding school students and, in many ways, this poem is a bit of boarding school nostalgia.

The first oral version is from Tohe's performance of this poem at the Native American Music Festival held at Diné College in Tsaile, Arizona, on June 8, 2001. Tohe had been invited to the festival by the president of the student-run Diné Music Club. The president of the club had met Tohe in January of 2001 when Tohe and three other poets had put on an impromptu poetry reading at Diné College. The president—Daniel[2]—had introduced her at that event. The organizing committee gave the music club one hour on the first night of the festival as a way to show support for the student organization. The music club had been quite active during the Spring 2001 semester at Diné College, organizing a biweekly open mic in the Student Union where music and poetry were performed.

The audience for Tohe's reading was still quite large by the 10:00 p.m. starting time. It included both young Navajos as well as "middle-aged" Navajos. The stage was in front of the Ned Hatathli building and the audience stood or sat in the parking lot. Lights shone on Tohe—making her visible, but the audience invisible. Or, as she stated, "Can't see you, but I'm glad to be here." Tohe was the only poet to read on the first day of performances; other performers had been a variety of musical genres.

The second oral version of "Cat or Stomp" was performed at the Navajo Nation Museum in Window Rock, Arizona, on July 18, 2001. The event was put on by Tapahonso and photographer and educator Monty Roessel in conjunction with a writer's camp that Roessel runs annually at Rough Rock Demonstration School. The writer's camp is for high school students and brings in a variety of writers including poets like Luci Tapahonso and Shonto Begay, but also journalists and academics like Mark Trahant and Peter Iverson.

This event brought together the largest collection of Navajo writers performing their work in a public forum. Writers who performed included Laura Tohe, Luci Tapahonso, Irvin Morris, Blackhorse Mitchell, Nia Francisco, Rex Lee Jim, Esther Belin, and Sherwin Bitsui. In the lobby of the museum you could purchase the various books written by the poets, and the poets also signed their works.

In attendance were a number of educators from the Navajo Language Academy, as well as Roessel and poets like Alyse Neundorf and Rutherford Ashley. The auditorium was packed with people. Some sat against the walls on the steps. In the audience were older Navajos, teenagers from the writers' camp, and young children. The audience, as at the Native American Music Festival, was overwhelmingly Navajo.

In the following presentations of these two oral performances, I begin before the actual poem is read. I do this because the poem is embedded within a certain performance style and narrative. The poem does not appear out of nowhere; rather a narrative is constructed that makes the appearance of the poem seem "natural." Lines have been separated based on breath-pause and intonation contours. Short pauses create lines. Longer pauses create stanzas. There is a general tendency for each new line to begin at a slightly higher pitch and then trend downward and coincide with a breath pause. Audience responses are in brackets. Initial particles such as "and," "then," and "now" are not used in the poem with great regularity nor are similar Navajo forms such as *'áádoo* (and [then]), *'áko* (then), or *k'ad* (now). This may be a by-product of writing (see Schiffrin 1987 on the use of these discourse devices). However, in the extemporaneous narrative introduction to the poem, initial particles in English like "and," "but," and "because" do occur.

Another reason to use pause as a line marker comes from an interview I did with Tohe. In that interview, I inquired into the motivations for segmenting units into lines. She responded that lines were segmented by a "feeling," a "sense of rhythm," "where to make breaks or pauses," and an "artistic sense." The breaks in lines could be based on pauses "or on something more, a pause in time, reflection." The line breaks in the orthographic version may represent places to pause, but they may also represent something else, a point of reflection or intensification. For purposes here, I follow the suggestions of Toelken and Scott (1981) and Benally (1994) concerning the segmenting of Navajo narratives into lines.

Joyce McDonough (2003b) has shown that Navajo appears to lack distinctive intonation contours for interrogatives and focus constructions. McDonough argues that this is likely a product of the confluence of three features of the language: (1) the verb stem is the most phonologically salient form in the language; (2) Navajo is primarily a Subject-Object-Verb language (SOV); and (3) Navajo is a pronominal argument language where pronouns are prefixed to the verb stem and independent nouns are optional in any clause. Thus there is great emphasis on the rightward placing of prominence (accent). This gives Navajo a relatively flat intonation contour. In poetry performances by Rex Lee Jim in Navajo it was often difficult to discern lines by intonation contours. Pause structure was the more salient feature for the structuring of poetic lines. This is also good evidence for the use of pause structure as the organizing principle behind line structure.

Finally, we can compare poetry as both a "visual" phenomenon and an "auditory" phenomenon. This is why I will maintain a classificatory stance here, with theoretical implications that regard all three examples as "versions." I give primacy to no single example. I also do not claim some "great divide" between some putative and naive division between "orality" and "literacy." Our understandings of the complexities of both oralities and literacies argue against any such straightforward dichotomy (see Collins and Blot 2003; Webster 2006b).

I also do not wish to reify a single version as the Ur-text. Far too often this has been done in the documentation of oral performances as written text artifacts. Thus we find a single performance standing for "the Navajo origin legend." This chapter is not about "the Navajo Cat or Stomp," it is instead about three particular performances by Tohe of her poem "Cat or Stomp." When I spoke with Navajo poets about their written poetry and its relationship to their oral performances, many Navajo poets suggested that the written form was a "way-station" on the road to reoralizing the poem. As Tohe suggested, "poetry is performance." More recently, Luci Tapahonso's (2008) newest book of poetry and stories includes a CD of her reading selected poems from the book as well as fan favorites (like "Hills Brothers Coffee") that she might be "scolded" for not reading.

"Cat or Stomp": Three Versions

WRITTEN VERSION[3]

    Cat or Stomp
    to all the former cats and stomps
                of the Diné Nation

    The first few days back at the Indian School
        after summer vacation
    you wore your new clothes wrangler tight jeans
        stitched on the side
    and boots (if you were lucky enough to have a pair)
    Tony Lama
    Nacona
    or Acme
    a true stomp listened to country western music
        Waylon and George Jones
    dying cowboy music and all that stuff

    you wore
    go go boots and bell bottoms if you were a cat
        and danced to the Rolling Stones
    even if you wore tennis shoes it was clear which side
        you were on

    Every year the smoking greyhound buses pulled up
        in front of the old
    gymnasium bringing loads of students
    fresh off the reservation dragging metal trunks,
        train cases and
    cardboard boxes precariously tied with string
        the word spread quickly
    of some new kid from Chinle or Many Farms
    "Is he a cat or stomp?" someone would ask
    "Stomp"
    and those with appropriate clothing
        would get their chance
                to dance with him that night
    (Tohe 1999:6)

ORAL VERSION ONE
    I wrote a book called No Parole Today
    and some of you might be familiar with it
    but if you're not
    ah I invite people to look at this
    cover and see people in there you might notice from the Indian school
    because I was there
    at the Albuquerque Indian school for a number of years
    and I call this my where's Waldo picture
    and if you've never been to any of my poetry readings I tell people
        if you can find me in this photo
    I'll give you five dollars

    um as I said I was at the Albuquerque Indian school
    and but I grew up right over here on the other side by
    a: at Crystal
    New Mexico
    and um
    I want to read just about three poems from this book
    ah first of all
    how many of you:
    a probably from a little bit older generation
    know cats or stomps
    if you do
    clap
    [clapping; laughter]
    okay great
    cat or stomp
    this for a
    all of you former cats and stomps of the
    Navajo Nation
    cat or stomp
    the fe: first few days back at the Indian School
    after summer vacation
    you wore new clothes
    wrangler tight jeans

stitched on the side
and boots if you were lucky enough to have a pair
Tony Lama
Nocona
or Acme
a true stomp listened to country western music
Waylon and George Jones
dying cowboy music
and all that stuff
you wore go-go boots and bell bottoms if you were a cat
and danced to the rolling stones
even if you wore tennis shoes
it was clear which side you were on

every year the smoking greyhound buses pulled up in front of the old gymnasium
bringing loads of students
fresh off their reservation
dragging metal trunks
train cases
and cardboard boxes precariously tied with string
the word spread quickly
of some new kid from Chinle
[cheering]
or Many Farms
[cheering]
is he a cat or stomp
someone would ask
stomp
[laughter]
and and those with appropriate clothing would get their chance to dance with him that night

ORAL VERSION TWO
    LT:
I have this book called No Parole Today
And um if you've ever been to any of my poetry readings
I call this my where's Waldo picture
And I always tell my audience if uh
If you can find me in here
Uh
Collage
I'll pay you five dollars
But it doesn't count if you already know where I am
Because I've been doing some readings this summer
A this book I wrote
Because I was in a boarding school
Uh on the reservation at Crystal
Uh where I lived for awhile and then was sent to the Albuquerque Indian School
And lived there for
Four years
A this
Title is called No Parole Today but I didn't know at the time that it's French
Uh word meaning no voice
Or no one to speak for you
Uh and for me that's what Indian schools were all about
Was was assimilation
And it was also the taking away of our language

How many of you a went to boarding schools
Just raise your hands

How many of you were cats
[laughter, raised hands]
How many of you were stomps
[laughter, raised hands]
Well I have a a poem here for you cats and stomps
[laughter]
You were a cat

Audience Member:
AIM
LT:
AIM
[laughter]
Okay
This is called cat or stomp

To all the former cats and stomps of the Navajo Nation

The first few days back at the Indian school after summer vacation
You wore your new clothes
Wrangler tight jeans stitched on the side
And boots if you were lucky enough to have a pair
Tony Lama Nacona or Acme
A true stomp listened to country western music
Waylon and George Jones
Dying cowboys music and all that stuff
You wore go-go boots and bell-bottoms if you were a cat
And danced to the rolling stones
Even if you wore tennis shoes
It was clear which side you were on
Every year the smoking greyhound buses pulled up in front of the old gymnasium
Bringing loads of students fresh off the reservation
Dragging metal trunks
Train cases and cardboard boxes
Precariously tied with string
The word spread quickly of some new kid from Chinle or Many Farms
[soft laughter]
Is he a cat or stomp
Someone would ask
[laughter]
Stomp
And those with appropriate clothing
Would get their chance to dance with him
(eight? or late?) [unclear]

Comparison of the Contexts of Performance of the Poems

CONTEXT VISITED: REQUESTS AND AUDIENCE

As mentioned, the first oral performance occurred outdoors at the Native American Music Festival in Tsaile. Tohe, who was an assistant professor at Arizona State University at the time, had been asked by a student organization to perform her poetry. Lights spotlighted her and prevented her from seeing the crowd. The shortness of lines and the increased use of pauses in this oral version may be results of a relatively informal performance situation and the inability to see her audience. They may also be because it was a relatively novel form of performance for her.

At the readings in Window Rock, the setting was different. In comparison to the standing crowd at Tsaile, the crowd at Window Rock was largely seated. Tohe had been asked to read by Luci Tapahonso and Monty Roessel. Luci Tapahonso is probably the most famous Navajo poet today. When I explained what I was doing on the Navajo Nation to various people I met, namely that I was interested in Navajo poetry, the vast majority of people told me I should talk to Luci Tapahonso. Other poets were mentioned far less often. Rex Lee Jim, because he wrote in Navajo and performed on KTNN, was the next most frequently mentioned poet. Tapahonso has published a number of books of poetry. Roessel is an award-winning photographer and the son of Robert and Ruth Roessel, important educators at Rough Rock Demonstration School for years (on Rough Rock see McCarty 2002).

Thus the requests to perform were from significantly different people. This is important because there was a time constraint on the poets at the Window Rock reading. Eight people read their work that night, all of whom had had a certain amount of "success" in terms of publishing. Each poet was given roughly "the same amount of time" (about fifteen minutes). This had been discussed before the performances and each performer knew he or she had only a limited amount of time. Furthermore, Tohe could see her audience. Included in this audience was Luci Tapahonso who operated as Master of Ceremonies and as informal timekeeper.

The setting and audience of the two performances may have led to different rhetorical structures. In one case, the structuring seems related to the novel situation, the inability to see the audience, and the power relations between herself as faculty at a university and the invitation to perform from an undergraduate student (Daniel, the music club president, who also acted as MC of the music club section). In the other case, the structuring seems a response to time constraints.

The insertion of the title into the poem a second time in the first performance may also be connected with the setting of the performance. As seen here in example 1, she seems to be slightly off balance at the beginning of the poem:

(1) *Oral Version One:*
Cat or stomp
This for a
All of you former cats and stomps of the
Navajo Nation

Cat or stomp
The fe: first few days back at the Indian School

After this beginning, with several false starts and the reinsertion of the title, she slows the poem down considerably. She pauses more often than in the second oral version and creates more lines than the written version. She also creates a number of rhythmic sections (the list of brand names or the three lines with four beats).

It should also be clear that all three versions of the poem are framed in some measure by "writing" and by Tohe's book. The written version is in Tohe's book of poetry, which clearly indexes Tohe's status as a published poet. Both oral performances, as seen in example 2 below, reference her book of poetry and place this poem within that context as well:

(2) *Oral Version One:*
I wrote a book called No Parole Today
and some of you might be familiar with it

Oral Version Two:
I have this book called No Parole Today

I will return to the introductory remarks in the next section; here, I want only to call attention to the undercurrent of writing and publishing.

CONTEXT REVISITED: DINÉ OR NAVAJO

I turn now to another contrast between the three versions that should be clear from looking at the dedication of this poem. In both oral performances Tohe states "Navajo Nation," but in the written version Tohe states "Diné Nation." I do not think this is a mistake. I argue that it is not a mistake because it occurs in both oral versions, but also because to call it a "mistake" would reify the written version as the "animating" version. Part of the point of this chapter is to cast that kind of reification of written forms into doubt.

I think the dedication "frames" the performance that is to follow (on framing see Goffman 1974). While "Diné" has grown in currency in public venues among Navajo (especially at Diné College), the tribe continues to be called the Navajo Nation in most public venues. For example, KTNN offers up the assertion in many of its promotions that it is, "the voice of the Navajo Nation." Furthermore, the tribal newspaper is still called the *Navajo Times*. Indeed, one of the primary public relations faces of Navajoness—iconic of and indexical of "tradition"—is "Miss Navajo" (see Denetdale 2006). When contests over Diné or Navajo occur, they may have political overtones. This was the case at Diné College in early 2001 when students argued that the initials for student organizations should be changed from NCC (Navajo Community College) to DC. Also, all during the fall of 2000 Navajo people had been posting signs concerning the impending vote on Proposition 203, "English for the Children." Such phrases as "Dooda prop 203" (no prop 203) or "Save Diné bizaad" (Save the Navajo language) appeared on a number of such signs. "Diné" had, to some degree, become politicized. Likewise, when driving from Flagstaff, Arizona, onto the Navajo Nation in 2000 and 2001, the sign stating "Welcome to the Navajo Nation" had been "corrected" to read "Welcome to the Diné Nation," Navajo having been crossed out by hand and replaced by Diné.

Diné is often used by poets as a way of indexing an identity that contrasts with Navajo. Diné is a term of self-reference for these poets and the poems are meant to circulate in these books beyond the Navajo Nation.

In fact many of these books are sold at tourists sites such as Canyon de Chelly, the Grand Canyon, and Mesa Verde.

Here is where "framing" comes into play. I use the term "play" on purpose, following Sherzer's discussion of the term (2002:2–3) and focusing on what exactly is being framed (see Sherzer 2002:96–106). I take this poem to be an example of speech play and, as such, it is "simultaneously humorous, serious and aesthetically pleasing" (Sherzer 2002:1). Like Basso's (1979) description of Western Apache imitations of "whitemen," in which jokes about Anglo ineptitude with Apache norms is both humorous and dangerous, this poem is both funny for many Navajo and also evocative of the cruelty of the boarding school system. In both of Tohe's oral performances laughter is heard when she introduces the terms "cat" and "stomp." She engages the audiences by asking either for a show of hands of former "cats and stomps" or by clapping. The audiences responded by laughing and raising hands or clapping.

Notice also the shift she makes in pronominal usage, which acts to engage and include the audience. In the first oral version, she changes "the" to "you" in the dedication:

(3) Cat or stomp
This for a
All of you former cats and stomps of the
Navajo Nation

In the second oral performance we have an interruption in the performance at just the point where Tohe has engaged the audience by asking them to self-identify as cat or stomp. An audience member, during the laughter, calls something out that Tohe could not make out. Tohe then addresses the audience member for clarification. Here is the relevant section:

(4) LT: Well I have a a poem for all you cats and stomps
[laughter]
You were a cat
AM: AIM

> LT: AIM
> [laughter]
> Okay
> This is called cat or stomp

The response that Tohe gets from one of the audience members is AIM (American Indian Movement). There is laughter after Tohe repeats "AIM." This includes the audience member. Even though AIM was a deadly serious organization at times, here it is juxtaposed against young students in boarding schools who were "cats" or "stomps." Because the audience has been engaged already, this potentially disruptive reference appears humorous to many (including the woman who made the insertion). But note that the insertion of AIM is meaningful because it draws into momentary relief the undercurrent of seriousness that is also a part of this poem and performance.

As stated above, this poem is not meant to be taken completely seriously, though there is an element of seriousness to it. It is a form of speech play. Tohe engages the audience as coparticipants in the performance. We see this again at the end of the poem when the areas known as Chinle and Many Farms are used. In both cases people responded to such place names. In the oral performance at the Native American Music Festival there was widespread cheering when both Chinle and Many Farms were mentioned. Geographically speaking, I should add, both Chinle and Many Farms are closer to Tsaile than they are to Window Rock. At the performance in Window Rock there is soft laughter after Chinle and Many Farms have both been mentioned. But in both cases there is a response. The responses are obviously conditioned by the type of event at which they were performed. The cheers came, after all, at a Music Festival that included rock and roll, country music, and heavy metal. The music festival is eclectic in its showcasing of music styles. The Window Rock performance was a more formal setting. It was held indoors in the Navajo Nation Museum's auditorium.

As with much speech play, there is also an undercurrent of seriousness (Sherzer 2002). For many Navajo the boarding school was not a pleasant experience. Many of the poems in Tohe's book focus on such issues as language loss, homesickness, racism, and the like. But there was something else going on, too. Something captured in this poem. People met people (including future spouses at dances). And while the poem draws you in, through the performance style of Tohe, it also contrasts with the current situation on the reservation where such boarding schools are far less common.

Finally, it is aesthetically pleasing. People I spoke with after Tohe's performances commented on how "good" her poetry was and how "funny." Some even stated that they had not expected to "enjoy a poetry reading."[4] I take this to contrast with a general tendency by some to view poetry as serious business. I initially found all Navajo poetry terribly serious. It was only at performances that I realized just how humorous many of these poems were for Navajo people. I had seen the undercurrent of seriousness, but I had missed the obvious humor of these poems. I missed the initial frame that this was speech play.

The poems in the oral performances are also embedded within a specific narrative, namely the narrative of Tohe having gone to boarding school; they are localized within the boarding school matrix of many Native American experiences. She attended the Albuquerque Indian School, not the Phoenix or Santa Fe school. This is a way of creating connections (both specific and general). In the performances, she indicates her own life story in relation to boarding schools in two ways. First, she does this is by simply stating that she had indeed attended the Albuquerque Indian School and prior to that a boarding school at Crystal, New Mexico. Note also that, in both oral introductions, Tohe also locates herself in relation to Crystal. This is another way of positioning herself within Navajo ethnogeography. Both the repeated use of the Albuquerque Indian School and Crystal, New Mexico, localize her.

The Albuquerque Indian School has yet to have an adequate history written about it, but the story of Clarence Hawkins's escape from the school and his subsequent 300-mile journey back to the White Mountain Reservation is telling (see Greenfeld 2001). Suffice it to say that the Albuquerque Indian School was not always the easiest place to live. Tohe says this about the school in oral performance version two:

(5) Uh and for me that's what Indian Schools were all about
Was was assimilation
And it was also the taking away of our language

Second, she engages the audience in her own narrative, her own story, in her "where's Waldo" picture offer. At every poetry reading I have seen her perform poems, she makes this offer. On the cover of her book is a collage of photographs from students at the Albuquerque Indian School. One of them is hers. If you can guess which photograph is her, she will give you five dollars. This rarely happens. However, her photograph from boarding school on the cover of her book validates her claim that she was there; essentially saying "I have the picture to prove it." The poems about the boarding school experiences are not just poems about the general boarding school experience. Her photograph on the cover validates these poems as poems about Tohe's *specific* boarding school experience. In other poems in the collection she makes this quite clear. In one poem concerning the arrogant mispronouncing of Navajo personal names, Tohe is careful to include her name in the list of names so mangled.

(6) Tohe, from T'óhii means Towards Water.
Tsosie. Ts'ósí means Slender.
And Yazzie, from Yázhí, means Beloved Little One/Son.
(Tohe 1999:5)

In a performance of this poem at Tsaile to a collection of Navajo students at Diné College and Navajo faculty, I could see Navajo faculty and older "returning" students nodding their heads in agreement as Tohe listed the ways that Navajo names had been mispronounced. Note that the visual form of this poem may reproduce the very mangling of pronunciation that Tohe is writing against, the sounds of the Navajo words become salient in the oral performance of this poem.

The photographs on the cover of Tohe's book show students in thick glasses, now out-of-fashion haircuts and clothes, and are—on the whole—less than flattering. Instead, they may remind Navajos who attended boarding school of an earlier time ("Ah I invite people to look at this / cover and see people in there you might recognize from Indian School"). For younger Navajo they are "old photos" of a time now largely gone, but a time that still circulates in stories and poems (like Tohe's work or Blackhorse Mitchell's reissued *Miracle Hill* [2004]). There is a feeling of nostalgia to this book, evoked through humor. But there is also a cautionary tale as well. That, I believe, is the significance of the twin functions (humor and seriousness) of speech play in her poems.

The written version of the poem also includes biography. Note that biography is important both in the oral and the written versions of this poem. In *No Parole Today*, Tohe includes an autobiographical introduction in the form of a letter to General Richard Pratt.[5] I quote it at length here because it has relevance to the politicizing use of "Diné" in this book and how this may contrast with the frame-creating use of "Navajo" in the oral performances, which are less outwardly politicized events.

> In the late 1950s I began school on the largest reservation in the United States, the Diné reservation. Although outsiders give us the name Navajo, we call ourselves Diné, *The People*. I prefer to call myself the name my ancestor gave us because I am trying to de-colonize myself. When I began school, the principal placed me in first grade because I was one of the few students who could speak English, though *Diné bizaad* was my mother tongue. All my classmates were Diné and most of them spoke little or no English.
>
> On the first day of school we found ourselves behind small wooden desks looking at the teacher who acted on behalf of your assimilation policies. Besides teaching us to read, write, and count in English, she was instructed to wipe out *Diné bizaad* through shame and punishment. We still bear painful memories for speaking our native language in school and that legacy is partly why many indigenous people don't know their ancestral language. I skipped Beginners class and went straight to first grade. My grandmother called me *hwiní'yu*, being useful, because I translated for my classmates. I felt helplessness when English sounds couldn't form into language that could save them. If I didn't help them, I felt I would be a participant in their punishment. We learned quickly that if we didn't want to be punished and shamed in front of our

classmates we had best speak our language far from the ears of the teachers, or stop speaking; most chose the latter. (Tohe 1999:x–xi)

Thus in both the oral performances and the written version of her poem Tohe situates herself as a participant in the boarding school. The poem is embedded within a story, her autobiography. I think it is important to recall the very narrative quality of "Cat or Stomp." The poem recounts a story. It has a beginning, "The first few days back," a turning point, "Every year the smoking greyhound buses," and a conclusion, "To dance with him that night."

The performances are situated in public venues; they are shared. Recent work by Julie Cruikshank (1998), for example, has stressed how such public performances aimed at both native and nonnative audiences create differing contexts. Thus, among Northern Athabaskan people verbal performances are both aesthetically pleasing and claims to place and tradition. The claims to place may at times be subtle and missed by nonnative audiences, but to the native audiences they are clear assertions. This has to do with Northern Athabaskan conceptions of knowledge and what is and is not considered legitimate forms of knowledge (see Cruikshank 1998; Rushforth 1992, 1994). Such multivoiced or polyphonic performances are also related to Australian Aboriginal art where again the audiences were at times decidedly nonnative, yet the communicative function was concerned with assertions of legitimacy and placedness via "the Dreaming" (see Myers 1991, 1994). Even if, to a large degree, such assertions were missed because of a need to fit Australian Aboriginal acrylic art into a frame of reference concerned with Western notions of "art" (see Myers 1991, 1994, 2002).

What is occurring with Tohe's three performances is similar in practice. Tohe is making certain assertions that may be missed by nonnative audiences in one context, but appreciated in other contexts. The written version, for example, makes a stronger political statement vis-à-vis Anglo/Navajo relations than do the oral performances. She pointedly articulates or creates a "voice" of anger at Richard Pratt and the politics of assimilation. Here we expect the politicized Diné form, not the form Navajo. We are not let down. In other contexts, the oral contexts, contexts that are more Navajo, such a form may be seen as too explicit, too obvious. The subtlety that an Anglo may believe they are gleaning from such a performance may be, instead, a lack of awareness of the stock of knowledge or of a misrecognition of a people as expressed and circulated through individual performances (the boarding school experience, for example). The performances, written or oral, play to the audiences, articulating a sense of Navajoness. They are, however, also (mis)interpreted by the audience (Fabian 2001:33–52).

When Navajo poets perform before audiences—audiences as diverse as Line Break on NPR or poetry readings at a person's house or poetry readings at the Native American Music Festival—many invariably introduce themselves via their clan relations in Navajo. This is true of both native Navajo speakers and nonnative Navajo speakers; it is a formula many Navajo learn (see Slate 1993; House 2002). To many Navajo people this locates a person within an existing clan structure, stating what relation they may or may not have with particular audience members. It is a specific kind of assertion or reckoning of Navajoness and resonates in a specific way for many Navajo. Laura Tohe, for example, introduces herself at the two performances by her clan relations. Tohe tells the audience, in Navajo, that her mother's clan is *Tsé Nahabiłnii* (Sleepy Rock People) and her father's clan is *Tó Dich'ii'nii* (Bitter Water People). Such introductions matter in making Tohe locatable within Navajo clan reckoning, though, to be sure, some Navajo poets like Esther Belin will play with the clan introduction formula. Sometimes at public performances, Belin will include as her fourth clan *hólahéi* (I don't know). The formula is not invariant.

For non-Navajo audience members such clan introductions are a display of Navajo as "other." Thus, such introductions also create an "other" for non-Navajo audiences, a different kind of Navajoness. The language of the introduction, even if it is formulaic (and to Navajo speakers *because* it is formulaic), is "different." The idea of clans is also different from the stock of knowledge of non-Navajo audiences but do fit a pattern of Navajo as "other." The introductions, while invariably in Navajo, are then "translated" or "explained" in English. Thus, one finds statements like the following in the transcripts from performances (the first is from Tohe): "I just introduced my mother's clan" or "that's the traditional way Navajos greet each other." These are metalinguistic cues (see Gumperz

1982) that frame a stretch of talk in Navajo as "traditional," as "Navajo," and, in so doing, index the position of the speaking subject. Creating, again, something we might term Navajoness.

But the key, thinking back to Cruikshank, is that Navajoness is not identical across audience members. It is not an immutable feature. It is, rather, co-constructed variously among variegated subjects. Non-Navajo audience members may appreciate certain cues as indexes of Navajoness in rather different ways than Navajos might. Navajoness is not just context-dependent (in the crude sense), but is rather co-constructed simultaneously in differing ways by speaker/writer and audience. On the one hand, Navajoness can be interpreted as "identity" by Navajo people and, on the other hand, Navajoness can be understood as "difference" by many non-Navajo audience members (this distinction is, of course, inspired by the work of Jameson 1979).

Conclusions

When Tohe performs her poetry, whether it is an oral or written performance, she is using language creatively and artistically. She is also playing out a tension between the oral traditions of Navajo expressive genres and her own unique creativity. For example, Tohe's use of formulaic clan introductions clearly taps into a larger recognized speech genre among Navajos. Her poetry about boarding schools also taps into an experience common to many Navajos of a certain generation. Likewise, her use of place names in the above poems connects it to Navajo narrative traditions that place a premium on the grounding of narratives within Navajo ethnogeography.

However, we cannot completely predict the form of this poem based on Navajo oral tradition. I have tried, where applicable, to note connections to Navajo oral traditions, but we need to also approach this narrative poem as a unique creation by an individual. There are influences from Navajo oral tradition to be found in this poem; there are also expressions of individuality. Likewise, the poem is meant to be performed and, as such, it is constantly remodeled and reshaped in relationship to the contexts of the performance, but it is also tied to Tohe's aesthetic sensibilities. This remaking and refashioning is, of course, a hallmark of certain genres of Navajo verbal art (Coyote stories, for example). By focusing on the individual we better understand the unique creativity of the linguistic individual (Johnstone 1996). It allows us to understand and appreciate how Tohe uses English to create, assert, and imagine Navajoness.

I am reminded of Samuels's (2004b:149–176) discussion of Boe Titla's "idiosyncratic authenticity" or the way the song "Mathilda" became "an artifact of social memory in the community, resonant and saturated with experiences and knowledge of the people who have heard it and sung it through the years" (Samuels 2004b:136). The differences we find in Tohe's poem reflect the differences in audiences as well in her own life story. Tohe is not just performing a poem about boarding school romances, she is also—as she makes clear through her "where's Waldo" introduction—sharing something of her own individual life story—a life story grounded in clan relations, the Albuquerque Indian School, and Crystal, New Mexico. The performances of this poem speak, then, to a myriad of felt connections. If you attended boarding school in the 1960s and 1970s you, too, may recall the distinction between "cat" or "stomp." Or, as the audience member inserts, you may remember the politics of the 1970s, when Navajo AIM leader Larry Casuse was killed in Gallup, New Mexico, and a memorial march was given in his honor through the streets of Gallup. This moment was memorialized in a poem by fellow Navajo Nia Francisco:

(7) horses that paraded during l. casuse's memorial march
(Francisco 1977a:349)

Included in this poem is Francisco's footnote:

(8) L. Casuse: A Navajo murdered in Gallup, New Mexico, in 1971.
(Francisco 1977a:349)

AIM is not in Laura Tohe's poem about cats and stomps. But, as an interactional performance, it can be. The politics of the 1970s and boarding-school life can be brought forward by this poem. The feelingful work of language, the creative use of language, can and does bring such images and remembrances into momentary focus. That is the felt power of language, evoked through the creative and individual use of language.

Finally, in all three of these performances, much of the identity work, the evocation of history, is done by Tohe through the localizing of the poem. In Tohe's performance we see that when poetry is a kind of storytelling, when it employs emotionally expressive language, and when it is shared, felt attachments to aesthetic forms evoking nostalgia for a prior here and now can be realized. It is in those moments that we glimpse a sense of "we-ness," of Navajoness. Contrary to House (2002), who describes "narratives of Navajoness," but does not focus on the poetics of actual discourse, this chapter has looked to individual and contextualized performances of narratives of Navajoness and the poetics of those performances to understand how that sense of we-ness is achieved. Narratives of Navajoness are not abstractions; rather they are localized moments of language in use. To appreciate the identity work of narratives of Navajoness, we must first appreciate the performances as the creative achievements of individuals. We must also appreciate them as narratives that emerge within meaningful contexts. Finally, we must appreciate the felt connections, the feelingful iconicity, that such narratives can and do evoke. In looking closely at individual voices we can learn a great deal about the concerns of peoples within communities, about identity as a kind of storytelling, and about how language use can frame contexts or become context creating.

FIVE

Narratives of Navajoness and Indigenous Articulations

Poetry, therefore, is something more philosophic and a higher thing than history.

Aristotle, *Poetics*

Narratives of Navajoness and Indigenous Articulations

In this chapter, I want to continue exploring the work that poetry and poetry performances do in constructing narratives of Navajoness. In the previous chapter I looked at how Tohe performed poetry that was connected to her own life story—"Cat and Stomp"—and the ways that such stories could reverberate outwards to audience members. In this chapter, I want to explore how Tohe performs narratives of Navajoness, through her poem "In Dinétah," that connect to a wider conception of Navajo historical consciousness. Here I again take up House's (2002) recent book on Navajo language shift and her initial discussions concerning "narratives of Navajoness." Part of understanding narratives of Navajoness, I argue, is to understand the particular poetic devices that connect one narrative of Navajoness with other narratives of Navajoness. That is, we need to understand how narratives of Navajoness are implicated and entangled within the specific poetic and narrative traditions of other Navajos and non-Navajos. Thus we need to move beyond merely accounting for narratives of Navajoness as the stories that Navajos tell about themselves, to investigate how narratives of Navajoness are actually structured and circulated. That is to understand the kinds of dialogue that such narratives are engaged in. In the following example, Tohe intertextually links to narrative traditions outside what we would term Navajo tradition as well as to Navajo formulaic devices. By intertextuality, I mean the ways that discursive resources interanimate each other (see Hanks 1999). As William Hanks (1999:13) notes, "each text is an intertext, an object whose meaning potential was realized in the context of other texts, under certain discursive conditions." Tohe has constructed this poem through "massive intertextuality" (see Sherzer 1994:922). The goal of this chapter is to understand Tohe's long narrative poem as embedded in "communicative processes in broader social fields" (Hanks 1999:13).

Denetdale (2006b, 2007b) offers a useful and insightful starting point for considering "narratives of Navajoness," the Long Walk, and their relationship with Western historical scholarship. As Denetdale (2006b:79) notes, "non-Navajo versions emphasize both the military actions that led to Navajo surrender and the role of Manuelito in the final defeat of the Navajos." In contrast to this, Denetdale (79) notes that Navajo oral tradition is focused on the "return from *Hwéeldi*, the prison camp, and emphasize[s] the reestablishment of life in *Diné bekéyah*." She further notes that such stories concerning the Long Walk and the return focus on the role of Navajo women as well. As Denetdale (2007b:41) argues, "Navajos' own stories about their identity and their past challenges established constructions of Navajos." Her recent interrogation of Navajo historiography echoes the work of Spicer, who noted, concerning the Long Walk, that,

> A Navajo is concerned, for example, with the meaning of the Long Walk. Was it something that happened to Navajos because they were resisting civilization and were defeated by that brave frontiersman, Kit Carson? Or was it an event in which Navajos were forcibly removed from their homeland, suffered deeply together, showed their spiritual strength, and won back possession of their own land? (Spicer 1975:50)

Identity, then, is also a part of history or tradition making. This is, I argue, a narrative view of identity construction (see also Erickson 2003). Following Rumsey's (2006) work on innovation of style and content in Ku Waru chants, we might ask, then, how poetic devices interanimate—that is make connections—with what James Clifford terms (2001) indigenous articulations. According to Rumsey (2006:50), indigenous articulations "draw selectively on their past to articulate a positively valorised position of difference." I argue that that is the identity work behind Tohe's poetry as narratives of Navajoness. Tohe's poetry and performances valorize Navajo history from a particular perspective. Her poetry and performances, as expressions of narratives of Navajoness, are then also indigenous articulations. One of the ways they accomplish that task is to intertextually connect with other Navajo verbal genres (by poetic forms, parallelism, tropes, and performance features). Another way is through Tohe's use of the rhetoric of movement and the projective "we." Here, Tohe's poetry performances are reminiscent of Yaqui narratives about movement to and from "the homeland" (see Erickson 2003). As Silverstein (2003b:538) notes, such narratives "are in effect anchored to an origin point where the display takes place, and they project a kind of radial geometry around the origin point, where the group's we-ness—instantiated in the first person display—lives."

A Brief "History" of the Long Walk

In 1864 the United States sent Kit Carson to capture and remove the Navajo from their traditional homeland. Thousands were captured; some managed to escape. Those who were captured were forced to march across most of the current state of New Mexico and across the Rio Grande to Fort Sumner (also known as Bosque Redondo and *Hwéeldi*). Many died on the walk, during the worst time of year, and many more died during their four years of internment. And while the Long Walk is a singular event in Navajo historical consciousness, it was not a singular event. There were a number of walks (see Denetdale 2007b; Iverson 2002). Finally, in 1868 Navajo leaders were able to negotiate a return to their traditional homeland. It is one of the rare cases in which a Native American group was able to return to their homeland and to negotiate an increase in their land base (see Parman 1994; Iverson 2002; Denetdale 2007b, 2007a; Johnson 1973). For many Navajos it is the defining moment in Navajo identity formation. Denetdale (2006b:79) describes the Long Walk, the internment, and *Hwéeldi* as "a trauma that remains etched in the collective Navajo memory." Indeed, it is not only etched but it is actively circulated in narratives of Navajoness in a variety of genres.

The Long Walk was a topic that was often brought up in discussions I had with Navajo poets. I also heard gifted narrators tell stories of the

Long Walk. Iconographic images of the Long Walk are often painted in schools on and around the reservation. Indeed, shortly after the return from *Hwéeldi* petroglyphs chronicling the events were created, thus encoding the event on the landscape (see Martineau 1973). In 1968, the Navajo Nation sponsored a literary contest for the 100-year anniversary of the return to *Dinétah*. More recently (May 15, 2003:A-6), Leandra Begay, an eighth grader, had a poem—"Heritage"—published in the *Navajo Times* that references the Long Walk. The Long Walk is still a salient moment for many Navajos. It should not be surprising that it is also a topic that many Navajo writers have explored. In this respect, the poems about the Long Walk, *Hwéeldi*, and the return are a part of the identity-creating use of narratives of the past that Spicer spoke of. The poems about the Long Walk are ways that Navajos circulate their past and imagine their past. It is how they create history (as the telling of the past) and an interpretation of that past.

There are other poetic forms that circulate stories about the Long Walk. For example, the Long Walk also recurs in the rap music of Mistic. Briefly, Mistic and his brother Shade are Navajo rappers who both rap in English and in Navajo. As they said in an interview with Red Nation.com, "we do our own thing—rappin one of the hardest languages to speak." On Mistic's album *Tribal Scars*, the title track concerns the Long Walk, the internment, and the return. The title track, however, is rapped in English. Rapping in English means that Navajos who do not speak Navajo will also have access to this story. This is similar to the use of English in the Laura Tohe poem to be discussed. Stories, *hane'*, about the Long Walk continue to circulate among Navajos and also outward to non-Navajo audiences. For most Navajos that I know, the events of the Long Walk are presupposed. That is, the stories of the Long Walk form the stock of knowledge that a Navajo listener brings to bear on any "new" narrative of the Long Walk. However, some Navajo poets and rappers are concerned that young Navajos are not fully aware of the events of the Long Walk. Here they see their work as educational. I will return to this topic in the conclusion of this chapter.

Stories of the Long Walk do not circulate in a vacuum and, as oral stories, they are potentially devalued or dismissed by non-Navajos who claim to be experts on Navajo history. While I was out on the Navajo

Nation in 2000–2001, self-styled historian Martin Link published a booklet about the Long Walk and internment that caused quite a sensation (see Link 2001). In the booklet, Link argued "that knowledge about the Navajo experience has been mythologized" (Denetdale 2007b:77). The booklet was popularized by reporter Bill Donovan in *The Gallup Independent* in an article that claimed that much of what Navajos thought they knew about the Long Walk and the internment was not "true" (Donovan 2001). In fact, Donovan and Link framed their argument as the search for "truth." Denetdale then wrote a response in the *Navajo Times* arguing for the value of Navajo oral tradition (Denetdale 2001). More recently she has returned to the issue and argued that Link's representations "reproduce colonial categories that justify conquest and dispossession and deny the horror, violence, and inhumane treatment of the Diné" (Denetdale 2007b:77). Link (2001) responded in the *Navajo Times* claiming that his "academic freedom" was being impinged by Denetdale and other Navajos who questioned his search for truth. Link and Donovan's argument was simple: The Long Walk and the internment at Fort Sumner were not nearly as bad as Navajos claim. The written record by U.S. officers contradicts the oral history of Navajos. The written records, Donovan and Link argue, offer a clearer and more accurate view of the events at Fort Sumner and during the Long Walk. The question, then, becomes one of epistemology and the primacy one is willing to give the written record.

The argument that Link and Donovan make is tied up with a linguistic ideology that understands literacy and those steeped in literate traditions as "the hallmark of rationality" (Collins and Blot 2003:161). Literacy, the writing of records by colonizers, then becomes a part of what James Collins and Richard Blot (2003:123) call, "legitimating the conquest." It privileges the colonizer's gaze as more accurate and more rational than that of those being colonized and erases the voices of the colonized from the Western historical imagination (see Hill 1988). It is thus legitimating of conquest in at least two ways. The first way, as Collins and Blot (2003) note, is through the legitimating logic of literate people "needing" (for one justification or another) to conquer nonliterate people to aid them in "civilization" (literacy here being understood as a hallmark of some putative civilization). The second way comes from the legitimating uses of written records as the accurate historical record (written by the colonizers) and the delegitimating of oral traditions of those who were colonized. As a number of scholars (Cruikshank 1998; Denetdale 2007b; Hanks 1999; Hill 1988) have shown, this, the idea that written records are innately more reliable than oral traditions, is simply false. It reifies literate practices as natural and not embedded in social fields. It is also naive history. As Jonathan Hill (1988:2–3) notes:

> History is not reducible to the "what really happened" of past events nor to global situations of contact but always includes the totality of processes whereby individuals experience, interpret, and create changes within social orders and both individuals and groups change over time as they actively participate in changing objective conditions.

Many Navajos challenge the primacy of a Western-controlled literate history. As one Navajo I knew pointed out, Link and Donovan's argument was essentially that, Navajos "needed to get over the Long Walk." That Navajo went on to say, that when Navajos had all their land back, had been reimbursed for the manifold injustices, and were sovereign, then they would consider getting over it. The Long Walk and the internment were a topic of discussion while I was on the Navajo Nation. One of the points of contention was over which historical perspective one aligned with. Tohe's poem "In Dinétah" is embedded within that social field. Tohe, in fact, through the use of a number of oral poetic devices, flaunts the oral tradition that she is connecting her poem with.

Laura Tohe's "In Dinétah"

Laura Tohe's poem "In Dinétah" forms the focus of this chapter. It was written to accompany the opening of a museum display commemorating the 130th anniversary of the signing of a "peace treaty" between the Navajos and the U.S. government. The poem is a long, complex one concerning, among other things, the Long Walk. The poem is not just a third-person description of the events; it is, at times, a first-person recounting of the events.

I first encountered this poem as an oral performance on January 18, 2001. That context was an informal poetry reading given by four poets who happened to be in Tsaile, Arizona, at the same time. They were there working on a collection of Native American women's poetry (Erdrich and Tohe 2002). The four poets were Esther Belin (Navajo), Heid Erdrich (Turtle Mountain Band of Ojibway), Laura Tohe (Navajo), and Venaya Yazzie (Navajo/Hopi). Each poet took turns reading their poetry in the auditorium on the first floor of the Ned Hatathli Center (Diné College, Tsaile Campus). The audience was largely Navajo. I had the opportunity to videotape and audio-record the performances. I say more about the performance context below. Tohe was kind enough to provide me with an unpublished version of the poem in late January 2001. I recorded a second performance of it in Window Rock, Arizona, on July 18, 2001. The poem was eventually published in 2002 (Erdrich and Tohe 2002:100–106). Here I present the published version. I provide the poem in full because I feel it is only by looking at it in its discursive entirety that we can understand the multiple intertextual, traditionalizing, and feelingful uses of language that Tohe employs.

In Dinétah
On this historic occasion 130 years after the signing of the peace treaty of 1868. Within Dinétah the People's Spirit Remains Strong 1998. These words are for my people, the Diné, who endured colossal hardship and near death and continue to endure.

In the people's memory are the stories
This we remember:

I
Ałkidą́ą́' adajiní nit'ę́ę́,'
They say long time ago in time immemorial:
the stories say we emerged from
the umbilical center of this sacred earth into
    the Glittering World
smoothed by Twin Heroes,
sons of White Shell Woman,

who journeyed to find their father
and aided by Spider Woman who taught them
how not to fear the perilous journey.
They say the sun father to the Twin Heroes.
gave them knowledge to slay the monsters
so that the world would be safe

We lived according to the teachings of the Holy People
to dwell within the sacred mountains:
Sisnaajiní rising to the east,
Tsoodził rising to the south,
Dook'o'osłííd rising to the west,
Dibé Nítsaa rising to the north
We raised our families,
planted our corn,
greeted the dawn with our prayers,
and followed the path of corn pollen
Everyday was a new beginning
... in Beauty
... in Beauty.

II
The ancestors predicted it would happen,
that the wind would shift and bring
light-colored men from across the big water
who would shatter our world.
They would arrive wearing metal coats
riding strange beautiful animals,
would arrive in clothes that brushed the earth
carrying crossed sticks to plunge into Dinétah.
In their zealous urge they sought cities of gold.
Later we learned they came to take
our land, our lives, our spirits.

Did they not know we are
all created from the same elements?

Rainclouds for hair,
fingernails formed from beautiful seashells,
the rivers flow through our veins, our lifeline,
from wind we came to life,
with thunder voices we speak.
We fought back to protect ourselves
as we had fought with other enemies.

The world changed when
the light-colored men brought their women.
It was then that we knew they meant to stay.
They invented ways to justify what they wanted,
Manifest Destiny, assimilation, colonization.
And, most of all, they wanted the land.
One day a man wearing red clothes appeared.
"Bi'ee' Łichii'í," Kit Carson, sent by Wáashindoon.
He brought many soldiers.
They spoke with thunder sticks
that tore into everything we loved
to burn our beautiful peach orchards
to slaughter our sheep in front of us,
to starve us out from Dinétah,
to do unspeakable things to us,
to wrench us from our land.
What strange fruit is this that dangles
    from the trees?
We feared for our lives
and hid among the rocks and shadows
gathering food and water when we could.

III
What was our crime?
We wanted only to live as we had
within our sacred mountains
seeking harmony, seeking long life

. . . in Beauty
. . . in Beauty.

Others had their death march:
The Trail of Tears, Auschwitz,
The Door of No Return in the House of Slaves.
We are Diné.
We too had our death march forced on us.
When The Long Walk began, we witnessed our women murdered and raped
our children and relatives swept away in the rushing currents
       of the Rio Grande river
We heard explosions that silenced mothers giving birth behind the rocks.
We saw the newborn and the elderly left behind.
We saw our warriors unable to defend us.
And even now the land we crossed still holds
       the memory of our people's tears, cries, and blood.
Kit Carson marched us three hundred miles away.
In the distance we saw our sacred mountains
       becoming smaller and smaller.
We were torn from the land that held our birth stems.
We were taken to the land that was not us.
We were taken to the desolate place without trees or vegetation.
Where the men picked out undigested corn from animal dung to eat.
Where young women were raped.
We called this place Hweełdi,
this place of starvation,
this place of near death
this place of extreme hardship.

IV
We returned to our land after four years.
Our spirits ragged and weary.

And vowed that we never be separated from Dinétah;
> the earth is our strength

We have grown strong.
We are the children of White Shell Woman.
We are the people of the original clans she created.
We are the female warriors and male warriors—Manuelito,
    Barboncito
We are the Code Talkers who used our language to save America.
We are Annie Wauneka who taught us to have faith in the white
    man's medicine.
We are the sons and daughters of activists and other unsung heroes
> "when Indian men were the finest men there were."

We are the hands that create fine turquoise and silver jewelry.
We are the women who resisted relocation when the government
    came
> with papers and fences.

We are teachers, cowboys, lawyers, musicians.
We are medicine people, doctors, nurses, college professors.
We are artists, soldiers, politicians, architects, farmers.
We are sheep herders, engineers, singers, comediennes.
We are weavers of baskets and exquisite blankets.
We are bus drivers, welders, ranchers, dishwashers.
We are the people who offer prayers during the cycles of the day.
We are Diné.
In Beauty it was begun.
In Beauty it continues.
> In Beauty,
>> In Beauty,
>>> In Beauty,
>>>> In Beauty.

(Tohe 2002:100–106)

The Long Walk as Hane'

In this poem, Tohe actively attempts to link her poem to Navajo traditional genres through her use of type and token intertextuality. As

Thomas Csordas (1999:4) notes, "'tradition' itself is a central orienting concept in everyday life for Navajos struggling for sovereignty as a fourth-world nation." The topic of "tradition" is a topic that many Navajos are actively concerned with. In this section, I describe some of the intertextual linkages that orient this poem toward tradition and traditional genres. Building on the work of Bauman (2004), as well as work by Briggs and Bauman (1992), I attempt to understand the linguistic and poetic devices that Tohe uses that create a sense of tradition and of Navajoness; that is, how does she articulate Navajoness in this poem? Also, on a non-trivial level, the topic of the Long Walk implicated her narrative of Navajoness within other narratives of Navajoness (see Bakhtin 1986:91). Narratives about the Long Walk are a recognized genre and various tropes are presupposed. Tohe has repeatedly stated that she sees her poetry as a part of Navajo tradition, the tradition from the elders. Or as she said about her poetry at a performance in Carbondale, Illinois: "This is not just my voice, but the voices of my ancestors." This is not unique to Tohe. Esther Belin (2007:73) has also noted, "I realize my voice is not just mine; I speak in a chorus of voices." Indeed, the mitigating of the individual's voice is a key function of the poetic and epistemic use of *jiní* in traditional narratives.

ON TITLES OR "IN DINÉTAH"

One day, in 2007, I was hiking down White House trail at *Tséyi'* (Canyon de Chelly), with Navajo poets Esther Belin and Venaya Yazzie and American Studies scholar Jeff Berglund. We were talking about poetry, history, the Navajo language, and the poetry of Laura Tohe. Our talk turned to "In Dinétah." Yazzie, who is from the Huerfano, New Mexico, region, pointed out that the title of the poem was not how she had learned the location of *Dinétah*. *Dinétah* is the name for the Navajo ancestral home located near Gobernador Knob near the Navajo Dam region. Some Navajos, like Yazzie, and some non-Navajo archaeologists (see Towner 1996) view *Dinétah* as being to the north and east of Farmington, New Mexico. Recall, also, the quote from Denetdale (2006b:79) at the beginning of this chapter about the return to *Diné bikéyah*. In this view, *Dinétah* is outside the four sacred mountains and not part of the current boundaries of the Navajo Nation. On the other hand, *Diné bikéyah* is used for the land between the four sacred mountains and for the current boundaries of the Navajo Nation. In Tohe's poem, *Dinétah*, the ancestral Navajo homeland, becomes the land between the four sacred mountains. Tohe is linking the current reservation with the ancestral homeland of the Navajos. Like the poetry of William Butler Yeats, which was overtly about constructing an Irish nationalism and "meant to educate, to remind its listeners of their heroic past and unite them in hope" (Aberbach 2007:93), Tohe's poetry is also linked with Navajo nationalism (see Denetdale 2006; Lee 2007). And like Yeats's "Irish Legend," Tohe is connecting the contemporary Navajo Nation with the ancestral *Dinétah*. The choice of *Dinétah* over *Diné bikéyah* is a powerful political and rhetorical move. Where Tohe differs from Yeats is that while his poetry is written in English (he glorified Irish ways at the expense of the Irish language), more recent poetry by Tohe is in Navajo. Here Tohe connects with a number of indigenous writers throughout the world, who have challenged the hegemony of the English language by using their indigenous languages for written poetry. Here she reminds us more of the late Irish poet Mícheál Ó hAirtneada (Michael Hartnett), who in 1975 wrote *A Farewell to English* and thenceforth (by degrees) wrote in Gaelic, than of Yeats. And here Gaelic, like Navajo as discussed in Chapter 3, is also not a unitary object; but in nationalist discourses it becomes an imagined unitary language (see Coleman 2004).

DEDICATION AND SECTION ONE: RECOUNTING THE ORIGINS OF THE NAVAJO

The dedication frames this poem within the sphere of meaningfulness of Navajo history. This poem is a commemoration of the endurance of the Navajo people, both in the past and in the present. This poem—as a form of *hane'*—is, after all, the story of the Navajos. There are four segments to this poem. Four is a key rhetorical number in Navajo. The Navajos went through four worlds until they emerged into the fifth, the "glittering world" (Morris 1997; see also Zolbrod 1984). Likewise, the poem goes through four "sections" or "worlds." The poem begins in the distant past—indicated by the use of the formulaic opening—and concludes in the here and now, 130 years after the Long Walk, in the reverberations of a chant-like conclusion.

The opening line of the first section sets the stage. *'Ałkidą́ą́' adajiní nít'ę́ę́'* (long ago, they used to say) is a frame-creating device. As we have seen, it is a formulaic opening phrase. This is the voicing of tradition. As such, it is also a token of traditional narrative (Silverstein 2005; Dunn 2006) in that it can be seen as the "quotation" of a conventionalized formula. But these conventionalized formulae, like the use of place names, are "quotations" of prior speech. They are understood as words coming from the ancestors. The formulas gain currency through the indexical link to the words of the ancestors. As Denetdale (2007b:43) notes,

> Ałk'idą́ą́' is also a reference point for storytellers. In stories about the past, the primordial time comes alive as storytellers reiterate accounts of the events that led to the establishment of the world, how the boundaries of Navajo Land were set and how the People learned the rules for proper living.

It is also a "type" interdiscursively in that it acts as a genre signature of traditional narratives. Again the traditionalizing of those narratives is understood as the quoting of prior speech. The poem begins, then, as a traditional Navajo narrative. The use of the Navajo language localizes this narrative and attaches it to other narratives.

In the opening section, Tohe makes abundant use of culturally specific mythic figures, prefigured by the use of the formulaic opening to this section. Thus Tohe comments on the "Glittering World," which is the current world inhabited by Navajos (see also Morris 1997); she mentions the "Twin Heroes," important mythic figures; she talks of White Shell Woman and Spider Woman, again important mythic figures in Navajo philosophy (see Farella 1984; Zolbrod 1984; Reichard 1997; Schwarz 1998), and the creatures that the twin brothers "slay" (Zolbrod 1984). The repeated use of "they say" in the first section connects this narrative with other traditional narratives. In many Navajo narratives—narratives and events outside the speaker's firsthand experience—the rhetorical poetic device *jiní* (they say) is used to mark discourse units and to provide epistemic distance for the narrator: this is what others have said, not what I have witnessed. For example, in a personal narrative told by Charlie Mitchell to Edward Sapir, when Mitchell begins the narrative talking about his birth, he uses *jiní* (Sapir and Hoijer 1942:338–339). Once he begins to remember, he drops the use of *jiní* (Sapir and Hoijer 1942:338–339). Navajos do encode epistemic judgments within their narrative traditions. Recall the example from Chapter 1, where Belin (2002a:58) uses *jiní* in connection with Western knowledge concerning a previous era when water covered the Southwest.

Section one can then be understood, through the poetic devices employed by Tohe, as a retelling of the Navajo emergence and of the mythic events that occurred within Navajo ethnogeography. It concludes with the repetition of "In Beauty" twice. This seems to suggest a partial completion. I will return to this point below. Tohe makes use of a number of Navajo proper nouns. Examples of the use of Navajo language citations include the four sacred mountains, Kit Carson's name in Navajo, *Dinétah*, *Diné*, and *Hweeldi*. These forms are Navajo linguistic citations and often act as quotations of the ancestors. Place names, for example, were named by the ancestors and to use a place name is to repeat prior utterances that can be associated with the ancestors (Basso 1996; Bakhtin 1986). The shift from English to Navajo with respect to place names—especially the four sacred mountains—is, as we have seen, quite common.

Tohe's use of Navajo place names helps form an indexical chain to the words of the ancestors. However, as implicated and entangled words—the utterances of compounding others (Bakhtin 1986)—they also gain feelingful iconicity to the associated reverberations that they evoke. For example, *Tsoodził* is the place name often associated with the sacred mountain of the south. As such it has a number of associated linkages with mythic narratives and religious beliefs (see Reichard 1950; Schwarz 1998). It gained further feelingful iconicity, however, with the events around the Long Walk. As Tohe notes, "in the distance we saw our sacred mountains becoming smaller and smaller." The last sacred mountain to disappear from sight was *Tsoodził*. However, as a number of Navajos also told me, *Tsoodził* was also the first mountain the Navajos saw on their return from *Hweeldi*. Here is how Bruchac (2002:42–43) describes the event (note that Mount Taylor is often associated with *Tsoodził*):

> The people were so filled with joy that the first sight of Mount Taylor, the easternmost of their sacred peaks, overwhelmed them.

"When we saw the top of the mountain from Albuquerque we wondered if it was our mountain and felt like falling to the ground, we loved it so." One old woman was so moved that she exclaimed, "Sacred mountain, I am home," and then she died.

The place name is thus evocative of the return. New feelingful associations accrue over time to these places. Marilyn Help (2001:61–62) has also written a poem about the Long Walk. Here is how she describes the return:

(1) It is said
When the Diné people were released,
it was a great day.
The Diné saw and recognized the peak
Mount Taylor and they wept.

Note here that like Tohe, Help intertextually connects this poem to narratives by the use of "it is said." Again, "it is said" is an English gloss for *jiní*, the epistemic modal that acts as a form of traditionalization of Navajo narratives. The use of this form places this poem within the voice of tradition. There is a subset genre of Navajo songs that concern the first views of *Tsoodził* by the returning Navajos. Individual Navajos often have a personal relationship to various places (see Mitchell 2004; see also Kluckhohn and Leighton 1962:204). Help's evoking of weeping links with Navajo ritualized or stylized weeping, such as the wailing that Nicole Walker engaged in at the dedication of the Bosque Redondo Memorial (Denetdale 2007a). When Walker wept at the dedication, her weeping indexed sincerity as well as linked her to the weeping of her Navajo ancestors who had endured the Long Walk and the internment.

In naming the mountains, Tohe follows the conventional Navajo formula that begins in the east and ends in the north. This metonymic structuring is the prescribed formula found among many Navajos. It creates a sense of surrounding and security. A Navajo that I knew, who had lived for a time off the reservation, once told me that he had returned to the Navajo Nation and the land between the four sacred mountains because he simply felt safer and more secure there. The formula is also a story, life begins in the east and death is associated with the north. This is why, according to Navajo consultants, Navajo houses have a door in the east and no door or window in the north.

SECTION TWO: PROPHECY COMES TO PASS

Section two is framed as the fulfillment of the ancestors' prophecy concerning the arrival of the "light-colored men from across the big water" (on prophecy see Schwarz 1998; Cruikshank 1994; Mould 2003). As Schwarz (1998:751) has noted concerning more recent prophecies on the Navajo Nation, "Navajo people use oral traditions to make connections between the past and the present as well as to establish the outlines of the future." Tohe does just that in this poem. The light-colored men arrived in Dinétah, the sacred homeland of the Navajo. Here Tohe is retelling the beginnings of the invasion of Navajoland. She also describes the basic unity of human beings. Note the contrast displayed, we are all people "with thunder voices we speak," and yet later, when Kit Carson invades Navajoland, they speak "with thunder sticks." According to Tohe it becomes clear to Navajos—the "we" of this narrative—that light-colored men are here to stay when they bring their women. They are colonizers. Tohe invokes Manifest Destiny at this point in the poem, connecting with larger Native- and Anglo-American conflicts. Manifest Destiny was not merely concerned with Navajoland, but was rather a goal of coopting or seizing all of North America under the auspices and control of the United States (Iverson 1998).

Tohe's use of "thunder sticks" is also of interest. First, it clearly echoes with "thunder voices" as noted above. Second, it appears on first analysis to be a stereotypical example of a naive view of American Indian English. However, "thunder sticks" is more likely a representation of *bee'eldǫǫh*, the Navajo word for "gun." Here *bee-* is an instrumental and glosses as "with it" and *-'aldǫǫh* glosses as a "booming sound is made." *-dǫǫh* is an ideophone for "booming." Thus the word for gun is composed of an ideophone for booming. Further, a gun or rifle is a prototypical example for the classificatory verb stem *-tą́, -tįįh* (a long rigid object, stick-like object, has position.) To talk about *bee'eldǫǫh*, one would normally use the stick-like object classificatory verb (e.g., *niyítįįh* (he/she puts down a long rigid object [a rifle])). Tohe's choice of "thunder sticks" then resonates both with the ideophony found in the Navajo word and in the way that

Navajos, speaking Navajo, would habitually attend to an object with that shape (see also Hoijer 1951, 1971).

It is also in section two where Kit Carson invades *Dinétah*. Tohe makes it clear, though, that Carson's actions are supported by "Wáashindoon." Here we see Tohe use the Navajo form for Washington, D.C., as a metonym for the U.S. government. One could argue that the use of the form Wáashindoon is again a form of quotation of the ancestors. This is the Navajo form for English "Washington," but using Wáashindoon resists an alien phonological system. This is re-analysis as resistance. It also connects the way the ancestors talked about Wáashindoon with her current usage. Kit Carson's appearance in this poem is also a form of quotation. Here his Navajo nickname is given, *Biʻéé Łichiiʻí* (red shirt). The translation, if we can call it that, comes prior to the Navajo form. The use of the Navajo term incorporates Carson into a Navajo universe. The nickname was given to Kit Carson by the ancestors who encountered him and first appraised him based on the red shirt that he wore. To use the Navajo term is to accept that naming practice and to quote the ancestors. Tohe puts *Biʻéé Łichiiʻí* in quotation marks as well.

Note again, that Tohe continues to use the first person plural form "we." This is not history from an outside observer's view. Rather this is a "we-centric" view. In repeating the form "we" throughout the poem she is aiding Navajo readers/listeners to imagine themselves in these moments. The linkage to the ancestors is made explicit. One is to imagine oneself from the perspective of their ancestors. These events did not happen to anyone. Rather they happened to "us." The "we-ness," the Navajoness, is thus explicitly asserted through the repeated use of "we."

Note that section two does not end with "in Beauty." Instead it ends with Carson invading *Dinétah* and the Navajos living in fear and hiding.

SECTION THREE: THE LONG WALK

Section three begins with the rhetorical question, "What was our crime?" Tohe, embodied now as the "we" of Navajo, argues that they, the Navajos, "wanted only to live as we had / within our sacred mountains / seeking harmony, seeking long life . . . in Beauty / . . . in Beauty." Here again the use of "in beauty" intertextually links this poem to Navajo chantways. This section is a recounting, from a Navajo perspective, from the perspective of "we-ness" of the Long Walk. However, the Long Walk as a historical event is connected to other historical events. Here a number of intertextual references come into play. Perhaps the most obvious intertextual reference (or token) being "strange fruit." Tohe quotes Billie Holliday's famous song "Strange Fruit" in the middle of her poem about the Long Walk. Strange fruit, of course, references the lynchings of blacks in the Dixiecrat South. The line "The Door of No Return in the House of Slaves," is an intertextual reference to Gorée Island and the Atlantic slave trade. Tohe is connecting the struggles of African Americans with the struggles of the Navajos through this recontextualized usage.

Tohe also relates the Trail of Tears with the Long Walk; it reverberates among the experiences of the displaced, the dislocated, the disenfranchised. The Trail of Tears was the forced march of Southeastern Native Americans (specifically the Cherokee) to Indian Country. Tohe is not the only Navajo poet to make this connection. Nia Francisco (1977a:349), in her poem "escaping the turquoise sky," also connects the Trail of Tears with the Long Walk. As we saw in the last chapter, Francisco also connects The Long Walk and the Trail of Tears with the politically motivated murder of Larry Casuse, a Navajo AIM leader, in Gallup, New Mexico. In effect, these poems reach beyond the confines of the Navajo experience to comment on the fate of the "other" in U.S. society.

Tohe also references Auschwitz. Here the connection is more complex. According to Tohe, in an interview I conducted with her, Hitler and the Nazis studied the camp at *Hweeldi*, and modeled the concentration camps on *Hweeldi*.[1] Here she connects the sufferings of Jews during the Holocaust with the suffering endured by Navajos. As I show below, she also invokes this connection in one of her introductions. Indeed, as the Holocaust has become a leitmotif of Jewish consciousness, so, too, has the Long Walk become the event that created a collective consciousness for Navajos. I have discussed this point above, and I will return to it in the conclusion. The Long Walk as a trope continues to circulate on and around the Navajo Nation.

Tohe makes the connections explicit, between the Long Walk and other peoples' displacements, when she writes "We are Diné. / We too had our death march forced on us." The use of *Diné*, as I argued in the last chapter, is often political, it is outward facing. It is a claim to a prior placement and knowledge base that rejects being labeled "Navajo." It is the Navajo term that references "the people" and its use indexes a particular stance by the speaker, often a politicized stance. This is the stance of self-naming, of self-determination.

There are other references found within Tohe's account of the Long Walk. The images of women being raped, men picking corn from the excrement of animals, pregnant women being killed behind boulders, and the elderly being swept away in the currents of the Rio Grande are recurring tropes in the oral narratives of the Long Walk. For example, in a collection of stories of the Long Walk, Howard Gorman (Johnson 1973:30) describes a pregnant young woman being taken behind a boulder and shot near *K'aałógii Dził* (Butterfly Mountain). In a recent Navajo-English bilingual children's book written by Evangeline Parsons Yazzie (2005), she writes of the elderly and sick being taken behind boulders and shot during the Long Walk. Shonto Begay (Bruchac 2002:28–29) provides a visually stunning painting of the Long Walk and of "the cries of children, moans of the dying, futile prayers uttered in the snow and mud along a blood-soaked trail" (Begay in Bruchac 2002:27). Elsewhere, Navajo poet Luci Tapahonso has also written about the Long Walk. Tohe and Tapahonso's poems are intertextually linked by means of the oral narratives about the Long Walk (stories that are still told today). Here are two excerpts from Tapahonso's poem "In 1864" that connect with both Tohe's poem and the oral stories about the Long Walk:

(2)   Two women were near the time of the births of their babies,
        and they had a hard time keeping up with the rest.
    Some army men pulled them behind a large rock, and we
        screamed out loud when we heard gunshots.
    . . . .
    When we crossed the Rio Grande, many people drowned.
    We didn't know how to swim — there was hardly any water
        deep enough
    to swim in at home. Some babies, children, and some
        older men
    and women were swept away by the river current.
    (Tapahonso 1993:7–10)

Notice that like Tohe's poem, Tapahonso's poem is in the first person. These are events that happened to "us." Tapahonso is also asking Navajos to imagine themselves from the perspective of their ancestors who witnessed and lived through these events.

Tapahonso and Tohe's poems also connect with a poem by Help concerning the Long Walk. Note again in the example the way that Help frames this portion by use of "it is said," the conventional gloss for *jiní*. Help places her poem within Navajo tradition through her use of the intertextual citation of "it is said."

(3) It is said,
     Many elderly, women,
     and children died because of Hwééldi;
     The elderly were left behind,
     Pregnant women were taken behind rock
     Boulders and a short while later the sound of
     A gunshot was heard.
     (Help 2001:61–62)

My point here is that certain images—pregnant women being shot behind boulders—are still in discursive circulation. These poets tap into those images in these poems.

Tohe also contrasts *Hweeldi* with *Dinétah* in sections two and three. In section two Kit Carson destroys the "beautiful peach orchards," and kills "our sheep" in *Dinétah*. The unstated assumption here is that *Dinétah* provided sustenance for the Navajo. The Navajos were able to raise sheep and cultivate peach orchards prior to their destruction by Carson. *Hweeldi*, in contrast, is seen as "this place of starvation / this place of near death / this place of extreme hardship." The image of the umbilical cord is important here. According to a number of Navajos I spoke with, after a child was born their umbilical cord was planted near the family home. This gave Navajos a lifelong attachment to their homes. When Tohe evokes the umbilical chord image in the first section, she is connecting it to the emergence of the Navajos into the "glittering world." The reference to the "glittering world" is also intertextually linked to Irvin Morris's (1997) novel *From the Glittering World*. The intertextual linkages compound, like ripples spreading over a shallow pond. Later, in section three, as the Navajos are forced-marched away from *Dinétah*, the land between the sacred mountains, they are "torn from the land that held our birth stems." As Tohe makes clear in the next line of the poem, "We were taken to the land that was not us." *Hweeldi* was not, and could not be, the homeland that *Dinétah* was. Implicitly Tohe is stating that the Navajo are their homeland, they are *Dinétah*. Tohe creates a tension between *Hweeldi* and *Dinétah*. The two are set in opposition throughout this poem.

SECTION FOUR: GETTING IN THE GROOVE OF "WE-NESS"

Section four begins with the Navajo return to their homeland. According to Tohe, it is the return to *Dinétah* that has resulted in the resurgence and growing strength of the Navajo. Again, the important cultural figure White Shell Woman is mentioned. Here it connects both with Navajo mythic tradition, but also to the first section of this poem. The first and fourth sections, then, align through the overlapping of White Shell Woman. At the end of the intense parallelism found in section four, Tohe will also link back to section III when she repeats the phrase "We are Diné." The first time this phrase is used is when Tohe contrasts the death marches of other displaced and oppressed people with the experience of the Diné. In both cases it reaffirms a unique politically conscious identity.

Notice still further the use of parallelism in this poem. Tohe employs several formulas. She repeats "We were taken" and "We are _____." It is this final parallel formula that concludes the poem. She tells of the accomplishments of the Navajo, listing famous Navajos such as Chief Manuelito, Chief Barboncito, and Dr. Annie Wauneka, building toward the future. The Navajo language and the Code Talkers are evoked. Note that it was Wáashindoon that had initiated the invasion of the Navajo, but that the Navajo language helped "save America." The parallelism continues, with Tohe using the formula "We are _____" to recount—with minimal discussion—key moments in Navajo history since the return in 1868. The reference to the women resisting relocation connects with the ongoing Navajo-Hopi land dispute (see Brugge 1999). Tohe then moves through the formulaic "We are _____" to a litany of the known, naming the various professions that Navajos are now engaged in. In effect, the use of the "We are _____" and its directed parallelism creates a "groove" of we-ness (Feld 1988).

Framing the Long Walk: Intracultural Performances

In this section, I look at how Tohe frames "In Dinétah" in two public performances of the poem. Tohe's performance connects with larger discussions of public performances of identity, both as intracultural and intercultural displays (see Myers 1994; Cruikshank 1997; Graham 2005). Both performances were related to education in one way or another. The first example occurred at Diné College and the audience was made up largely of Navajo college students. The second performance was initiated at the behest of Monty Roessel and Luci Tapahonso to coincide with a writer's camp being held at Rough Rock Demonstration School (as discussed in Chapter 4). These were both largely intracultural performances of Navajoness, aimed largely at Navajo audiences. Though, as Tohe makes clear in both introductions, the original impetus for this poem was a request from the U.S. Government and Northern Arizona University. And as the intertextual citations noted above suggests, Tohe and this poem are not just in dialogue with Navajo poets, but with a larger poetic horizon.

PERFORMANCE ONE: TSAILE

I first recorded "In Dinétah" on January 18, 2001, at Tsaile, where Tohe was performing for an audience of students at Diné College along with Venaya Yazzie (Navajo/Hopi), Esther Belin (Navajo) and Heid E. Erdrich (Turtle Mountain Band of Chippewa). Each of the poets read, sometimes twice, and then answered questions from the audience. Students filtered in and out as classes entered and left. In what follows, I present Tohe's introduction and framing of the poem. Here is the introduction:

(4) um, in um 1998 1999 the original, um, treaty that was
signed between the Navajo, um, people that were incarcerated at Fort Sumner and the United States government was brought to Northern Arizona University. It was on display in the library for a year and, I don't know, some of you probably

saw that you went to see it. It was a very historic event, ah, because the group of people got together and they had a, um, a celebration, well not really a celebration, a commemoration, ah, reading the original treaty, and I was asked to write a poem and, ah, I didn't really know if I was up to writing this poem because it seemed like this was such a monumental event historic event in our Navajo history, but I, I thought, I'd go ahead and try it and, ah, it came out that I have four pages in this poem and so I'll read this and, ah, just one last poem after this. This is called, ah, oh this poem is about the long walk and it's called within Dinétah the people spirit remains strong

"these words are for my people the Diné
who endured colossal hardships and near death
and continue to endure
in the peoples memory are the stories
this we remember"

one

Tohe performs the dedication and then goes into the poem. Both the dedication and the section numbers are included in both performances that I recorded of Tohe's poem. They are thus a part of both the written text artifact and the performance of the poem.

Tohe introduces the poem by laying out the history of its conception, thus giving it its own "origin story." Tohe was asked to write a poem about the Long Walk in honor of the "treaty" being displayed at Northern Arizona University in Flagstaff, Arizona. The significance of the treaty being the original is important to Tohe (she will mention it again in the next example). At first, Tohe suggests she was reluctant to write the poem, it being such a "monumental" task. Notice, that the poem is to commemorate a "monument"—the treaty—being put on display. According to Tohe it was an "historic" event, and she draws the audience in by suggesting that they may have gone to the event. When she said this, some in the audience nodded their heads in what I took to be affirmation. Indeed, the Long Walk is a historic event (by Navajo standards) in that it has been inscribed by Navajos from roughly 1868 onwards and the narratives of the Long Walk have continued to circulate and continue to be used to comment on the present.

Note further that Tohe presents herself as the "reluctant" poet. The task—the creation of a poem commemorating the Long Walk, the internment, and the return—is made even more important by Tohe's display of deference. The creation of a poem of commemoration would not be easy because of the "historic" import of the events to be commemorated. She thus mitigates her role in relationship to the event to be commemorated. It is the event, and not her, that is of importance. Her framing of this poem thus ratifies the "historic" nature of the event by signaling her own acknowledgement and limitations of the task of commemoration. Such modesty, the not calling attention to oneself, is often highly valued among Navajos. The mitigating of one's own importance was something that many Navajo poets often did during performances.

It should not be surprising that the poem has four sections that connect with the importance of the number four in Navajo ritual or that Tohe points out that the poem took up "four pages." Four is an important rhetorical number for many Navajos. Things happen in fours, there are four sacred mountains and the four directions, and many tasks are completed on the fourth iteration. Tohe connects her poem to the logic of Navajo four. And this logic of four, "it came out," is naturalized in the creation of the poem by Tohe.

Tohe also ends the poem with the repetition of "in Beauty" four times. The pause structure here was quite marked. Tohe takes her time enunciating "in Beauty" four times; she lets the phrase linger in silence for a moment and then repeats the phrase. She is drawing attention to the lines. It appears then, because of its intertextual and poetic linkages, to be a "natural" conclusion.

PERFORMANCE TWO: WINDOW ROCK

The second performance I recorded of this poem was at the poetry reading at Window Rock on July 18, 2001, at the Navajo Nation Museum, a point that Tohe indexically locates in her introduction: "next door there is a . . . now an exhibit." The audience was largely Navajo and a number of young aspiring Navajo writers who were attending a writer's camp at

Rough Rock were also in attendance (I discussed this event in more detail in Chapter 4), as well as a number of Navajo scholars from the Navajo Language Academy. This was the largest performance event featuring Navajo authors that any of the Navajo performers could remember. In fact many of the writers remarked on what a special event it was that was taking place. As such it was an overt display of Navajoness; the event was repeatedly called attention to. Besides Tohe, Belin, Sherwin Bitsui, Nia Francisco, Rex Lee Jim, Blackhorse Mitchell, Irvin Morris, and Luci Tapahonso also performed (see Chapter 4). Here is the introduction:

(5) I was asked to write a poem for the commemoration of the treaty that was signed between the Navajo na: ah Navajo people when they were incarcerated at Fort Sumner um in 1864 through 1868 and this commemoration of the signing of the peace treaty took place in Flagstaff in 1998 and the original treaty was brought and it was kept there at the library for a year and at the beginning of that year 1998 and 199– and also at the end year 1999, um, there was a commemoration. I was asked to write this poem and I think next door there is a, a, a, now an exhibit of the, um, of the incarceration, um, and it's interesting that a, um, that Hitler studied what took place at Hwééldi at Fort Sumner when the Navajo people were incarcerated [poem begins]

ON "TREATIES" AND "OLD PAPER"

Tohe again introduces the poem by discussing the events that led up to the writing of the poem. Again, notice that Tohe once again states that "the original treaty" was being displayed. The "original treaty" reminds us of the reification of the text artifact in history. Such originals act as validation of the past. Copies do not have the same evocative force. They are fabrications, indexing the original, and there must be an original. As Collins (1998) has pointed out for the Tolowa (Pacific Coast Athabaskans), the power of the "written" word is often used in discourses about U.S. responsibilities toward indigenous groups. The Tolowa tell of a "treaty" or "deed" that has been "lost" or "hidden." In that "original" document is the evidence for Tolowa claims to their land, acknowledged by the U.S. government. The Navajo have the "peace treaty" and a copy is on display at the Navajo Nation Museum. They can validate that copy by reference to a publicly circulated and displayed original. An original, I should add, that Tohe's introduction confirms. Note, also, that when Tohe performed at Window Rock, the display of the treaty was in the exhibit next door.

The treaty is important and was commented on by a number of Navajos. First, it is one of the rare times that a Native American group was allowed or negotiated the return to their homeland. The Navajos had been removed via the Long Walk to *Hwéeldi*, but they returned to *Dinétah* because of the peace treaty. They, in effect, negotiated a return home. This is a point of pride for many Navajos I talked to, and it is a point of pride reiterated in many of the poems I have been discussing. Also as pointed out above, the treaty is on paper and, as such, can be put on display. Its presence validates—through complex ideologies about the import of the printed word—the place of the Navajo. As Tohe pointed out to me in 2003, some Navajos refer to the treaty as the "old paper" or the "old document." In doing so, they affirm the temporal aspect (the time perspective) of this treaty. The very age of the paper (treaty) is iconic of its meaningfulness and an index to a prior here and now. It is a continual reminder of a longstanding obligation/relationship between the Navajo and the U.S. government.

HITLER AND *HWEEŁDI*

Tohe also explicitly links the concentration camps of Nazi Germany and Hitler with the events that occurred at *Hweełdi*. The Navajo experience resonates with and informs other world historical events. The Navajo and their experience at *Hweełdi* have interdiscursive links to events outside *Dinétah*. Recall, again, that, according to Tohe, the Navajo code was used in the Pacific Theater during World War II and thus helped "save America." While Hitler modeled the incarceration camps of World War II on the internment at *Hweełdi*, the Navajo language was used in helping to "save America" in World War II despite the prior actions of Wáashindoon. The important point here is not whether or not the Navajo language "saved" the United States or whether Hitler did or did not model the concentration camps on *Hweełdi*, but rather on the identity work that such assertions accomplish. They are Tohe's (and other Navajos I have spoken with) ways of connecting Navajo history (from a Navajo perspective) with larger world historical events.

NARRATIVES OF NAVAJONESS AND THE PROJECTIVE WE

That Tohe performs this poem orally for two largely Navajo audiences, predominately student audiences, is not surprising. As an indigenous articulation aimed at the valorizing of key moments of Navajo history, such audiences are one of the central locations for the reproduction of narratives of Navajoness. Likewise, Tohe links her performance (a kind of education) with the Treaty of 1868, which was also about education and the promotion of education. She is helping to continue a tradition of talking about the Long Walk, both as an immense tragedy and as a point of pride. She is creating a frame by which to recognize and interpret the Long Walk, the internment, and the return. According to Tohe, then, the Navajos have become—in part—a people because of the Long Walk. And they continually become re-unified through performances of this poem. As she argues, it was a unifying moment in Navajo history. It is one of those stories, told from a particular perspective, that helps reinforce an identity. This is not an abstracted narrative of Navajoness. Rather, it is a feelingfully evocative narrative of Navajoness. It is a narrative that overtly links the listener with the struggles of their ancestors. The Long Walk permeates a variety of discourses, a variety of settings; it reaffirms a collective sense of identity. They are not simply a recounting of the events. Instead, they are the experiences of the narrator. Listeners are drawn into both the horror and the redemptive and revitalizing potential of the experience. "We lived according to the teachings of the Holy People." "We fought back to protect ourselves." "What was our crime?" In such ways, Tohe draws the listener into a prior here and now. At the performance at Window Rock, one older Navajo woman softly wept as Tohe read her poem. Her weeping validated the sincerity of Tohe's poem. Tohe evokes the past, engaging the listener to imagine themselves in the situation of their ancestors. She is, then, giving "an imagination to the listener."

By understanding the opening phrase in Navajo—the frame-creating device—one can also understand the use of the first-person plural as a kind of "projective we" (Urban 1989; Rumsey 2000). The use of the first-person plural is thus synecdochic. Not only does it index the Navajos who suffered the Long Walk, but it also connects with Navajos today and with those Navajos in the audience as well as to Tohe. It indexically projects both the Navajos of the past and the Navajos of the present under the rubric of "we." This is the "we" of an "imagined community" (Anderson 1991). It is a making of that shared sense of "we-ness" (Silverstein 2003a). It is the momentary valorization of Navajoness. One can see this most clearly when Tohe performs this poem for a Navajo audience, drawing them into the "we" of the poem. Here, Tohe's performance of this poem to largely Navajo audiences creates that grounded point of origin for extending the sense of we-ness outward to encompass the audience as well. It is in such moments that a shared sense of Navajoness, of we-ness, is accomplished and achieved.

This can also be seen in the progression of the "we" from the past to the present. In section four of the poem, the "we" begins at the return and then moves forward in time to "bus drivers" and "college professors." Tohe is a college professor and is thus indexing herself here. In fact, in both performances she was introduced as a professor at Arizona State University. Thus the audience can recognize the self-referential linkage that she is accomplishing. The "we," then, is the "we" of Navajoness. The parallelism thus aids in the feelingful iconicity that the poem evokes. The merging of a prior "we" with the listening "we" is feelingfully iconic. Navajos can recognize themselves inhabiting the "we" that Tohe creates. This is, again, especially and most forcefully done at the performances of this poem. Through performances of this narrative of Navajoness before Navajo audiences, Tohe creates that sense of we-ness that she is describing.

Through the formulaic "We are _____," Tohe is able to move through directed parallelism from the past (the people who returned to *Dinétah* after four years) into the present (see Jakobson 1960). All the while, the repeated use of "we" creates that shared sense of "we-ness" for Navajo peoples. The final lines point to the future, "it continues." And the last four lines echo the endings of a number of Navajo chants. It is thus also an intertextual reference. The repetition of "in beauty" four times is also meaningful. It suggests completion and surrounding (see Field and Blackhorse 2002). Notice again that the poem begins as a story and ends as a chant. It crosses genres. It also crosses languages. It is also important, I think, to take note that the poetry about the Long Walk is largely in English; as such it allows Navajos who do not speak Navajo to be included in the sense of historical memory, the sense of we-ness. But there are enough displays of Navajo to remind Navajos of the Navajo language as well.

Conclusions

In this chapter, I have examined Laura Tohe's poem "In Dinétah." I have shown how she uses a number of Navajo poetic devices to traditionalize her poem. First, she overtly connects the poem to oral narratives by using the formulaic opening device *ałkidą́ą́' adajiní nít'ę́ę́'* (long ago, they used to say). She also connects to oral poetics by her repeated use at the beginning of the poem of the phrase "they say," this matches the use by Navajo narrators of the epistemic modal *jiní* in a number of Navajo narrative traditions. Here it primarily functions to indicate that the events that one is describing are not from firsthand experience, but rather are implicated in the iterative transmission of knowledge; the voicing of tradition. She also cites a number of Navajo mythic characters and gives a minimal retelling of the Navajo emergence. She uses Navajo place names for the Navajo sacred mountains, signalling that Navajo names, not English names, are the legitimate names. Her use of *Dinétah* as the land between the four sacred mountains and for the current boundaries of the Navajo Nation explicitly links it with the ancestral homeland of the Navajos, which some Navajos do not see as being in the current location of the Navajo Nation (some do). The use of "in Beauty" four times at the end of the poem connects the poem to Navajo chantways and thus crosses genres from narrative to chant. In all of this, she positions her poetry, her narrative of the Long Walk, as being from a Navajo perspective, a particularly situated Navajo perspective, and not a Euro-American perspective.

In the introductions to the two public performances of this poem, I have attempted to show how Tohe then actively engages in the circulation of a narrative of Navajoness. This poem is a narrative and as such it tells the story of the Navajo people, however, it tells that story from the inclusive "we" perspective. Tohe wants Navajos to engage in imagining and reimagining the Long Walk from the perspective of their ancestors. She is encouraging Navajos to identify with their ancestors, ancestors who suffered during the Long Walk but were ultimately able to negotiate their return from *Hweełdi* and who "saved America" through their language and have continued to grow strong. Her poem then is an attempt to link younger Navajos with their tradition. As such this poem is an active and self-conscious attempt to circulate and recreate a sense of Navajoness. It is a narrative of Navajoness that is connected with the Long Walk. Note that the context of performing before Navajo students is also relevant to the circulation of these narratives of Navajoness. The use of parallelism and the use of "we" are ways to feelingfully connect audience and poet with the ancestors. This is the feelingful iconicity of Navajo poetics in the expression and circulation of narratives of Navajoness. It allows Navajos to imagine themselves in the place of their ancestors who suffered the Long Walk, the internment, and the return. Like the nationalist poetry of Yeats, Tohe's poem is enmeshed in rhetorics of Navajo nationalism. As David Aberbach (2007:94) argues, "Poets use myth and mythical history as a shifting tapestry of national identity." It is also, following Clifford (2001), an indigenous articulation whereby Tohe valorizes certain features of Navajo history as being enduring links to Navajo identity. She does this by the use of feelingfully evocative poetic forms that create a sense of continuity between her performances of her poetry and another set of genres.

The oral tradition, the discursive circulation, concerning the Long Walk is not new, as this quote from the 1940s by Kluckhohn and Leighton suggests:

> Even today it seems impossible for any Navaho of the older generation to talk for more than a few minutes on any subject without speaking of Fort Sumner. Those who were not there themselves heard so many poignant tales from their parents that they speak as if they themselves had experienced the horror of the "Long Walk," the illness, the hunger, the homesickness, the final return to their desolated land. One can no more understand Navaho attitudes—particularly toward white people—without knowing of Fort Sumner than he can comprehend Southern

attitudes without knowing of the Civil War. (Kluckhohn and Leighton 1962:41)[2]

Tohe's poem challenges the monologic Western historical narrative of the Long Walk, and rather embeds her poetry within another narrative tradition that stands in opposition to that Western historical imagination. When Tohe performs "In Dinétah," she is actively engaging Navajo poetic traditions. Tohe's poem actively engages recurrent tropes and images, creating a feelingful sense of continuity with oral traditions. When she evokes images of pregnant Navajo women being taken behind boulders to be shot, she is re-voicing an image that can be found in other narratives and poetry about the Long Walk. Her poem is thus thoroughly enmeshed in the voices and words of others and that, of course, is part of the rhetorical and feelingful power of this poem. But it is a selective sampling of voices. It works to valorize a sense of Navajo history that challenges a Western history overly focused on battles and leaders and the naturalizing course of Navajo assimilation (Denetdale 2007b). As Mistic raps in his song "Tribal Scars" about the Long Walk and Navajo history:

(6) Do you know what our people been through?
     Do you really know?
     Do you really know what went down?
     Forget the history books because they don't tell you nuthin
     (author's transcription)

Notice the inclusive use of "our" here. According to Mistic, this rap is aimed at educating young Navajos about their history. A historical perspective he fears they are forgetting. It explicitly rejects the history told in Western history books and instead posits an alternative history of, as Mistic says, "genocide." Like much hip-hop, Mistic sees his work as having an educational element as well.

Tohe's poetry, like the rap of Mistic and the poetry of Tapahonso, Help, and other Navajo poets, offers an alternative history to the Western literate gaze. This is a narrative that is deeply embedded, often explicitly so, within Navajo narrative traditions. They interanimate each other. Indeed, they gain their rhetorical force through such interanimating discursive strategies. Done in English, the poetry and rap reaches out not just to Navajos who speak Navajo, but also to Navajos who do not speak Navajo, and, of course, it circulates still further into the Western literate gaze. This is the ongoing circulation of discourse, made recognizable through and by Navajo ethnopoetics, implicated and entangled in the voices and words (if not images) of others. This is the identity work of telling and re-telling, imagining and reimagining histories. For Navajo poets (rappers included) the Long Walk can be continually reimagined, recirculated.

SIX

Intercultural Performances and the Dynamics of Place

> The understanding of a simple poem, for instance, involves not merely an understanding of the single words in their average significance, but a full comprehension of the whole life of a community as it is mirrored in the words, or as it is suggested by their overtones.
>
> Edward Sapir, "The Status of Linguistics as a Science"

Introduction

Up until now, I have been largely concerned with intracultural performances. In this chapter, I analyze portions of an intercultural performance by Laura Tohe to a non-Navajo audience in rural Illinois. By analyzing Tohe's metalinguistic commentaries about the use of Navajo, as well as her actual uses of Navajo in her performance, I argue that Tohe presents a metasemiotic stereotype of Navajo language users. In performing such stereotypic displays, Tohe also indexes her own Navajo identity and becomes iconic of it. Paying close attention to the uses of Navajo language place names also reveals how Tohe connects her performance with larger concerns about Navajo claims to place and language shift.

This chapter again takes a discourse-centered approach to language and culture following Sherzer (1987, 1994). Here, however, I focus less on the performance of poetry, and instead focus on how Tohe frames her performance. In focusing on a single discursive event and how it interconnects outwardly (both to the Navajo Nation and to more global concerns), I argue that we can begin to see how Native American intercultural performers lay the groundwork for future encounters with outsiders. That is, how do Navajos, and Native Americans more generally, create links between themselves and non-Native Americans about issues of import both locally and globally? It also should remind us that while Native American poetry is sometimes superficially valued for its aesthetic qualities as icons of quaint Indian-ness or New Age spirituality, political claims to place are often essential to understanding both Navajo poetry in particular and indigenous intercultural performances more generally (see, for useful discussions of representations of Native Americans, Deloria 1998, 2004, and chapters in Biolsi 2004 and Kan and Strong 2006).

Indexing Identity in Intercultural Performances

Tohe gave her performance on October 9, 2006, as a part of the annual Indigenous Peoples' Day celebration at Southern Illinois University at Carbondale (SIUC). Besides Tohe there were no other Navajos in the audience. Yet, this performance has a number of uses of Navajo language. Such uses of Navajo can be understood as "emblematic identity displays." As Silverstein (2003b:538) explains:

> It is important to realize that the key identity-relevant attributes of such cultural texts are not necessarily anything like represented "content" as such, but rather all the verbal and nonverbal signs that, displayed by and around the self, in effect wrap social personae, social spaces, moments in the social-organizational time, even institutional forms, with "in-group" (versus "out-group," of course) status.

In a more recent article Jocelyn Ahlers (2006:62) has insightfully described a speech style used by nonfluent Native Americans in California that she terms Native Language as Identity Marker (NLIM). Ahlers (2006) discusses how nonfluent Native American speakers' displays of Native language use—formulaic displays at that—come to formulate a shared Native American identity. The forms are spoken in the speakers' "heritage language" by a nonfluent speaker to an audience often committed to learning their own heritage languages (which may be different than the speakers') (Ahlers 2006:65). As Ahlers (2006:65) points out, "neither the speaker nor the audience can be assumed to have a native, or even a working knowledge of the language used." They act as emblems of identity. Such uses also create a "Native discourse space" (Ahlers 2006:71), so that what follows in English is recognized as "coming from a Native perspective" (Ahlers 2006:72) to a Native audience.

In Carbondale, on the other hand, we had an "intercultural" performance more akin to the discussions by Cruikshank (1997), Myers (1991, 1994), and Laura Graham (2002). As I discussed in Chapter 4, Cruikshank (1997) has described the Yukon International Storytelling Festival as an intercultural performance. There Yukon elders must delicately calibrate their performances in relationship to their audiences. They must balance assertions of place that may go unrecognized by outsiders, with assertions that will challenge public law in subtle ways. The use of place names, for these elders, then becomes a potent—if potentially obscure—way of making claims about connections to place (see also Dinwoodie 1998). Likewise, Myers (1991, 1994) has discussed the intercultural performances behind Australian Aboriginal acrylic art. There Aboriginal acrylic art, based on The Dreamings, can be misrecognized by outsiders as traditional without any understanding of what the linkages to The Dreamings are and how, in some cases, these are political claims to place. The political linkages to place in such intercultural performances are not always—intentionally or unintentionally—clear or overt. More recently, as Graham (2002:203) writes concerning Yanomami displays in intercultural performances, we see the way linguistic practices are enmeshed in such displays of identity:

> Here the words and gestures index "Yanomaminess" for outsiders, rather than calling forth particular spiritual or mythological referents as they would do for fully traditional Yanomami listeners who understand the way these propositions and imitated supernatural gestures index traditional beliefs underlying them.

In this chapter, I argue that Tohe's performance acts as a form of "second order indexicality" (Silverstein 2003) as well, one that indexes a Navajo identity to "outsiders." That is, while many of the poetic and linguistic devices Tohe uses in this performance clearly are linked with recognizable Navajo genres, indexing links to kinship and landscape to the mythic in the context in which they were performed, they often became referentially empty to non-Navajo audience members who did not understand

Navajo. The indexical linkages were not to a stock of Navajo knowledge, but rather these indexical linkages were to an *assumption* of a stock of Navajo knowledge. For many audience members, then, Tohe becomes an index and an icon of Navajoness (here understood as an indigenous articulation). Tohe's continued use of the Navajo place names and of poetic forms of Navajo, throughout the night, reinforced the importance of the use of Navajo that Tohe was describing. They also became emblems of Navajo identity.

As we have seen throughout this book, Navajo poetry written predominately in English will, at times, use Navajo lexical items and code-switch into Navajo. This code-switching often clusters around Navajo kinship terms, place names, mythic figures, emotions, ideophones, and other poetic devices that many Navajos consider incommensurate with English. These forms become emblematic of what Navajo poets consider to be important about the Navajo language. They become an affective register in and through poetry. Tohe's use of Navajo in this intercultural performance, and in the kinds of Navajo she uses, is thus consonant with the practices of other Navajos who write poetry in both Navajo and English.

Indigenous Peoples' Day, Carbondale, Illinois

Carbondale is a small college community in rural southern Illinois. It is about a two-and-a-half-hour drive from St. Louis and about five hours from Chicago. Tohe had flown into St. Louis and had been ferried to Carbondale by the president of the Native American Student Organization (NASO), which sponsored the event. Through my contact with Tohe, she had been invited by NASO to talk on "the importance of place among Indigenous Peoples" (flyer for Indigenous Peoples' Day, personal collection of author). The event was metapragmatically labeled by the flyer produced by NASO as "speaking on the importance of place among Indigenous Peoples." Tohe was identified as a "Diné Poet and Writer." It was her decision to be labeled "Diné," the Navajo language ethnonym, and not Navajo. In my experience, when Navajo poets perform in front of non-Navajo audience they tend to use Diné more than they use Navajo. She performed at the Student Center auditorium beginning around

7:30 p.m. The performance, followed by questions from the audience, lasted for over an hour.[1]

NASO's Indigenous Peoples' Day event acts as a counter-discourse to the more widely celebrated Columbus Day. In 2006 NASO was a small but active organization. Traditionally, Southern Illinois University has had a small Native American population (between 60–100). Most of these students come from Chicago or the surrounding area around Carbondale and St. Louis. As a faculty member who had worked with Native Americans and taught courses about Native Americans, I was recruited into helping with the planning for Indigenous Peoples' Day 2006 by the NASO's president, who had also been in a class that I taught on Native American verbal art. Not only did she recruit me to help with Indigenous Peoples' Day, but I was also recruited to help with the annual Native American heritage month (every November) and with the organization of what would become SIUC's Native American Studies minor in the summer of 2008.

The audience consisted of around fifty to sixty undergraduate students, graduate students, faculty, and community members. The audience was largely sympathetic to issues concerning Native Americans, including faculty concerned with indigenous issues, students that had taken or would take courses on Native American issues, as well as students from NASO. None of the students in NASO was Navajo. Tohe was the only Navajo in the Student Center auditorium that night. The event was also covered by the campus newspaper, but not by the local newspaper.[2]

The audience was significantly different from those in my previous experiences videotaping and audio-recording as Tohe performed her poetry. I had videotaped and audio-recorded her performances before largely Navajo audiences. Indeed, one of the poems she performed in Carbondale, "Cat or Stomp" (Tohe 1999), forms the basis of an article I have published elsewhere (Webster 2008a; also Chapter 4, this volume). In fact, Tohe had read and commented on that article for me and she knew that poem was a particular favorite of mine. Her performing it that night was, I believe, partly due to my presence. This was the first time I had videotaped her performing before a non-Navajo audience. Her performance differed from the previous performances I had documented in the explicit focus on the Navajo language and Navajo places. It was also more explicit concerning the brutality of the boarding school experience. This is something she has written about (see Tohe 1999), but in many performances before Navajo audiences she did not go into the details of the brutality (see example 6 below).

Though the event took place on Indigenous Peoples' Day, Tohe's performance was very much about being Navajo. Tohe had also originally planned to do a PowerPoint presentation showing pictures of the Navajo landscape. However, the technology did not oblige that night and Tohe could not use her slideshow, making this performance in some ways more spontaneous than it might otherwise have been.

As mentioned previously, Tohe is an associate professor of English at Arizona State University, has published several books of poetry (Tohe 1999, 2005), and has co-edited a volume of Native American women's poetry (Erdrich and Tohe 2002). She mentioned all of these things later in her introduction, after she had introduced herself by clan, first in Navajo and then in English. She has performed her poetry before a variety of audiences. This includes largely Navajo audiences, such as those at performances I recorded while doing fieldwork, and non-Navajo audiences such as those she performed for in Lima, Peru (as she notes in this Carbondale performance). Such statements vouchsafe her legitimacy as a poet and seem targeted for a non-Navajo audience that might be overly concerned with credentials. She also speaks Navajo and she places that ability and her early childhood within the reservation context early on during the performance.

(1)		grew up on the Reservation	297
		born on the Reservation	298
		I spoke Navajo	299
		as my first language and then learn	300
		English	301

During my time doing fieldwork in the summer of 2000, she was taking classes at Diné College, the Navajo tribal college, to learn to write Navajo (on Diné College see House 2002). The fruits of those classes can be seen in her most recent book of poetry *Tséyi': Deep in the Rock* (Tohe

2005). Not only is the title in Navajo, but there are several poems that are written entirely in Navajo. *Tséyi'* is an important geographic location in Navajo ethnogeography and has been transformed phonologically into the "Chelly" of Canyon de Chelly (see Kelley and Francis 1994; Jett 2001 on Navajo ethnogeography). The book also contains photos taken by Stephen Storm of *Tséyi'*. These photos visually link the written poetry with places in *Tséyi'*. That a Navajo place name, in Navajo, forms the title of this book becomes a point for Tohe to talk about land and language. She is also clearly knowledgeable about the ethnographic and linguistic literature that has been written about Navajos.

I Just Gave You an Introduction

On a mild October evening, Tohe climbed onto the stage, and when she began speaking she said:[3]

(2) Yá'át'ééh   1
    Shí éí Laura Tohe   2
    Shí éí Tsénabahiłnii   3
    Tódích'íinii éí bá shíshchíín   4

The audience in Carbondale, Illinois, almost to a person, did not understand the language that was being spoken. The language was Navajo, and Tohe was beginning to introduce herself in Navajo and by her clans. As she explained after the introduction in Navajo:

(3) I just gave you   14
    an introduction   15
    language   16
    which is what we do   17
    when we   18
    speak before an audience   19
    we let   20
    people know   21
    that   22
    uhm   23

we	24
are	25
members	26
of our clans	27
and	28
uhh	29
there's anyone in the audience	30
who might be a member of my clan	31
will be	32
considered relatives	33

I had seen Tohe perform this introduction several times before (Webster 2008a), but I had never seen her perform this introduction to an entirely non-Navajo audience. During my fieldwork on the Navajo Nation from 2000–2001, I had recorded numerous examples of this introduction in Navajo to largely Navajo audiences. As Tohe explains, later in her performance:

(4)	Tony	179
	uhm	180
	he was on the Navajo reservation my reservation	181
	for about a year and a half and	182
	he was	183
	everywhere that we went	184
	and I	185
	als	186
	almost like my own personal stalker	187
	[LAUGHTER]	188
	but	189
	he was on the reservation so long that	190
	we started to call him our in-law	191
	[LAUGHTER]	
	and we used to tea:se him that	192
	maybe you would find a Navajo woman on	
	the reservation	193
	[LAUGHTER]	

Tohe's use of "Tony" here indexes for the audience her familiarity with me. It establishes a link for the audience to understand her presence in southern Illinois. The vowel lengthening in *tease* adds an affective quality to the phrase again indexing familiarity. Indeed, not only is Tohe's discussion of teasing about me, it is also a form of teasing itself. Such teasing often creates affective bonds among Navajos and sometimes non-Navajos. I was told on more than one occasion by Navajos that it was a good thing that Navajos teased me relentlessly while I was doing fieldwork.

In the performance by Tohe here of her clan relations, there was little chance for the audience to understand the referential content of the opening use of Navajo. Instead, it had the pragmatic effect of indexically locating her as Navajo. Behind this use of Navajo and other uses of Navajo, as well as discussions about Navajo, was an implicit theory about languages (Navajo and English). The Navajo language forms precede the English forms. Tohe must explain to a non-Navajo audience what is and is not important for Navajos. She uses language as one way of indexing her status as a Navajo and of indexing the importance of the Navajo language to Navajo identity. However, she does more than merely describe such linguistic behavior. She also performs them as well.

I have recorded similar introductions by Tohe and a number of other Navajo performers to largely Navajo audiences. When Tohe performs before largely Navajo audiences, her opening in Navajo and by her clans is, on the one hand, referentially informative. Navajos can reckon their clan relations with her. On the other hand, it also serves the indexical function of indicating that Tohe is the kind of Navajo that speaks Navajo and knows the Navajo names for her clans. It thus places her within a sphere of meaningful indexical linguistic practices. Even Navajos who are not fluent in Navajo will perform this greeting and introduction in Navajo. For example, at the Diné Language Fair in 2001 at Diné College in Tsaile that I attended, elementary- and middle-school students were judged on how easily they were able to introduce themselves in Navajo. The second-order indexicality here is that students who use such forms index that they are the kind of Navajos who learn the language and traditional greetings. Diné College, as well as middle schools and elementary schools, actively promote this modeling of Navajo identity through linguistic practice.

Such uses of Navajo formulaic introductions are, then, in some ways similar to Ahlers (2006) discussion of the use of Native language by non-fluent speakers. They aid in creating a Navajo discursive space that is akin to Ahlers (2006:70) "Native discourse space." It frames that what will follow, even if in English, will be from a Navajo perspective. It differs, however, in that there is also a referential component to this introduction. Navajos can and do reckon whether or not they are related to the speaker by way of this introduction. It also differs in that Tohe is a competent speaker of Navajo. Her use of the opening here grounded her in a Navajo identity and highlighted the importance of the Navajo language to that identity.

We Were Not Allowed to Speak the Language at School

Knowing the Navajo language is not a neutral proposition. It is, as Tohe notes, not a given for Navajos. As I discussed in Chapter 1, the Navajo language has recently been described as a "threatened language" or a language shifting to English. Indeed, there is evidence that the number of children speaking or understanding Navajo entering elementary schools has dramatically decreased in the last twenty years (Holm and Holm 1995; see also Crawford 2008:426). Tohe brings this point up early on in her poetry performance. She does this in connection with the Navajo code talkers. Tohe's father had been a Navajo code talker, and she had written a poem about her father and the other code talkers. In bringing up the Navajo code talkers, she also attempts to establish a shared (or potentially shared) background knowledge based on U.S. pop culture. She does this by referencing the 2002 big budget film *Windtalkers*, which ostensibly was about the Navajo code talkers.

(5)	some of you have probably seen	453
	the film *Windtalker* which is based	454
	there's a story	455
	in there	456
	about	457
	uhm	458
	one of the characters or	459

two of the characters are	460
are Navajo code talkers	461

Linking to a wider, non-Navajo movie about the Navajo code talkers is one way that Tohe can validate the global value of the Navajo language. Tohe then turns to discussing her father's service as a code talker. She then turns to the "ironic thing" about the use of the Navajo language as a code during World War II. Namely, that while the United States was using Navajo as a code during World War II, the language was simultaneously being actively suppressed on the Navajo Nation. On the one hand, the United States could appropriate the Navajo language for its purposes in war abroad. On the other hand, the United States could actively suppress the Navajo language in the Navajo homeland.

(6)	back on the reservation	499
	back on	500
	at ho:me	501
	we were not allowed to speak the language at school	502
	we were not allow:ed	503
	to	504
	uhm	505
	speak in our classrooms	506
	uhm	507
	if you did	508
	you were punished for it	509
	so our language was	510
	a lot of ways	511
	during that assimilation era was	512
	uhm	513
	beaten out of us	514
	if you spoke your language	515
	you'll end up standing in a corner	516
	facing the wall	517
	you had your hand slapped	518
	with a ruler	519
	sometimes your mouth was washed out	520

with soap and water	521
and as a result	522
you know [LOW and SOFTER]	523
what you do when that happens you don't speak	524
you don't wanna speak	525
because you are afraid	526
you'll be	527
punished for it	528
so while the	529
war was using the Navajo language	530
as code	531
on the reservations we were not allowed	532
to speak our native language and I think	533
for	534
for that reason an and other	535
reasons	536
uhm	537
many of the	538
generation of Navajo people after	539
after me	540
don't speak the language	541
and so we are though	542
trying to	543
sa:ve our language	544

Tohe presents this time on the Navajo Nation as one of active suppression of the language. She highlights the violence that was often involved with the suppression of Navajo. As she states, the language "was beaten out of us." Notice the use of the exclusive first person here. Tohe is linking herself with the experiences of other Navajos. She is excluding members in the audience. She has done this previously when she stated that, "We'll always use our own names." In both cases, Tohe speaks for the Navajo "we-ness." Notice that this contrasts with her inclusive construction of the projective Navajo we discussed in the previous chapter. She again uses "we" for Navajos when she discusses the efforts to "save" the Navajo language. Notice in line 523 that she quiets her voice and speaks softly when she says "you know" after she has described the punishments. There is an affective quality here as she then turns to the results of such punishments.

She also connects the violence of the "assimilation era" to the current language shift from Navajo to English. She has already established her own Navajo credentials earlier by opening the performance speaking in Navajo. Her choice of connecting the current language situation with the well-known Navajo code talkers is instructive. She clearly links the Navajo language with, as she says earlier, "when the Navajo language was being used to help save America." Note the lexical parallelism:

(7) when the Navajo language was being used 482
    uhm 483
    to help sa:ve America 484

(8) and so we are though 542
    trying to 543
    sa:ve our language 544

The lexical item "save" recurs. In both cases the vowel is elongated, calling into relief the utterance. In the one case, the Navajo language helped "save America" and now Navajos must try to "save" the Navajo language. The recurrent use of the lexical item "save," then, echoes between the use of the Navajo language for the code talkers and the current language situation that Navajos face. It puts the two propositions into relief together.

The trope that the Navajo language helped "save America" is in wider circulation on and around the Navajo Nation. For example, it was often repeated at public meetings concerning Arizona Proposition 203, which meant to restrict bilingual education and which many Navajos I spoke with saw as an affront to the Navajo language. As I noted earlier, I attended a number of local meetings on the Navajo Nation that were held to discuss the potential ramifications of Proposition 203 and how to oppose the passage of the proposition. At a number of meetings the audience usually was composed of Navajos from a community, and elder Navajo men and women speakers wept as they spoke about their devotion and respect for their language, "*Diné bizaad.*"

Such a comparison as Tohe draws clearly taps into a wider discourse that can be found in the United States on "fairness" and "hypocrisy." It is that discourse that Tohe seems to be accessing in her discussion of the suppression of the Navajo language while it was simultaneously "saving America." This is a critique of assimilation policies, policies that did not recognize the importance of the Navajo language to the survival of the United States. This trope, that Navajo helped "save America," elevates the Navajo language to global importance. It also rhetorically obligates the non-Navajo American audience to the "debt" they owe the Navajos and their language.

We'll Always Use Our Own Names

Basso (1996) opened new ground in Native American studies and in linguistic anthropology more generally with his careful studies of Western Apache place names in didactic and other morally, interpersonally potent discursive events. Since then, a number of insightful discussions of Native American place-naming practices have appeared, building on Basso's work (Cruikshank 1990, 1998; Kelley and Francis 1994; Dinwoodie 1998; Jett 2001; Samuels 2001; Cowell 2004; Collins 1998; Thornton 2008; Nevins 2008). A number of these works have focused on the tensions between indigenous place-naming practices and Euro-American inscriptive practices (Collins 1998; Samuels 2001; Cowell 2004). James Collins (1998), for example, discusses the use of Tolowa (Pacific Coast Athabaskan) place names as a way of asserting a prior placement to English or Spanish place-naming practices. As Collins (1998:150) explains, "*Xus We-yó'* [Tolowa Language] argues for the ancientness of Tolowa occupation of that region. But it also argues for a link between that archaicness and the present period."

Samuels (2001:289), in discussing what he terms the "phonological iconicity" (similarity of sounds across languages) of place names, points out that Britton Goode, a Western Apache linguist, had attempted to discern an Apache etymology for what is often regarded as a Tohono O'odham–inspired place name: Tucson. As Samuels (2001:290) argues, "finding an Apache meaning in the English name *Tucson* denies whites the final right of denotation and insists that the meaning of any such name is not closed but rather contains its own response." Samuels shows how Western Apaches have actively engaged in the decoding of place names and the inherent ambiguities that such punning creates and sustains.

Eleanor Nevins (2008) describes how Western Apaches use contemporary English language pop-culture place names (see also Basso 1996:151–152; Samuels 2004b). As Nevins (2008:200) notes, however, these, "media-derived names are not used for established residential communities on the reservation but are applied only to newly constructed housing developments." Nevins (2008:207) argues that the use of English "highlights their difference from more 'traditional' residence patterns" because English acts as an icon of difference with Apache norms (see also Basso 1979). Navajos also name residential neighborhoods after popular culture references. For example, when I lived in Chinle, Arizona, I lived in a government-built duplex complex named "Beverly Hills" by local Navajo residents. Chinle is a population center in the central area of the Navajo Nation. It abuts Canyon de Chelly National Monument and is a tourist destination. Three hotels cater to both national and international tourists. However, "Beverly Hills" is a relatively impoverished housing neighborhood of an otherwise impoverished region of the Navajo Nation. The use of the name Beverly Hills stands in stark contrast to the poverty all around. To echo a point made by Nevins (2008), many non-Navajos were unfamiliar with the use of Beverly Hills for the neighborhood. One acquaintance of mine, who worked for the National Parks Service at Canyon de Chelly and had lived in Parks Service housing outside Chinle for years, was unfamiliar with the use of Beverly Hills for the area.

Andrew Cowell (2004) has discussed how Euro-Americans in Colorado reimagined Arapaho place names and reinscribed them onto the landscape, especially Rocky Mountain National Park, in a manner that is contrary to Arapaho naming practices and, in effect, removing the Arapaho from the lowlands of Colorado (where they lived) and placing them in the mountains (where they did not live). As Cowell (2004:29) notes, "The specific Arapaho names now on the map reflect white interests and conceptions of exoticism in the twentieth century." Cowell's analysis reminds us that even the appearance of indigenous names can be fraught with complexities that, in fact, erase the presence of indigenous people as they reinscribe and reimagine.

Tohe (2005) titles her most recent book *Tséyi': Deep in the Rock*. She does not provide the English place name Canyon de Chelly in the title. Rather she glosses the Navajo form into English. *Tsé* is a noun and can be glossed as "rock" in English; *-yi'* is a postpositional and can be glossed as "between, inside, on the interior." *Tséyi'* is both the conventional word for "canyon" and the place name for what is commonly referred to by non-Navajos as Canyon de Chelly (Jett 2001:190); *Chelly* (še'i or še) is the phonologically reanalyzed form of *Tséyi'*.[4] This is phonological iconicity that obscures indigenous placement. Note that even the phonologically altered (and redundant) Canyon de Chelly reinscribes the place with an indexical link to Spanish influences on the Southwest. Tohe's book also intertextually taps into Navajo "genres of place," much Navajo verbal art begins at named and knowable ethnogeographical locations (see Thornton 2008:23 on genres of place).

Toward the middle of her performance at Carbondale, Tohe discusses the title of the book and her use of Navajo. Here Tohe explains how the use of Navajo in her title and the use of Navajo place names are important to her and Navajos. Notice that she presents this discussion as a series of reported speech events. She first quotes herself in lines 1056–1057. She then uses quoted speech to report the response of the press in lines 1060–1066. Such uses of quoted speech make the performance of the discussion more vivid for the audience.

(9) Tséyi' 1039
is our name for this place that Navajo Canyon de Chelly 1040
printed on the map 1041
"Canyon de Chelly" 1042
uhm 1043
that work 1044
was al 1045
we'll 1046
always use our own 1047
na:mes 1048

for the places on our homeland	1049
so when I was uhm	1050
gonna publish this book I was asked	1051
what I want to	1052
title this book	1053
and so I said	1054
like	1055
"Tséyi'	1056
deep in the rock"	1057
but the press	1058
came back	1059
and said "we prefer	1060
deep in the rock	1061
Tséyi'	1062
for marketing purposes	1063
people will be able to understa:nd that	1064
uhm	1065
better"	1066
and	1067
I was	1068
very insistent	1069
that	1070
uhh	1071
we have	1072
Tséyi' first because	1073
Navajo language was here	1074
before	1075
co:ntact	1076
and	1077
so	1078
they pu	1079
they	1080
uhm	1081
they were convinced by that	1082
so that's why it is called	1083
"Tséyi' deep in the rock"	1084

Notice that Tohe contrasts the name "printed" on a map with the Navajo name. Thus while the maps may have the name "Canyon de Chelly" on them, the Navajo "always use our own names for the places on our homeland." Here she signals that Canyon de Chelly is not a Navajo name, and that *Tséyi'* is a part of the Navajo homeland. Her statement that Navajos always use their own names for places is reminiscent of comments a number of Navajos made to me while I was doing fieldwork, namely that Navajo place names could not be translated into English; one had to use the Navajo place names for Navajo places.

Navajos that I know occasionally play with Navajo place names and phonologically "translate" them into English. For example, *Lók'a'ch'égai* (normally written *Lukachukai* on maps) was sometimes called "Luckychucky" by Navajos that I knew who lived in Chinle and Lukachukai, Arizona. Here they played on what they said were tourists' mispronunciations of *Lók'a'ch'égai*. Or take a more pertinent example, *Tséyi'* was sometimes called Disney by a Navajo neighbor I had in Chinle. Following Samuels (2001), I argue that some of the pleasure that my neighbor had in using Disney was from the phonological iconicity between *Tséyi'* and *Disney*. According to my neighbor they "sound alike." Another Navajo I knew said that rather than *Tséyi'* being Disney, it was instead *Tsé Ná'áz'élí* (the rock that water flows around). This place is also in *Tséyi'*. That Canyon de Chelly is now a tourist stop for both U.S. and international tourists brings a relevance to the verbal play by Navajos of *Tséyi'* or *Tsé Ná'áz'élí* as Disney. These places are like Disney in that they attract U.S. and international tourists. But Chinle and the surrounding area, including *Tséyi'*, are also impoverished places as well. And in this way it is very much *not* like Disney. Here linguistic play can call attention to social realities such as the influx of tourists onto the Navajo Nation and to the economic disparities between Navajos and non-Navajo tourists. Navajos would not confuse *Tséyi'* with a tourist attraction such as Disney, and the pun here suggests that Navajos are not convinced that non-Navajo tourists do not see *Tséyi'* as simply a tourist attraction and not home to many Navajo families and an important historical and mythic place. Indeed, my neighbor still had a sheep camp in *Tséyi'*. When Navajos pun *Tséyi'* as Disney, they are challenging *de Chelly* as phonologically iconic of *Tséyi'* and offering their own substitution with its attendant social commentary. Here such punning resonates with discussions concerning Western Apache punning—especially place-name punning—by Samuels (2001, 2004b). This is punning as resistance, in the sense of James Scott's (1990) "arts of resistance," and social critique.

Note that this commentary about *Tséyi'* differs from the practice described by Nevins (2008) and the example of Beverly Hills I discussed above, however, in that the media-derived name Disney is used not for a new housing development, but rather for an important place in Navajo ethnogeography. Yet this place now has a National Park Service Visitor Center, complete with a mock-*hooghan* to greet tourists. It is reminiscent of the Western Apache practices described by Nevins in that the use of the English language media-derived place-name Disney indexically links with the oppositional language ideology toward the English language that I described in Chapter 3. Thus the use of English acts as an icon of difference with Navajo norms.

The importance of writing, suggested in Tohe's reference to maps, becomes more important once she recounts the story concerning the press wanting to use the English glossing first and not the Navajo place name. Tohe must convince the people at the press that they should use the Navajo place name and that it should come first. She argues this by pointing out that the Navajo language precedes "contact" (the time when Europeans and Native peoples encountered each other). The use of the Navajo place name indexically links the Navajos to a prior placement, but it also reasserts the Navajos current placement. Inscribing it on the cover of her book of poetry only further validates both the currency and the primacy of Navajos. Note also that by placing the Navajo place name before the English glossing, it is iconically connecting with the Navajos being here before Europeans and their languages. Thus the title iconically maps out the historical order: first Navajos and then English (and both present).

She makes the point concerning maps again when she discusses a poem about the Long Walk and the internment at *Hwéeldi* (see Tohe 2007 for her view of the importance of remembering *Hwéeldi*).

(10) I make some references also to   1254
    Hwéeldi   1255
    which   1256
    is a pla:ce   1257
    for   1258
    it's at   1259
    southcentral New Mexico where the Navajo people were   1260
    incarcerated for four years   1261
    from 1864 to 1868 just around   1262
    uhm   1263
    the time of the civil war   1264
    uhm   1265
    that the Navajo people were   1266
    for:ced ou:t of this ho:meland ou:t of Tséyi'   1267
    and other places of our reservation   1268
    o   1269
    other places on our ho:melands   1270
    and for:ced to   1271
    Hwéeldi   1272
    which is a Navajo wor:d but   1273
    uhm   1274
    in   1275
    again   1276
    in the map   1277
    see it as   1278
    Fort Sumner   1279

Note again the contrast that Tohe creates between the Navajo form and the "map" form. Again we see the Navajo form as the "prior" or "legitimate" form and the English form as somehow inauthentic or inaccurate. In line 1267, Tohe draws out and lengthens the vowels in *o:ut*, *ho:meland*, and *o:ut* again, and in the retroflex in *for:ced*. In doing so, she calls attention to *for:ced ou:t* and *ho:meland ou:t*. She is emphasizing that this was a forced removal. They did not leave willingly. She repeats this emphasis on both *homeland* and *forced* in lines 1270 and 1271 respectively. Note also that in line 1267 she uses *Tséyi'* here without further explication. Her use of the Navajo word links back to her earlier discussion of the importance of using Navajo place names.

Implicit in her discussion is a view that argues that since the Navajo language preceded European languages, they are not equivalent. Navajo and English are not equivalent precisely because Navajo was here before English. The place name in Navajo is thus a better fit to the place than any English place name would be. This, I might add, fits a trend on the Navajo Nation where Navajo Chapters (regional political units) are changing their names from English names to traditional Navajo names. For example, the chapter formerly named "Hogback" has legally changed their name to the Navajo place name Tse' Daa' Kaan (*Tsétaak'ą́* [rock that slants into the water]). This place name was originally used for a prominent place near the current community in northern New Mexico and was and continues to be the Navajo alternative to the English place name. In such ways, Navajo place names have different indexical linkages because, as Navajo Nation Council Speaker Lawrence Morgan stated, "Most of those are names [English names] given by the early settlers, and then they moved away . . . The Navajo names have always been there" (Whitehurst 2007).

I Wanted to Become Literate in My Own Language

As I discussed above, during my fieldwork on the Navajo Nation, Tohe was taking classes at Diné College in Tsaile to learn how to read and write Navajo. As she explained earlier in the performance (lines 299–301), she is a Navajo speaker. However, like many Navajo speakers, she was not literate in Navajo. In this example, Tohe describes her own attempts to learn to read and write Navajo. She also connects the Navajo language to Navajo ceremonies.

(11)	I wanted to become literate	1438
	in my ow:n	1439
	la:nguage	1440
	uhm	1441
	I wanted to	1442
	learn how to rea:d in my	1443

so I took courses at Diné College	1444
uhm	1445
for four summers	1446
and uhh	1447
I learn how	1448
to	1449
rea:d and write	1450
my language	1451
I'm still lea:rning	1452
I won't say that	1453
I'm	1454
uhm	1455
perfect in it but	1456
uhm	1457
I'm trying to	1458
to rea:d	1459
and write	1460
in my own language so that	1461
uhm	1462
other	1463
Navajo speakers can	1464
rea:d this	1465
and uh	1466
this	1467
I	1468
I love	1469
the stories	1470
I love to hear the stories	1471
in Navajo language I think	1472
because I think the language	1473
is a way	1474
to	1475
connect to	1476
uhm	1477
the worldview	1478
of the Navajo people	1479

it's a way to become intimate	1480
with the worldview of the Navajo people	1481
and it's a way to participate	1482
in the ceremonies	1483
of the Navajo people which I have done I	1484
I've participated in	1485
the Blessing way	1486
ceremonies	1487

Here I want to call attention to how Tohe defines the importance of the Navajo language. First, writing in Navajo becomes a way for Tohe to speak directly to other Navajo speakers. This is so even though most Navajo speakers do not also read the language. But the ideal is that Navajo speakers will be able to read her poetry in Navajo.

However, Tohe's book is sold on the Navajo Nation. In 2007, I saw copies of it at Gloria Emerson's 'Ahwééh/Gohwééh Coffee Place in Shiprock, New Mexico. 'Ahwééh and Gohwééh are two Navajo words for "coffee." Emerson is a Navajo educator, painter, and she also writes poetry and has had her own book of poetry and painting published (Emerson 2003). It was also sold at Cool Runnings in St. Michaels, Arizona, which is a music store that also produces Navajo musicians (like Blackhorse Mitchell) and has published Navajo poetry (for example, by Ford Ashley). Both of these are locally controlled businesses and are frequented by a Navajo clientele. However, during the summer of 2007, late fall of 2007, and the summer of 2008, Tohe's book was not sold at the Visitors Center at Canyon de Chelly National Monument, which sells a number of books about Canyon de Chelly and is frequented largely by non-Navajos.

Second, with reference to her use of Navajo, Tohe argues for a felt attachment to the Navajo language. Tohe "love[s] to hear the stories in the Navajo language." As a number of Navajos told me at different times, for some things, Navajo is just a "better" or "more accurate" language than English. This is the felt attachment to language. There is a pleasure in hearing and using the Navajo language. To know the Navajo language, for these Navajos, then, is to become "intimate with the worldview of the Navajo." This is an essentialist discourse and has been documented for Navajo educators at Diné College by House (2002).

Third, following on that point, the use of the Navajo language is connected to a Navajo "worldview." The term "worldview" echoes the work of Gary Witherspoon (1977). Witherspoon created a largely idealized and decontextualized perspective on Navajo language and culture. It assumes a homogenous Navajo worldview and homogenous "the Navajo universe." In my experience, however, Navajos tend to disagree on a number of points. In fact, Tohe directly engaged that topic during her performance when she discussed the "fourth world / or fifth world depending on / who is / telling the story" (lines 127–130). When she was asked about the variation between fourth and fifth worlds during the Q&A, she replied with what I have come to expect from Navajo consultants when I try to pin them down on a topic, "It depends" (line 1973).

However, as a trope, the idea that the Navajo language connects with an entire worldview or philosophy, is quite common among Navajo educators. Some argue that the use of Navajo connects to an entire philosophy, an entire way of understanding the world (see House 2002). Consider, for example, a recent discussion at a conference involving Navajo educators and community members, where some self-identified Christian Navajos did not want the Navajo language taught to their children because they believe that Navajo philosophy (i.e., religion) and the Navajo language cannot be separated. Indeed, some non-Christian Navajos agreed with this perspective as well. This, I might add, is the logic that undergirds the phrase *Dinék'ehjí yáłti'* (he/she is talking the Diné way). Living the Navajo way is intimately linked here with speaking Navajo. English lacks the connection to Navajo religion that the Navajo language has. As one Navajo explained to me, English is more powerful in the secular world, Navajo is more powerful spiritually. That is why—according to him—English and Navajo cannot be translated, the one into the other or vice versa. In such ways, Navajo and English are said to be not equivalent because they tap into two entirely different stocks of knowledge (compare with Richland 2007 on similar linguistic sentiments among the Hopi).

Nihik'inizdidláád (Luminescence Is All Around)

Throughout the night, Tohe repeatedly mentioned that Navajo is a "poetic language." She discussed the poetic uses of repetition in Navajo songs and the use of repetition in other Navajo poets' poetry. Again, this idea that the Navajo language is a poetic language was an idea that many Navajo poets often expressed to me during fieldwork. Indeed, this was one of the key places where Navajo poets expressed incommensurability between Navajo and English. The Navajo form, they said, is just more "poetic" or "better." These were feelingful associations. That is, Navajos couched these statements in emotional terms. Navajo "felt" better than an English form. Navajo and English then are not equivalent, because they do not have the same felt attachments.

To get a sense of that I want to provide another example. This example concerns a discussion by Tohe about her attempts to translate a poem written entirely in Navajo into English. This example is from late in the performance.

(12) the Navajo language is very poetic 2211
when I first started writing 2212
I used to think about poems in Navajo 2213
and then write 2214
turn them into English 2215
and I guess maybe in some ways I still do that 2216
because like I said the language is very poetic 2217
the way it looks at the world 2218
the world in terms of dualities 2219
and even that 2220
there's this line in that poem about female rain 2221
about how the luminescence is all around 2222
it took a long time to try 2223
to find an equivalent in English 2224
because the word itself a:h 2225

there's that one word 2226
I love that word in Navajo 2227

/nihik'inizdidláád which	2228
it's an action	2229
you know in Navajo it's verb based	2230
and so /nihik'inizdidláád means you know	2231
this light	2232
just	2233
poured over us	2234
or among us	2235
and there's this relationship you have with the light	2236
but in the English it seems a little flat	2237
when you say luminescence all around	2238
it's just like a reporting about what happened	2239
and there's none of that	2240
personal connection	2241
to light	2242

First notice that when writing poetry, Tohe states that the Navajo language form comes before the English form. Navajo again precedes the English form. Navajo is thus the prior condition. Navajo poetic forms begin in Navajo and then must be translated into English. In that translation they lose something. Notice also that Tohe frames the poetic nature of Navajo as a general condition of the Navajo language. Notice still further that Tohe connects the language with a way of looking at the world. This is done indirectly when she states that, "Navajo, it's verb based." Many Navajos, Navajo academics, and Navajo non-academics often pointed out to me that one of the major differences between English and Navajo was that English is "noun based" and Navajo is "verb based."

This kind of vernacular categorization of the Navajo language as a verb-based language was a widely held position among Navajo writers and educators that I worked with. This is no doubt based on the importance of the verb in the Navajo language and a familiarity about the linguistic literature on the importance of the verb in Navajo (see, for example, Witherspoon 1977 and Young 2000). Navajo novelist Irvin Morris (1997), in his book *From the Glittering World*, writes this about his language and in particular the movement-based nature of place names:

The word and name *Tséhílí* [Where it flows into the canyon] refers simultaneously to the locality and the act of the creek entering the canyon there. The language is like that, full of motion. *Diné bizaad* [Navajo language] is verb-based, whereas English is noun-based. (Morris 1997:99)

Tohe also makes a feelingful connection to the Navajo language. She explains how she "love[s] that word in Navajo." She highlights *nihik'inizdidláád* with a slight rise in pitch when she produces the Navajo form. The word *nihik'inizdidláád* can be morphologically analyzed as follows:

(13) nihi-   cessative or termative prefix
      -k'i-   straight
      -niz-   faraway
      -di-   extending along a line
      -dláád   shine a light

Tohe poetically glosses this as "luminescence is all around." But note that Tohe considers this glossing to be incomplete. It misses something. It "seems a little flat." Rather than evoking the moment, it is rather merely a report of what has happened. The pragmatic relationship between language use and language form is missing in the English gloss. This relationship, as Tohe mentions, is a "personal connection to light" that is evoked by *nihik'inizdidláád*. Part of that personal connection may arise from the homonymy, that is words that sound the same but differ in meaning, between *nihi-* the cessative or termative prefix and the first person possessive plural prefix *nihi-* (our) (e.g., *nihizaad* [our language]). Structurally the termative *nihi-* and *nihi-* (our) do not align (the termative prefix is attached to verbs, the possessive prefix attaches to nouns). However, as potentially evocative, the homonymy here adds another layer of resonance. For Tohe, Navajo and English are incommensurate because English lacks the feelingful attachment between linguistic form and speaker.

This case of phonological iconicity, between *nihi-* and *nihi-*, where the two senses reverberate off of each other, was something that other

Navajos and Navajo poets often commented on. For example, Luci Tapahonso (2008:18), in her most recent book *a radiant curve*, notes that, "the word for mountain, *dził*, is very much like *dziil*, which means 'to be strong' or 'to possess strength.' Thus mountains serve as literal reminders that, like our ancestors, we can persevere in difficult situations." While, we might consider this a "secondary rationalization" (see Silverstein 1979), it certainly motivates certain poetic expressions in Navajo. Indeed, many Navajo consultants I have worked with have enjoyed speculating on various homonyms and near homonyms, attempting to find semantic links between iconic forms. As Kluckhohn and Leighton (1962:260) note, "homonymous words and syllables gives rise to the many puns in which the Navahos delight. For instance, *ha'át'íishą́ nílį́* means either 'what is flowing?' or 'what clan are you?' and The People [Navajos] tell stories with many embellishments about this question's being asked of a man who was standing beside a river."

The poetry of Rex Lee Jim is especially appreciated by Navajos for its homonyms and semantic ambiguity, its polyvalent nature. For example, one late autumn evening in 2000, I was interviewing Jim at an overlook at *Tséyi'* under a starlit night, and he told me a poem that he had been thinking about writing. He performed the poem in a soft voice. Each word a single line marked by a breath pause. My tape recorder running, Jim was illuminated by the headlights of my car. Here is the poem:

(14) Náhookǫs
 Náhookǫs
 Náhookǫs

Now *náhookǫs* can be conventionally glossed at least three ways that I know of. First, however, I should note that *náhookǫs* is actually a verb that can be glossed as "one stiff slender object makes a revolution." *Náhookǫs* is frozen etymologically; that is, most Navajos that I spoke with about this form could not segment the form into its constituent parts. However, it is one term for the Big Dipper. Beyond that, it is also the directional used for "north." The north is often associated by some Navajos with death and, hence, danger. Finally, it can mean something akin to "swirl" or "gyre." However, this swirling or gyring is always from east to west, which is often associated with the movement of sacred eventings. There is an implied movement within this poem. And, of course, on that night *Náhookǫs* (the Big Dipper) was within our visual field. It was, quite literally, moving above us. All of those associated meanings are evoked by degrees in Jim's poem. Yet none is privileged. When I talked with another Navajo poet about this poem, he pointed out that it was one of his favorites because it was, in his words, "ambiguous." It made him think.

Panel Wants Tséyi' Back in Navajo Hands

I have presented several snippets of an intercultural performance in Carbondale, Illinois, by Navajo poet Laura Tohe to a non-Navajo audience. I have focused primarily on snippets that concern Tohe's metalinguistic discussions concerning the Navajo language and her displays of the Navajo language. I have also attempted to connect her performance to other performances I recorded where she performs before largely Navajo audiences. Her opening frame in Navajo is done in both circumstances. In Tohe's performance in Illinois, it indexically linked her to a Navajo identity, an identity she aided in constructing through metasemiotic stereotyping; that is, she is constructing a stereotype of how Navajos use the Navajo language on the reservation. Here we have an intercultural performance of a metasemiotic stereotype. A part of that stereotype is that Navajos always introduce themselves by clans and in Navajo.

Another part of that metasemiotic stereotype is that Navajos "always use" Navajo place names on the Navajo Nation (lines 1046–1049). Her claim here is not so much about actual linguistic practice, but rather about the importance of Navajo language place names. Place names in Navajo are important emblems of Navajo identity and they are repeatedly used in Navajo written poetry. Tohe performs both these idealized ways of speaking at her performance in Illinois. That is, she is not just describing how Navajos should speak, she is actively performing such idealized ways of speaking for a non-Navajo audience. In doing so, she becomes not just an index of these idealized ways of speaking, but an icon of them.

Her book and her performance are an attempt to reestablish the indexical linkage between place and placement. In this way, the uses of such place names in her performance in Carbondale are reminiscent of the use of Tsilhqut'in place names in public discourse in Canada (Dinwoodie 1998). David Dinwoodie (1998) has described the debates that concerned the use of Native names for a Canadian park and how they were entangled in concerns with recognition. As Dinwoodie (1998:212) notes, "The selection of the park name registered continuing Tsilhqut'in presence in the area. For the Tsilhqut'in people of Nemiah Valley and, whether reluctantly or not, for the government too, the choice indicated a degree of political recognition." Dinwoodie's position assumes recognition that an indigenous language is indigenous and of indigenous placement. But as Cowell's (2004) discussion of Arapaho place names in Colorado parks reminds us, this may not always be the case. Note also the way that *Tséyi'* has been phonologically reanalyzed as *Chelly* in "Canyon de Chelly," thus obscuring Navajo placement and substituting Spanish placement. It marks *Tséyi'* foreign as the "Chelly" of *de Chelly*.

There are other discourses that attempt to remove Native American languages from the "native" category and make them foreign. Discourses that Tohe's performance is in a delicate dialogue with. As Barbra Meek (2006:120) thoughtfully shows for "Hollywood Injun English," "representing the speech of Native Americans as substandard and foreign portrays Native American speakers as foreign, as NOT native" (emphasis in original). I argue that not only can so-called Hollywood Injun English index foreignness, but the use of a Native language, such as Navajo, can be read as "foreign." Thus, for example, it is still the case that people like conservative pundit Phyllis Schlafly (2002) can decry the use of Navajo in ballots in Colorado as "foreign language ballots." In an article published in 2002 on her website Eagleforum.org, titled, "Foreign Language Ballots a Bad Idea," Schlafly lists ballots written in Navajo and Ute as examples of these "Foreign Language Ballots." Navajo, for Schlafly, is a "foreign," non-native language. It cannot be assumed that Navajo, or any indigenous language, always indexically links to "native-ness." Thus, Tohe must remind the audience that Navajos were here before contact. Tohe is challenging a linguistic ideology that naturalizes English with being "native born" to America. She is arguing for a prior placement and a continued placement. Furthermore, she also taps into a recurring trope among Navajos that the Navajo language helped "save America." At the same time, she notes that the Navajo language was actively and violently being suppressed. This is a powerful rhetorical gambit.

Dinwoodie's (1998) article also raises the issue of "going public" with Native language place names and the politics of recognition. Tohe's use of *Tséyi'* both in her book and in her performance links with larger concerns about land claims (both locally and more globally). On the one hand, her uses of the Navajo language place name for *Tséyi'* links with a whole clustering of associations that Navajo place names can evoke for Navajos (see Kelley and Francis 1994; Jett 2001). This clustering is largely outside the awareness of those in the audience. Place names are also aesthetically pleasing uses of language. On the other hand, my neighbor, who used to call *Tséyi'* Disney, was also one of the first people to alert me to the idea that Navajos would like Canyon de Chelly National Monument returned to the control of the Navajo Nation. In fact, an article in the *Navajo Times* on April 6, 2006, runs the headline "Panel Wants Tséyi' Back in Navajo Hands" (Yurth 2006a; see also Yurth 2006b). I do not think it surprising that the *Navajo Times'* headline also uses the Navajo name *Tséyi'* here. In Chinle, which abuts Canyon de Chelly National Monument, there is a shopping center that has a sign that combines the Navajo place name *Tseyi'* (without the tone marking) and the imprint of capitalism.[5] One can hear on KTNN at various times, live remotes from the Bashas store at, "the Tséyi' shopping mall in Chinle, Arizona" (recorded August 27, 2000). *Tséyi'* is a recognizable form both visually and aurally.

Some Navajos do want Canyon de Chelly National Monument, an important historical and mythic place (see Kelley and Francis 1994; Jett 2001), returned to the Navajo Nation, as the article from the *Navajo Times* makes clear. The U.S. Park Service currently manages Canyon de Chelly National Monument (see Keller and Turek 1998). Not all the residents that live there are pleased with how the park service has managed the monument (Yurth 2006a, b; see also Keller and Turek 1998). There is now a debate concerning legal rights to place between Navajos and the U.S. government over *Tséyi'*. Tohe's use of the Navajo form in the title of her book and in her performance in Illinois can then be linked to concerns about the control and management of *Tséyi'*.[6]

Conclusions

The Navajo language and Navajo place names are subjects of continued discussion on and around the Navajo Nation. Whether it is the recent discussion concerning the banning of employees speaking Navajo at RD's Drive In and the subsequent lawsuit (see Zachary 2005), or debates on the Navajo Nation concerning whether or not to use Navajo in an educational setting, or the attempt by some chapters to reinscribe their names with traditional Navajo language place names, or about the felt attachments that speakers have to their language, they continue and expand apace.[7] There are playful and politically salient puns of Navajo place names as English-language place names. Signs in Navajo were more common on the reservation in 2007 than they were when I first did fieldwork in 2000–2001. There is also discussion concerning who controls *Tséyi'*, the U.S. government or the Navajo Nation. There is still lingering resentment about Arizona Proposition 203, expressed to me in 2007. Public displays of the Navajo language matter in all of this as well.

Such discussions are also, and clearly, moving beyond the Navajo Nation and its surrounds. Tohe must negotiate these debates as she engages in an intercultural performance. They are a social field in which her intercultural performance and her book are now entangled. As the work by Graham, Cruikshank, and Myers suggests, these kinds of performances are more and more common throughout the United States as well as beyond. For example, Tohe has performed her poetry in Peru, Rex Lee Jim has performed in New Zealand, and Blackhorse Mitchell has performed in the Czech Republic. These performances are enmeshed in both local and global discourses, discourses concerning the control of *Tséyi'* and the infusion of tourists on the Navajo Nation as well as in discourses about language endangerment and what it means to be Navajo and who defines that. These are all part and parcel with larger global debates about identity, language rights, indigenous rights, and land claims (see Hill 2002; Errington 2003). Bonnie Urciuoli (1996:35) has noted that many displays of ethnic difference (including languages other than English) revolve around dominant attempts at "ethnification" where difference is sanctioned by making it "cultural, neat, and safe." These are the regularly scheduled displays of ethnic identity that once displayed can be ignored. I have argued that Tohe has challenged such "neat and safe" compartmentalizations by extending the indexical linkages beyond the here and now of the performance to a wider set of social and discursive fields. By paying attention to both the metalinguistic commentary and to the metasemiotic stereotypes that she both describes and displays, we can begin to understand the ways that some Native American performers attempt to speak to larger political issues (such as land claims and language shift) as well as how they simultaneously construct their own identity within such performances. That is, we can begin to understand how individuals locate themselves in relation to others.

Conclusion
Multiplying Glimpses of Navajo Poetics

How do I know when I know my language is no longer English or Navajo?

Esther Berlin (2007:74)

Ronald and Suzanne Scollon (1981:53) once argued that, "an Athabaskan cannot, as an Athabaskan, write easily about Athabaskan things." I think many Navajo poets would disagree with that statement.[1] Esther Belin (2007) recently titled an article in *Wicazo Sa Review*, "Contemporary Navajo Writers' Relevance to Navajo Society." In that piece she talks about traveling around the Navajo Nation and surrounding area and speaking to students of all ages about poetry and being a Navajo poet. Navajo poetry is grounded in the lived realities of Navajo people. The focus on the loss of language, the importance of place, or the boarding school experience all informs Navajo poetry. Concerns about how Navajos are represented inform the ways that Navajo poets present themselves and their work. The image of a singular Navajo language, uninfluenced by English, is an image that many Navajo poets help to circulate.

Another image, for example, of Navajos as borrowers—so usefully challenged by Erica Bsumek (2004), Jennifer Nez Denetdale (2007b), and James Faris (1990)—may rear its metaphorical head again at the thought of Navajo poetry. The trope of the Navajo as borrower, as Denetdale and Bsumek have shown, has vacillated with the interests of Euro-Americans. When it was in Euro-American interests to present Navajos as recalcitrant, they were represented as unwilling to learn from outsiders, trapped within tradition. When it was in Euro-American interests to highlight Navajos' willingness as co-participants in their assimilation, Navajos became borrowers. My argument is for neither Navajo primordialism or essentialism nor Navajos as ubiquitous borrowers. Rather it is to understand how Navajo poets actively engage tradition. I argue, instead, that Navajo poetry is an indigenous articulation (Clifford 2001) whereby Navajos use narrative—*hane'*—to reckon their place in the world. Navajo poetry is about reckoning, reckoning both one's place in the world and coming to terms with that place. Contemporary Navajo poetry is a narrative tradition. There has been an active and selective persistence.

As Chapter 6 showed, Navajo poets are not confined to the Navajo Nation. Instead they perform around the country and, indeed, around the world. As such, their performances are active displays and assertions of Navajoness. That Navajo poets create positively valorized images of Navajoness should not be surprising. However, as the example from Chapter 6 concerning Tohe suggests, there is often more going on than mere displays of Navajoness. There are also, I argue, subtle and not so subtle claims about place and identity as well. Navajo scholar Lloyd Lee (2006, 2007, and 2008) has recently made a number of powerful arguments in favor of Navajo nationalism, linking nationalism with the promotion of "the Diné language." Some Navajo poetry resonates with the rhetoric of Navajo nationalism and with Navajo sovereignty as well.

Paying attention to the specific forms of Navajo poetry and poetry performances helps reveal how Navajo poets actively engage in narratives of Navajoness and in the construction of imagined (language) communities. Ultimately, Navajo poets, through their poetic displays, help create and maintain narratives of Navajoness. These narratives of Navajoness are not, however, abstractions. Rather they are grounded in specific discursive practices. By paying attention to the poetic forms of such narratives, we also begin to appreciate the voices of individual Navajos. We move beyond abstractions, to an understanding of particular ways that Navajo poets connect with the oral tradition and the audiences that they perform before. Oral tradition and the poetic devices associated with traditional narratives become mechanisms for indigenous articulations.

When I first did research on the Navajo Nation in 2000–2001, there were no regular venues for Navajo poets to perform there. The closest thing to such an opportunity was the "open mic" at Diné College in the spring of 2001. When I returned in 2007, Gloria Emerson had opened a coffee shop in Shiprock, New Mexico, that irregularly featured Navajo poets, writers, and artists (see www.falconlabs.com/ahweehgohweeh/culture.htm). At the coffee shop, Navajo books of poetry are now for sale. Likewise, Cool Runnings has now opened a cafe that adjoins the music store. Here, Navajo poets like Blackhorse Mitchell have performed. Such locally controlled means of poetry and expressive production are, I believe, vital to the continuing relevance of Navajo poetry to Navajos. Many Navajo poets, poets like Sherwin Bitsui, Esther Belin, and Venaya Yazzie, work with school children to encourage them to engage in creative activities and to reflect upon their lives as Navajos and indigenous peoples. Navajo poetry is relevant.

The importance of local control of expressive genres resonates with recent developments in Internet technology. When I first began videotaping Navajo poets, few objected. Often I made copies of the videos for them. More recently, when I asked to videotape one poet I have known for years and videotaped numerous times, he agreed for purposes of my research, as long as it did not end up on YouTube. He then told me about finding video on YouTube of him performing, video he had not authorized and that I had not taken.

Poetry, as a number of poets explained to me with due patience, is a social act. Navajo poetry is a kind of storytelling. One afternoon in February of 2001, I (AKW) was interviewing an older Navajo woman (ONW) who wrote poetry in a journal that she planned to give to her grandchildren. Here is a segment of our conversation:

AKW: Do you think poetry has to be written?

ONW: No
    poetry can be your
    trip down memory lanes some what
    and then when it becomes paper then we call it poetry
    but it doesn't have to be
    on paper
    it's like me and my sister laughing
    about silly things we did
    instead of talking [weeping begins]

> in the two weeks before my sister's death
> our evenings were full of reminiscences about things we
>   did together
> a:h
> throughout
> our childhood

Poetry is the human relations, the intimacy, between individuals. As this woman said, poetry is a "trip down memory lanes." The Navajo woman then read me a poem that she had written about her sister in Navajo. As she read the poem, she wept. I did not understand much of the content of the poem at that time. Her weeping I now understand as a metasignal of sincerity that linked her to a whole clustering of feelingful connections. Similar in practice to the weeping Elsie May Cly Begay did when her long lost brother returned in the movie *The Return of Navajo Boy*, or the wailing of Nicole Walker when she interrupted Senator Pete Domenici at the dedication of the Bosque Redondo Memorial, or when older Navajo women wept as they spoke about their attachments to the Navajo language during community meetings on the Navajo Nation about Proposition 203, or like Navajo grandmothers did when they first saw *Tsoodził* after four years of internment at Bosque Redondo.

At the time this older Navajo woman read me her poem, I was a young anthropologist with limited proficiency in Navajo. But I was not there to understand the referential content of that poem; rather, what mattered were the feelings that the poem evoked, the felt pragmatic iconicity of the moment. For me, more than any other experience, that was the moment I understood the feelingful relationship between individuals and poetry, the way that felt relations can be evoked through the performance of poetry.

I have argued that an ethnopoetic and a discursive perspective on Navajo poetry and poetry performances allows us to better understand Navajo poetics, the voices of creative individuals, and something of the ways that Navajo poetry creates feelingful iconicity, both to language and to the emotions that poetry can evoke. In looking at the poetics of Navajo poetry, we also begin to understand something about how individual Navajo poets create felt attachments both to Navajo and to English. Understanding how Navajo poets talk about political and emotional topics may yet inform how outsiders understand what Navajos are talking about. In understanding Navajo narratives, outsiders may learn to respect the ways Navajos express themselves. Ethnopoetics is about respecting the voices of others.

Language is more than mere reference. It is more than a communicative tool. Rather, it is also a set of poetic, aesthetic, and expressive potentials that individual speakers delight in. Language is pleasurable and sensuous. This is because individuals create language through use, and such uses create felt attachments to linguistic forms. They pun and play with their language, putting it in dialogue with other languages. One of the ramifications of language shift is not just that words for things are lost (the referentialist fear), but that ways of being intimate with others and the world are lost (this is the iconism of language). If reference is meaningful, then iconicity is feelingful.

Moreover, as the discussion concerning Navajo ideophony suggests, certain poetic forms may be fragile when they confront a Western linguistic ideology that devalues their use. As one Navajo consultant forcefully told me, they would not use ideophones in their writing and they would discourage others from using such forms. According to some Navajos, ideophones did not match expectations of Western literary conventions. Poets like Rex Lee Jim and Gloria Emerson, as well as students in Navajo writing courses, do use ideophones in their written poetry, and here we can understand such uses as forms of resistance that stand in contrast to prevailing Western linguistic ideologies. So, too, the centering of a poem on the page can act as a form of resistance to perceived Western literary traditions, as understood through the prism of BIA schooling. On the other hand, *jiní* seems to be used less and less in contemporary written versions of Navajo Coyote narratives. Its repeated use, its epistemic stance, seem counter to Western linguistic ideologies concerning written forms. In understanding the language shift from Navajo to English that is occurring, it is important to take note of poetic forms, to those forms that create delight, involvement, and stand in opposition to perceived Western literary norms.

Navajo language becomes real in use, in Navajo poetry and poetry performances. A focus on discourse allows us to avoid the false dichotomy between "language" and "culture" and rather focus on what people are actually doing. One thing that they are doing is bringing delight and evoking feelings through poetic expressions. They are also constructing images about *Diné bizaad* and *Bilagáana bizaad*. They are reckoning their place in this world through poetic means. Navajo poetry also offers multiplying glimpses of Navajo identity. Navajo poetry, as a form of discursive reckoning, is both emplacing and empowering. Understanding how Navajo poets give voice to such discursive reckonings, then, becomes a crucial goal of ethnopoetics. Far from being marginal to anthropology, ethnopoetics becomes a crucial site for understanding the relationship between the individual, the world in which he or she lives, and the ways they orient to that world.

In the multiplying glimpses that have made up this book, I have suggested that an ethnopoetic and discourse-centered approach allows us to understand something of the ways that Navajos engage in positively valorizing their past to create a stance of difference. That is, a discourse-centered approach and a focus on poetics allow us to understand how narratives of Navajoness, as an indigenous articulation, are actually circulated. Metasemiotic stereotypes about identity, because they are reportable and discussable, become a crucial locus in understanding the discursive strategies of self-presentation. One discursive strategy—the primary focus of this book—is through the poetics of Navajo poetry. Here I argue for the value of a broadly ethnopoetic perspective that focuses on aesthetic practices, feelingfully iconic aesthetic practices, that aid in the construction and circulation of metasemiotic stereotypes of identity. Ethnopoetics is very much about identity.

Recent work in anthropology has argued for a more dialogic perspective (see Tedlock and Mannheim 1995; Van Vleet 2008), forefronting the discursive interactions—the voices—between and of interlocutors (including the anthropologist). A discourse-centered approach and an ethnopoetic approach, because they take care to look at the words of those we work with, have, I argue, been at the forefront of such dialogic perspectives. Hymes's (1981) early work to simply include the names—

Victoria Howard or Louis Simpson—of narrators in the titles of his publications is one simple but important example. People tell stories. Here I have attended to the voices of individual Navajo poets. In this book, I have also put my work in dialogue with the work of contemporary Navajo scholars. Lloyd Lee (2007) and Jennifer Denetdale's (2006b, 2007b, 2007a) recent analyses of the emergence of Navajo nationalism have informed my understanding that contemporary Navajo poetry has important links with Navajo nationalism. Martha Austin-Garrison's (1991) work on *hodiits'a'* (sound symbolism) in Navajo poetry has enhanced my understanding of ideophony in Navajo poetry. Galena Sells Dick's (1998) concern with the individual in Navajo language shift has influenced my own thinking on the applicability of an ethnopoetic perspective on Navajo language shift.

Navajo poets also read what I write and what others write about them. Many Navajos have consistently asked me when I was going to write my book on Navajo poetry. Tohe, for example, read and commented on my dissertation and on various chapters in this book. In the summer of 2008, I interviewed Zoey Benally (Twyla Zoann Benally) at Emerson's coffee shop. Zoey Benally had been active in the slam poetry scene around the Four Corners region and Shiprock, New Mexico. During our interview she told me about a recent book she is in. She kindly lent me Lesley Wheeler's (2008) *Voicing American Poetry: Sound and Performance from the 1920s to the Present*, which has a chapter focused on Benally and her poetry slam team. It would be a mistake to think that this book will not also be read by Navajo poets.

In this book, I connected contemporary Navajo poetry, through a series of multiplying glimpses, to a wider horizon of linguistic practices and linguistic ideologies among Navajos. I also suggested something of the intertextual work that Navajo poetic devices do, linking it with forms of traditionalization, affective registers, the replication of linguistic ideologies about proper ways of speaking, and the ways such displays place the individual poet within a broader voice of tradition. Navajo poetry is, however, not unitary and Navajo poets do disagree on the uses of Navajo in their poetry. Navajo poetry is also not static. It is a dynamic process. There are tensions: tensions between an idealized view of Navajo in the world and the sociolinguistic realities of the Navajo Nation, tensions concerning the role of Navajo in contemporary Navajo life and its relationship to English, and tensions between idealized views of the relationships between language and identity as well. It is also important to remember that Navajo poetry is not simply read by outsiders, but that Navajo poets do perform their poetry before Navajo audiences on the Navajo Nation. As Tohe once explained to me about Navajo poetry, "poetry is performance." It is in such performances that we can begin to understand contemporary Navajo poetry as fully entangled in Navajo linguistic ideologies about the form, function, and proper uses of—the proper ways of speaking—"the Navajo language" and its relationship to Navajo identity. Navajo poets, through their poetry and poetry performances, are attempting, as one Navajo consultant remarked about the use of sound symbolism, "to give an imagination to the listener." Contemporary Navajo poetry, as a form of a *hane'*, gives an image of Navajo and Navajo identity; however, it does not yet impose an interpretation on a singular image.

APPENDIX A

Navajo Books of Poetry Consulted
(number of bilingual Navajo examples per work are in parentheses)

Allen, Terry, ed. 1972. *The Whispering Wind*. Garden City, NY: Doubleday. (0)
Ashley, Rutherford. 2001. *Heart Vision 2000*. Window Rock, AZ: Cool Runnings. (1 p. 350)
Begay, Shonto. 1995. *Navajo Visions and Voices Across the Mesa*. New York: Scholastic. (0)
Belin, Esther. 1999. *From the Belly of My Beauty*. Tucson: University of Arizona Press. (0)
Bitsui, Sherwin. 2003. *Shapeshift*. Tucson: University of Arizona Press. (0)
Browne, Vee. 2000. *Ravens Dancing*. Bloomington: AuthorHouse. (0)
Chee, Norla. 2001. *Cedar Smoke on Abalone Mountain*. Los Angeles: UCLA. (1 p. 6)
Emerson, Gloria. 2003. *At the Hems of the Lowest Clouds*. Santa Fe: School of American Research Press. (0)
Erdrich, Heid, and Laura Tohe, ed. 2002. *Sister Nations*. St. Paul: Minnesota Historical Society Press. (1 p. 8)
Evers, Larry, ed. 1980. *The South Corner of Time*. Tucson: University of Arizona Press. (0)
Francisco, Nia. 1988. *Blue Horses for Navajo Women*. Greenfield Center, NY: Greenfield Review Press. (0)
Francisco, Nia. 1994. *Carried Away by the Black River*. Farmington, NM: Yoo-Hoo Press. (0)
Frank, Della, and Roberta Joe. 1993. *Storm Patterns: Poems from Two Navajo Women*. Tsaile, AZ: Navajo Community College Press. (0)
Jim, Rex Lee. 1989. *Áhí Ni' Nikisheegiizh*. Princeton: Princeton Collections of Western Americana. (0)

Jim, Rex Lee. 1995. *saad*. Princeton: Princeton Collections of Western Americana. (o)

Jim, Rex Lee. 1998. *Dúchas Táá Kóó Diné*. Beal Feirste, Ireland: Au Clochan. (o)

John, Hershman. 2007. *I Swallow Turquoise for Courage*. Tucson: University of Arizona Press. (o)

Milton, John. 1969. *The American Indian Speaks*. Vermillion: University of South Dakota Press. (o).

Tapahonso, Luci. 1987. *A Breeze Swept Through*. Albuquerque: West End Press. (o)

Tapahonso, Luci. 1993. *Sáanii Dahataał: The Women are Singing*. Sun Tracks. Vol. 23. Tucson: University of Arizona Press. (o)

Tapahonso, Luci. 1997. *Blue Horses Rush In*. Tucson: University of Arizona Press. (o)

Tohe, Laura. 1999. *No Parole Today*. Albuquerque: West End Press. (o)

Tohe, Laura. 2005. *Tséyi': Deep in the Rock*. Tucson: University of Arizona Press. (o)

Walters, Anna Lee, ed. 1993. *Neon Pow-Wow*. Flagstaff: Northland Publishing. (o)

Yazzie, Venaya, ed. 2006. *Saad ak'e'elchi': Navajo/English Poetry*. Farmington: Northwest New Mexico Arts Council. (o)

Yazzie, Venaya. 2006. *Livin' Matriarchal: Chapbook I*. Farmington, NM: Venaya Yazzie. (o)

APPENDIX B

Regular Venues for Navajo Poetry Performances (that I attended)
    Central Navajo Fair, Chinle, AZ
    Diné Language Fair, Tsaile, AZ
    Fandango, Bluff, UT
    Flagstaff Book Festival, Flagstaff, AZ
    Shiprock Fair, Shiprock, NM
    Navajo Nation Fair, Window Rock, AZ

The Navajo Nation Museum, Window Rock, AZ; Edge of Cedars Visitors Center, Blanding, UT; Gohwééh/'Ahwééh Coffee Shop, Shiprock, NM; The Phil, Shiprock, NM; San Juan College, Farmington, NM; and Diné College, Tsaile, AZ, also periodically have poetry readings. As poets explained to me in 2008, Shiprock has become the hub of Navajo poetry in recent years.

NOTES

Chapter 1

This chapter was previously published as "'Ałk'idą́ą́' Mą'ii Jooldlosh, Jiní': Poetic Devices in Navajo Oral and Written Poetry," *Anthropological Linguistics* 48, no. 3 (fall 2006): 233–265. Reproduced with permission from the University of Nebraska Press. Copyrighted by the Trustees of Indiana University.

1. The literature on language shift and both the macrolevel and microlevel analysis of that shift is extensive. On Athabaskan language shift, see Eung-Do Cook (1989, 1995); Clifton Pye (1992); Guy Lanoue (1991); Eleanor Nevins (2004); and Barbra Meek (2007).

2. The phrase glosses as "may I be everlasting and beautiful living" (Jim 2000:232). For discussions concerning this phrase, see Rex Lee Jim (2000); Gary Witherspoon (1977); and John Farella (1984). For general discussions concerning the Navajos and the language/culture nexus among Navajos, see Kluckhohn and Leighton (1962).

3. I thank Leighton C. Peterson for helping to clarify my thinking on the distinction here. See also Peterson (2006).

4. I want to thank Jonathan Hill for pointing me in the direction of Navajo ritualized or stylized weeping. In October 2007, Bennie Klain screened *The Return of Navajo Boy* at Southern Illinois University, Carbondale, with the support of John Downing and his Global Media Research Center. Hill and I both attended the screening and after the final scene with Elsie May Cly Begay reuniting with John Wayne Cly, Hill noted the similarities of her weeping to South American examples of ritual wailing he was familiar with. Having seen this stylized weeping a number of times by older Navajo women, Hill's comments immediately led me to review tapes I had recorded of this weeping. I thank Leighton C. Peterson for reminding me that Navajo men also weep

publicly. Let me add that saying that Navajos have a "stylized weeping" is not to say that it is not sincere, but rather to say that the form of weeping and the public displays of weeping are cultural and can be understood as indexing sincerity and tradition.

5. Navajos are not the only Native Americans writing poetry. Ronald Snake Edmo, for example, has published a collection of poems in both Shoshoni and English (Edmo 2001). He clearly sees one of the goals of his poetry as creating a corpus of written materials in the Shoshoni language. I thank Edmo for many useful conversations concerning his poetry. See also Ofelia Zepeda (1982, 1997, 2000) for examples of Tohono O'odham poetry as well as linguistic and autobiographical information. Colleen Fitzgerald (2003) has analyzed the word order in some of Zepeda's poetry. Margaret Bender (2002:155), only too briefly, describes an example of a poem written in Cherokee and in the Cherokee syllabary by a Cherokee educator.

6. In Navajo, ways are known as follows:

Hózhǫ́ǫ́jí	Blessingway
Tł'éé'jí'	Nightway
'Anaa'jí'	Enemyway
Mą'iijí	Coyoteway

In all of the above cases, the forms are morphologically segmentable. In the first example *Hózhǫ́* is the form for "blessing" (among other things) with the enclitic *-jí*. Likewise, in the second example, *Tł'éé'* glosses as "night" and again we have the enclitic *-jí*. This enclitic glosses as "in the direction of" or "way."

7. Let me be clear here about what I mean by "traditional Navajo poetic devices." I mean only those formal devices that have lingered in the text-artifact documented by linguists, folklorists, and anthropologists. For a quite useful discussion on this topic, see Dinwoodie (1999).

8. Barre Toelken suggested in his review that *-dlosh* is only used for Coyote as far as he knew. As far as I know that is the case. However, Coyote does take other verbs of "running." In the Watchman narrative titled "Horned Toad and his Corn Patch" (Sapir and Hoijer 1942:16), Coyote makes his appearance in association with the verb form *-ghod* (to run). So it appears to be the case that *-dlosh* almost, if not always, occurs with Coyote and that Coyote can appear with both *-dlosh* and *-ghod*.

9. Hoijer (1945) claimed that final /n/ in *jin* was actually a syllabic /ń/ and thus *jiń* and that there was no form *jin* in Navajo. Hoijer was critiquing the work

of Gladys Reichard. Reichard (1947:194) responded by pointing out that "most of my informants and many of the casual speakers I know use *jin*, as well as *jiní* and, more rarely, *jiń*" (I have updated Reichard's orthography by changing /dj/ to /j/). Toelken and Scott (1981) point out that the form can be reduced to *jn*. While I have not looked at this completely, I suspect the form is both *jn* and *jń*. Likewise, I agree with Reichard's estimations concerning the distribution of the forms *jin*, *jiní*, and *jiń*. Most often the form *jiní* is being reduced to a single-syllable morpheme in narratives (*jin*, *jn*, or *jń*). My reading of McDonough (2003a:106) is that the process of /n/ + /i/—> /ń/ was a "tendency" and not an absolute. If that is the case then *jin*, *jn*, and *jń* are all plausible realizations of *jiní* in causal speech. The debate between Hoijer and Reichard is interesting both in what it suggests about Navajo phonemics, but also as it relates to the creation of "standard orthographies."

10. Nicholas Mirkowich (1941:313–314) was one of the first to note the perduring nature of Navajo place names in the face of Spanish and English incursions. Mirkowich notes Navajos used Navajo names for towns that had English or Spanish names and were founded by Spaniards or Americans. Thus Navajos renamed, for example, Flagstaff, Arizona, *Kin Łání* (Many Houses). The importance of place names in Navajo, then, seems to be a perduring feature. See Chapter 6.

11. Barre Toelken suggests that not only does Laura Tohe evoke *hózhǫ́*, but in the very act of repeating "In beauty" four times she "produces" *hózhǫ́*. I take this suggestion quite seriously. For more on the creative power of language see Witherspoon (1977).

Chapter 2

1. An earlier tradition of anthropologists wrote Navajo as "Navaho." However, the Navajo Nation prefers the spelling "Navajo." I oblige their preference. However, when quoting earlier sources I keep the author's original spelling. Some Navajos that I know find it insulting when contemporary authors use "Navaho" outside such quotations. Here we see the ways that orthographic decisions can be seen as assertions of Navajo sovereignty. For an interested history of Navajo writing, see Young (1993). See also Webster 2006a.

2. I note here that both automobiles and airplanes can be described using the animate object classificatory verb stem. As Witherspoon (1977:121) writes, "*Sizį́* is said to refer to a living being but that does not explain why it also refers to iconic representations of animate beings [i.e., dolls] and to such things as cars, trucks, and airplanes." According to Witherspoon, cars and airplanes are classified as

animate objects because of their potential for movement. I find it interesting that the noun for automobiles is an ideophone. See also Alyse Neundorf (1982) on body part terms for car parts in Navajo (see also Basso 1967; Young 1989).

3. I thank Leighton C. Peterson for reminding me about this.

4. Compare with James Faris (1994:184) who argues for the Nightway that,

> Any concrete circumstance may demand and involve more or less of the specific learned practices: excessive snowfall or insufficient rainfall, or the medical history and gender of the afflicted person . . . the specific time of year, the number of previous Nightway in the specific season . . . all contribute to determinations of specific concatenations of Nightway practices. None of these versions are or can be wrong; none are or can be incomplete, since context is bounding and framing, and there is no possible deviation. But context is contingency, and contingency bears on the infinite ever-changing details of ordinary life, for which any given Nightway is designed.

I take this as a clear statement concerning the felt pragmatic iconicity of Navajo chantways. Navajo forms gain meaning from the felt connection to what is being done and the moment that it is being done. This is again the precision of iconicity; an utterance bears a naturalness of fit to that moment and the moment that it evokes.

5. Paul Zolbrod (2004:687) cites Pearl Sunrise giving a gloss of *hazéíts'ósii* as "little chatterbox." Zolbrod (2004:687) goes on to note that Sunrise further stated that chipmunks normally produce "a chattering sound." It is likely that the *ts'os, ts'os, ts'os, ts'os* in example 11, is precisely that "chattering sound." Note also that while Zolbrod glosses *-ts'ósii* as "little," the form reverberates with the ideophone used in example 4. Thus Chipmunk produces a sound linked to its very name. This is the interweaving of ideophones. See the example concerning *na'asts'ǫǫsí* (mouse) later in this chapter.

6. For non-Athabaskan examples of Native American (Seneca and Nakota) interlingual punning, see Chafe (1998:189) and Farnell (1995:136). For a useful discussion of punning more generally, see Sherzer (1978). See now also Sherzer (2002:29–37).

7. The five-senses approach to creative writing is not unique to Navajos. It is one way that written poetry is often taught in the United States. From a tentative survey of some examples of English-language five-senses poetry on the Internet, it appears that Navajos are more likely to use sound symbolism, such as in

example 16, while the English-language poems describe the sounds (i.e., "the sound of a bus running along a gravel road"). Navajo poems tend to evoke the sound (i.e., "I hear the **tł'ish, tł'ish, tł'ish** sound of someone"). This impression needs to be confirmed.

Chapter 3

An earlier version of this chapter appeared as "'Plaza'góó and before he can respond . . .': Language Ideology, Bilingual Navajo and Navajo Poetry," *Pragmatics* 18, no. 3 (2008): 511–541.

Chapter 4

1. This sense was discovered by Tohe in the following manner: In an interview I conducted with Alyse Neundorf I pointed out that "parole" could be understood in two senses, with the French sense of the word resonating with the theme of Tohe's book. Alyse Neundorf then told this to Laura Tohe and Tohe then stated that she had just found out about this second sense of the word—which she thought fit nicely—at a poetry reading in Window Rock, Arizona, July 18, 2001.

2. "Daniel" is a pseudonym.

3. Laura Tohe, "Cat or Stomp" from *No Parole Today*. Copyright © 1999 by Laura Tohe. Reprinted with the permission of West End Press, Albuquerque, New Mexico.

4. Comments on the performances were usually collected directly after it by going up to various people and inquiring about their impressions. This was usually done without a tape recorder and so my notes often have very short quotes, as above. I also interviewed people days later that had been at a poetry reading. I prefer, in some measure, the off-the-cuff feeling of the remarks recorded at the performance.

5. Pratt, as is well known, began the Carlisle Institute, Carlisle, Pennsylvania, as a progressive way to "civilize" Native Americans. Many Native Americans were taken from their homes to a far different climate where they suffered and died. Many students attempted to escape. For a brief overview of this project see Iverson 1998.

Chapter 5

1. In this chapter I use *Hwééldi*, *Hweeldi*, and *Hwéeldi* interchangeably. Tohe writes *Hweeldi*, other poets write *Hwééldi*. When I am quoting the actual speech of Tohe, I present it in the form that I heard. The issue concerns the fact that Navajo poets spell the word a variety of ways and I want to acknowledge that fact. Denetdale writes it *Hwééldi*. Tapahonso writes it *Hwéeldi*. Help writes it *Hwééldi*. Tohe writes it *Hweeldi* in the poem and *Hwéeldi* in the article. It would appear that the word is becoming standardized as *Hwééldi*.

2. I have heard Navajos compare the Long Walk with many other world historical events, such as the Trail of Tears, the Holocaust, and the Japanese internment during World War II. I have never heard it compared by Navajos to the Civil War. The Japanese internment camps were also suggested to me as being modeled on *Hweeldi*. Feel the interdiscursive reverberations as the Navajo were using their language to "save America" from the Japanese, while Wáashindoon was re-creating *Hweeldi* and internment on Japanese Americans.

Chapter 6

1. There was approximately twenty minutes worth of questions. This portion of the transcript begins after line 1941. The questions ranged from the bizarre (a question about the Navajos and the television show *The X-Files*) to the more obvious (a question about "Navajo shamans") to those that dealt with language (the question on the Navajo writing system). During this time she was also asked to read another poem in Navajo. She read that poem and then discussed it (see lines 2211-2242). She read eleven poems in total that night. The first one, "Gallup Ceremonial," dealt with "Midwesterners" misrecognizing Navajo tradition (lines 380-405) and aided in establishing Tohe as "the" cultural authority. The second one concerned the Navajo code-talkers (lines 549-726). The third poem (lines 843-888) concerned the riots at the Santa Fe state prison in 1980 and the boarding school experience (see Tohe 1999:38). The fourth poem (lines 935-987) was "Cat or Stomp" (see Tohe 1999:6; Webster 2008a). The fifth poem (lines 1330-1356) concerns *Hwééldi* (see below) and is also a "love poem" (see Tohe 2005:3). The sixth poem (lines 1542-1578) is a bilingual poem in Navajo and English and is titled "Many Horses" (Tohe 2005:7). In that poem, Tohe performed both in English and in Navajo. The seventh and eighth poems (1669-1696) are the English-language versions of "Female Rain" and "Male Rain" (Tohe 2005:26-27). The ninth poem (lines 1804-1875) contains some Navajo, which she performed that night as well (Tohe 2005:17). The tenth poem (lines 1891-1940), which was the final poem before the Q&A, is titled "Poem about You" (Tohe

2005:39) and in it Tohe says the Navajo word *nidlohísh* (are you cold) in an affective manner. The switch here to Navajo is very similar to Irvine's (1990) discussion of affective registers. Here Navajo becomes the affective register. The eleventh poem, *Niłtsą́ Biką́* (Male Rain), was the Navajo version of an earlier English-language poem and came at the request by an audience member for her to read another poem in Navajo.

2. Oddly, the local newspaper, as well as the campus newspaper, did cover a presentation of an earlier version of this chapter that I gave in 2007 for Native American Heritage Month. Neither covered, however, a "reading" (as it was billed) by Navajo poet Sherwin Bitsui for the 2007 Native American Heritage Month at SIUC. Nor did they cover screenings by Navajo film-maker Bennie Klain, also in 2007 at SIUC. It is interesting that the metatalk, the talk about a talk by a faculty member, would draw the attention of both the campus newspaper and the local newspaper. On a purely aesthetic level, my performance style suffers mightily in comparison to Tohe, Bitsui, or Klain. We should also note that the local newspaper here replicates my role as "anthropologist," "cultural broker," and "expert." They do not need to cover the actual event, because I will explain it for them. My talk was meant to promote the pending establishment of the Native American Studies minor.

3. The transcript that follows presents individual lines based on pause structure. In presenting the transcript, I hope to present something of the cadence and rhythm of the performance. In general, I follow the transcript formatting as used by Evers and Molina (1998:39) in presenting a Yaqui lecture or *hinivaka* on "the flower world." Lengthening has been indicated by : and a rise in tone is indicated with /. I will have more to say about these stylistic devices later in this chapter. The slowness of cadence aids in the construction of the metasemiotic stereotype of the carefulness of Tohe's speech. The entire transcript runs to just over 2,500 lines. The opening lines gloss as follows:

> it is good
> I that one Laura Tohe
> I that one Sleeping Rock People
> Bitterwater People that for them I was born for

Yá'át'ééh is a conventional Navajo greeting. *Tsénabahiłnii* and *Tódích'íinii* are Tohe's maternal and paternal clans respectively.

4. *de Chelly* is also a regional diacritic for in versus out groupness in the Southwest more generally. A pronunciation of *de Chelly* as either [di šɛli] or [di čɛli] clearly indexes an out group status.

5. The tone marking on the /e/ is not included on the sign, but the glottal stop is included. Dinwoodie (1998) discusses the role of the representations of glottal stops in relation to the Tsilhqut'in the place name for the Canadian park.

6. While Tohe does not live on the Navajo Nation she does keep abreast of the issues circulating there and she does return periodically. Tohe, for example, was the person who told me that KTNN could be heard on the Internet and emailed me the link.

Conclusion

1. For a more sustained and pointed critique of the Scollons's statement and the logic that underlies it, see Webster 2006b.

BIBLIOGRAPHY

Aberbach, David.
    2007.   Myth, History and Nationalism: Poetry of the British Isles. In Nationalism and Ethnosymbolism: History, Culture and Ethnicity in the Formation of Nations. Athena S. Leoussi and Steven Grosby, eds. Pp. 84-96. Edinburgh: Edinburgh University Press.

Agha, Asif.
    1998.   Stereotypes and Registers of Honorific Language. Language in Society 27:151-193.

Ahlers, Jocelyn.
    2006.   Framing Discourse: Creating Community Through Native Language Use. Journal of Linguistic Anthropology 16(1):58-75.

Anderson, Benedict.
    1991.   Imagined Communities. Rev. edition. London: Verso.

Anderson, Myrdene.
    2005.   The Saami Yoik: Translating Hum, Chant, or/and Song. In Song and Significance. Dinda Gorlée, ed. Pp. 213-234. Amsterdam: Rodopi.

Aoki, Haruo.
    1994.   Symbolism in Nez Perce. In Sound Symbolism. Leanne Hinton, Johanna Nichols, and John Ohala, eds. Pp. 15-22. Cambridge: Cambridge University Press.

Ashley, Rutherford.
    2001.   Heart Vision 2000. Window Rock: Cool Runnings.

Atsitty, Tacey.
    1999.   Song of a Great Nat'aannii—Shímásaní. Eagle's Eye 30(2):34.

Auden, W. H.
    1990.   The Dyer's Hand. New York: Vintage Books.

Austin-Garrison, Martha.
    1991.   Bee Ákohwiinidzinígíí Binahjį' Ak'e'alchí Bíhoo'aah. Journal of Navajo Education 9(1):43–50.
Axelrod, Melissa.
    1993.   The Semantics of Time: Aspectual Categorization in Koyukon Athabaskan. Lincoln: University of Nebraska Press.
Bahe, Maggie.
    1971.   Prayer for a Brother in Vietnam. Arrow III:5–6.
Bahr, Howard.
    1994.   Multiplying Glimpses, Gleaning Genres: A Multidisciplinary Approach to the Study of Change among Navajo Peoples. Human Organization 53(1):55–73.
Bakhtin, Mikhail.
    1981.   The Dialogic Imagination. Austin: University of Texas Press.
    1986.   Speech Genres and Other Late Essays. Austin: University of Texas Press.
Baldinger, Jo Ann.
    1992.   Navajo Poet Tapahonso Holds Home in Heart. New Mexico Magazine 70(8):31–35.
Bartelt, H. Guillermo.
    1981.   Some Observations on Navajo English. Papers in Linguistics 14(3):377–385.
    2001.   Socio- and Stylolinguistic Perspectives on American Indian Texts. Lewiston, NY: Edwin Mellen Press.
Basso, Keith.
    1967.   Semantic Aspects of Linguistic Acculturation. American Anthropologist 69(5):471–477.
    1979.   Portraits of "The Whiteman." Cambridge: Cambridge University Press.
    1990.   Western Apache Language and Culture. Tucson: University of Arizona Press.
    1996.   Wisdom Sits in Places. Albuquerque: University of New Mexico Press.
Basso, Keith, and Nashley Tessay Sr.
    1994.   Joseph Hoffman's "The Birth of He Triumphs Over Evils": A Western Apache Origin Story. In Coming to Light. Brian Swann, ed. Pp. 636–656. New York: Vintage Books.
Bauman, Richard.
    1984.   Verbal Art as Performance. Chicago: Waveland Press.

1986. Story, Performance, and Event. Cambridge: Cambridge University Press.
2004. A World of Others' Words. Malden, MA: Berg.

Bauman, Richard, and Charles Briggs.
1990. Poetics and Performance as Critical Perspectives on Language and Social Life. Annual Review of Anthropology 19:59–88.
2003. Voices of Modernity: Language Ideologies and the Politics of Inequality. Cambridge: Cambridge University Press.

Bauman, Richard, and Joel Sherzer, eds.
1989. Explorations in the Ethnography of Speaking. London: Cambridge University Press.

Becker, Alton.
1995. Beyond Translation. Ann Arbor: University of Michigan Press.

Begay, Lydia Fasthorse, ed.
1998. Hane' Naach'ąąh. Tsaile: Diné Teacher Education, Diné College.

Begay, Shonto.
1995. Navajo Visions and Voices Across the Mesa. New York: Scholastic.

Belin, Esther.
1999. From the Belly of My Beauty. Tucson: University of Arizona Press.
2002b. Dootłizh. Frontiers 23(2):57–58.
2002b. First Woman. In Sister Nations. Heid Erdrich and Laura Tohe, eds. Pp. 8–9. St. Paul: Minnesota Historical Society Press.
2007. Contemporary Navajo Writers' Relevance to Navajo Society. Wicazo Sa Review 22(1):69–76.

Benally, AnCita, and Denis Viri.
2005. Diné Bizaad [Navajo Language] at a Crossroads: Extinction or Renewal. Bilingual Research Journal 29(1):85–108.

Benally, Timothy.
1994. Ma'ii Jooldloshí Hane: Stories about Coyote, the One Who Trots. In Coming to Light. Brian Swann, ed. Pp. 601–613. New York: Random House.

Bender, Margaret.
2002. Signs of Cherokee Culture: Sequoyah's Syllabary in Eastern Cherokee Life. Chapel Hill: University of North Carolina Press.

Binder, Wolfgang, and Helmbrecht Breining, eds.
1994. Luci Tapahonso. In American Contradictions. Pp. 111–123. Hanover, NH: Wesleyan University Press.

Biolsi, Thomas, ed.
2004. A Companion to the Anthropology of American Indians. Malden: Blackwell Publishing.

Bitsui, Sherwin.
    2003.   Shapeshift. Tucson: University of Arizona Press.
Blommaert, Jan.
    2006.   Ethnopoetics as Functional Reconstruction. Functions of Language 13(2):255–275.
Blot, Richard, ed.
    2003.   Language and Social Identity. Westport: Praeger.
Boas, Franz.
    1966.   Introduction. *In* Handbook of American Indian Languages & Indian Families of America North of Mexico. Pp. 1–79. Lincoln: University of Nebraska Press.
Brenneis, Donald, and Alessandro Duranti, eds.
    1986.   The Audience as Co-Author. Text 6(3):239–347.
Briggs, Charles.
    1992.   Linguistic Ideologies and the Naturalization of Discourse. Pragmatics 2(3):387–404.
    1993.   Personal Sentiments and Polyphonic Voices in Warao Women's Ritual Wailing: Music and Poetics in a Critical and Collective Discourse. American Anthropologist 95(4):929–957.
    1996.   The Meaning of Nonsense, the Poetics of Embodiment, and the Production of Power in Warao Healing. *In* The Performance of Healing. Carol Laderman and Marina Roseman, eds. Pp. 185–232. New York: Routledge.
Briggs, Charles, and Richard Bauman.
    1992.   Genre, Intertextuality, and Social Power. Journal of Linguistic Anthropology 2(2):131–172.
Bright, William.
    1993.   A Coyote Reader. Berkeley: University of California Press.
Brill de Ramirez, Susan.
    1997.   Ałk'idáá' jiní ... Luci Tapahonso, Irvin Morris, and Della Frank. Cimarron Review 121:135–153.
    1999.   Contemporary American Indian Literatures & the Oral Tradition. Tucson: University of Arizona Press.
Browne, Vee.
    2000.   Ravens Dancing. Bloomington: AuthorHouse.
Bruchac, Joseph.
    2002.   Navajo Long Walk. Washington, D.C.: National Geographic Society.

Brugge, David.
:   1999.   The Navajo-Hopi Land Dispute: An American Tragedy. Albuquerque: University of New Mexico Press.

Bsumek, Erika.
:   2004.   The Navajos as Borrowers: Stewart Culin and the Genesis of an Anthropological Theory. New Mexico Historical Review 79(3):319–351.
:   2008.   Indian-Made: Navajo Culture in the Marketplace, 1868–1940. Lawrence: University Press of Kansas.

Bunte, Pamela.
:   2002.   Verbal Artistry in Southern Paiute Narratives: Reduplication as a Stylistic Process. Journal of Linguistic Anthropology 12(1):3–33.

Canfield, Kip.
:   1980.   A Note on Navajo-English Code-Mixing. Anthropological Linguistics 22:218–220.

Casaus, Bernice.
:   1996.   Nihizaad, T'áá Diné Bizaad. Journal of Navajo Education 13(3):3–10.

Chafe, Wallace.
:   1998.   Polysynthetic Puns. *In* Studies in American Indian Languages: Description and Theory. Leanne Hinton and Pamela Munro, eds. Pp. 187–189. Berkeley: University of California Press.

Chee, Melvatha, Evan Ashworth, Susan Buescher, and Brittany Kubacki.
:   2004.   Grammaticization of Tense in Navajo: The Evolution of nt'éé. Santa Barbara Papers in Linguistics 15:76–90.

Chee, Norla.
:   2001.   Cedar Smoke on Abalone Mountain. Los Angeles: UCLA.

Childs, G. Tucker.
:   1996.   Where Have All the Ideophones Gone? The Death of a Word Category in Zulu. Toronto Working Papers in Linguistics 15:81–103.
:   2001.   Research on Ideophones, Whither Hence? The Need for a Social Theory of Ideophones. *In* Ideophones. F. K. Erhard Voeltz and Christa Kilian-Hatz, eds. Pp. 63–73. Philadelphia: John Benjamins Publishing.

Clifford, James.
:   2001.   Indigenous Articulation. The Contemporary Pacific 13(2):468–490.

Coleman, Steve.
:   2004.   The Nation, the State, and the Neighbors: Personation in Irish-Language Discourse. Language & Communication 24(4):381–411.

Collins, James.
- 1985. Pronouns, Markedness, and Stem Change in Tolowa. International Journal of American Linguistics 30:368–372.
- 1987. Reported Speech in Navajo Myth Narratives. *In* Linguistic Action. Jef Verschueren, ed. Pp. 69–85. Norwood, NJ: Ablex Publishing.
- 1998. Understanding Tolowa Histories. New York: Routledge.

Collins, James, and Richard Blot.
- 2003. Literacy and Literacies: Text, Power, and Identity. Cambridge: Cambridge University Press.

Cook, Eung-Do.
- 1989. Is Phonology Going Haywire in Dying Languages? Phonological Variations in Chipewyan and Sarcee. Language in Society 18:235–255.
- 1995. Is there Convergence in Language Death? Evidence from Chipewyan and Stoney. Journal of Linguistic Anthropology 5:217–231.

Cowell, Andrew.
- 2004. Arapaho Placenames in Colorado: Indigenous Mapping, White Remaking. Names 52(1):21–41.

Craig, Vincent.
- 1998. Yer' Jus' Somehow: Recorded Live at San Juan College. CD. Mutton Man Productions.

Crawford, James.
- 2008. Endangered Native American Language: What Is to Be Done and Why. *In* Language: Introductory Readings. Virginia Clark, Paul Eschholz, Alfred Rosa, and Beth Lee Simon, eds. Pp. 424–439. Boston: Bedford/St. Martin's.

Cruikshank, Julie.
- 1990. "Getting the Words Right": Perspectives on Naming and Places in Athapaskan Oral History. Arctic Anthropology 27(1):52–65.
- 1994. Claiming Legitimacy: Prophecy Narratives from Northern Aboriginal Women. American Indian Quarterly 18(2):147–167.
- 1997. Negotiating with Narrative: Establishing Cultural Identity at the Yukon International Storytelling Festival. American Anthropologist 99(1):56–69.
- 1998. The Social Life of Stories. Lincoln: University of Nebraska Press.

Csordas, Thomas.
- 1999. Ritual Healing and the Politics of Identity in Contemporary Navajo Society. American Ethnologist 26(1):3–23.

DeLisle, Helga.
    1980.   Consonantal Symbolism in American Indian Languages. Journal of the Linguistic Association of the Southwest 4:130–142.

Deloria, Philip.
    1998.   Playing Indian. New Haven: Yale University Press.
    2004.   Indians in Unexpected Places. Lawrence: University Press of Kansas.

Denetdale, Jennifer Nez.
    2001.   The Long Walk: A Response to an Amateur Historian. Navajo Times, March 8, 2001.
    2006a.   Chairmen, Presidents, and Princesses: The Navajo Nation, Gender, and the Politics of Tradition. Wicazo Sa Review 21(1):9–28.
    2006b.   Remembering Our Grandmothers: Navajo Women and the Power of Oral Tradition. *In* Indigenous Peoples' Wisdom and Power: Affirming Our Knowledge through Narratives. Julian Kunnie and Nomalungelo Goduka, eds. Pp. 78–94. Burlington, VT: Ashgate Publishing.
    2007a.   Discontinuities, Remembrances, and Cultural Survival: History, Diné/Navajo Memory, and the Bosque Redondo Memorial. New Mexico Historical Review. 82(3): 295–316.
    2007b.   Reclaiming Diné History. Tucson: University of Arizona Press.

Dick, Galena Sells.
    1998.   I Maintained a Strong Belief in My Language and Culture: A Navajo Language Autobiography. International Journal of the Sociology of Language 132:23–25.

Dick, Galena Sells, and Teresa McCarty.
    1997.   Reclaiming Navajo. *In* Indigenous Literacies in the Americas. Nancy Hornberger, ed. Pp. 69–92. Berlin: Mouton de Gruyter.

Diglot Favorites.
    n.d.   Diglot Favorites Navajo and English. Colorado Springs: Listen Press.

Dinwoodie, David.
    1998.   Authorizing Voices: Going Public in an Indigenous Language. Cultural Anthropology 13(2):193–223.
    1999.   Textuality and the "Voices" of Informants: The Case of Edward Sapir's 1929 Navajo Field School. Anthropological Linguistics 41(2):165–192.

Doke, Clement.
    1935.   Bantu Linguistic Terminology. London: Longmans and Green.

1948. The Basis of Bantu Literature. Africa: Journal of the International African Institute 18(4):284–301.

Donovan, Bill.
2001. Long Walk Steeped in Myths. Gallup Independent, Jan. 30, 2001, A6.

Dunn, Cynthia.
2006. Formulaic Expressions, Chinese Proverbs, and Newspaper Editorials: Exploring Type and Token Interdiscursivity in Japanese Wedding Speeches. Journal of Linguistic Anthropology 16(2):153–172.

Durbin, Marshall.
1973. Sound Symbolism in the Mayan Language Family. *In* Meaning in Mayan Languages. M. S. Edmonson, ed. Pp. 23–49. The Hague: Mouton.

Edmo, Ronald Snake.
2001. Spirit Rider. Pocatello: Idaho State University Press.

Emerson, Gloria.
1971. The Poetry of Gloria Emerson. The Indian Historian 4(2):8–9.
1972. Slayers of the Children. The Indian Historian 5(1):18–19.
2003. At the Hems of the Lowest Clouds. Santa Fe: School of American Research Press.

Erdrich, Heid, and Laura Tohe, eds.
2002. Sister Nations. St. Paul: Minnesota Historical Society Press.

Erickson, Kirstin.
2003. Moving Stories: Displacement and Return in the Narrative Production of Yaqui Identity. Anthropology and Humanism 28(2):139–154.

Errington, Joseph.
1998. Shifting Languages. Cambridge: Cambridge University Press.

Evers, Larry, and Felipe Molina.
1998. "Like This It Stays in Your Hands": Collaboration and Ethnopoetics. Oral Tradition 13(1):15–57.

Fabian, Johannes.
2001. Anthropology with an Attitude. Stanford: Stanford University Press.

Farella, John.
1984. The Main Stalk: A Synthesis of Navajo Philosophy. Tucson: University of Arizona Press.

Faris, James.
    1990.   The Nightway: A History and a History of Documentation of a Navajo Ceremonial. Albuquerque: University of New Mexico Press.
    1994.   Context and Text: Navajo Nightway Textual History in the Hands of the West. Resources for American Literary Study 20(2):180–195.

Farnell, Brenda.
    1995.   Do You See What I Mean: Plains Indian Sign Talk and the Embodiment of Action. Austin: University of Texas Press.

Fast, Robin Riley.
    2007.   The Land Is Full of Stories: Navajo Histories in the Work of Luci Tapahonso. Women's Studies 36:185–211.

Feld, Steven.
    1988.   Aesthetics as Iconicity of Style (Uptown Title); or (Downtown Title) "Lift—up-over sounding": Getting into the Kaluli Groove. Yearbook for Traditional Music 20:74–113.
    1990.   Wept Thoughts: The Voicing of Kaluli Memories. Oral Tradition 5:241–266.
    1996.   Waterfalls of Song: An Acoustemology of Place Resounding in Bosavi, Papua New Guinea. *In* Senses of Place. Steven Feld and Keith Basso, eds. Pp. 91–135. Santa Fe: School of American Research Press.

Field, Margaret.
    2001.   Triadic Directives in Navajo Language Socialization. Language in Society 30:249–263.
    2007.   Increments in Navajo Conversation. Pragmatics 17(4):637–646.

Field, Margaret, and Taft Blackhorse Jr.
    2002.   The Dual Role of Metonymy in Navajo Prayer. Anthropological Linguistics 44(3):217–230.

Fitzgerald, Colleen.
    2003.   Word Order and Discourse Genre in Tohono O'odham. *In* Formal Approaches to Function in Grammar. Andrew Carnie, Heidi Harley, and Maryann Willie, eds. Pp. 179–189. Amsterdam: John Benjamins.

Foster, Susan, Gloria Singer, Lucy Benally, Theresa Boone, and Ann Beck.
    1989.   Describing the Language of Navajo Children. Journal of Navajo Education 7(1):13–17.

Francisco, Nia.
    1977a.   escaping the turquoise sky. College English (November):348–349.
    1977b.   táchééh. College English (November):346.

1988. Blue Horses for Navajo Women. Greenfield Center, NY: Greenfield Review Press.
1994. Carried Away by the Black River. Farmington, NM: Yoo-Hoo Press.

Frank, Della, and Roberta Joe.
1993. Storm Patterns: Poems from Two Navajo Women. Tsaile: Navajo Community College Press.

Friedrich, Paul.
1979. Language, Context, and the Imagination. Stanford: Stanford University Press.
1986. The Language Parallax. Austin: University of Texas Press.
1996. The Culture in Poetry and the Poetry in Culture. *In* Culture/Contexture. Daniel Valentine and Jeffrey Peck, eds. Pp. 37–57. Berkeley: University of California Press.
2006. Maximizing Ethnopoetics: Fine-Tuning Anthropological Experience. *In* Language, Culture, and Society. Christine Jourdan and Kevin Tuite, eds. Pp. 207–228. Cambridge: Cambridge University Press.

Frisbie, Charlotte.
1980. Vocables in Navajo Ceremonial Music. Ethnomusicology 24(3):347–392.

Gal, Susan, and Judith Irvine.
1995. The Boundaries of Languages and Disciplines: How Ideologies Construct Difference. Social Research 62(4):967–1001.

Goddard, Pliny.
1933. Navajo Texts. Anthropological Papers of the American Museum of Natural History. Vol. 34, Part 1. New York: The American Museum of Natural History.

Goffman, Erving.
1974. Frame Analysis. New York: Harper.

Goodfellow, Anne.
2003. The Development of "New" Languages in Native American Communities. American Indian Culture and Research Journal 27(2):41–59.

Graham, Laura.
2002. How Should an Indian Speak? *In* Indigenous Movements, Self-Representations, and the State in Latin America. Kay Warren and Jean Jackson, eds. Pp. 181–228. Austin: University of Texas Press.
2005. Image and Instrumentality in a Xavante Politics of Existential Recognition. American Ethnologist 32(4):622–641.

Greenfeld, Philip.
    2001.   Escape from Albuquerque: An Apache Memorate. American Indian Culture and Research Journal 25(3):47–71.

Gumperz, John.
    1982.   Discourse Strategies. Cambridge: Cambridge University Press.

Haile, Fr. Berard.
    1984.   Navajo Coyote Tales. Lincoln: University of Nebraska Press.

Hale, Ken.
    1973.   A Note on Subject-Object Inversion in Navajo. *In* Issues in Linguistics, Papers in Honor of Henry and Renée Kahane. B. Kachru et al., eds. Pp. 300–309. Chicago: University of Illinois Press.

Hamill, James.
    1983.   Navajo Syllogisms: Structure and Use. Central Issues in Anthropology 5(1):43–57.

Hanks, William.
    1999.   Intertexts. New York: Rowman and Littlefield.

Hartnett, Michael.
    1975.   A Farewell to English. Dublin: Gallery Books.

Help, Marilyn.
    2001.   It Is Said. *In* We'll Be in Your Mountains, We'll Be In Your Songs: A Navajo Woman Sings. Ellen McCullough-Brabson and Marilyn Help, eds. Pp. 61–62. Albuquerque: University of New Mexico Press.

Hill, Jane.
    1985.   The Grammar of Consciousness and the Consciousness of Grammar. American Ethnologist 12(4):725–737.
    1990.   Weeping as a Meta-Signal in a Mexicano Woman's Narrative. *In* Native Latin American Cultures Through Their Discourse. Ellen Basso, ed. Pp. 29–49. Bloomington: Folklore Institute/Indiana University.
    2002.   Expert Rhetorics in Advocacy for Endangered Languages: Who Is Listening, and What Do They Hear? Journal of Linguistic Anthropology 12(2):119–133.

Hill, Jonathan, ed.
    1988.   Rethinking History and Myth: Indigenous South American Perspectives on the Past. Urbana: University of Illinois Press.

Hill, W. W.
    1943.   Navajo Humor. Menasha, WI: George Banta.

Hill. W. W., and Dorothy Hill.
    1945.   Navaho Coyote Tales and Their Position in the Southern Athabaskan Group. Journal of American Folklore 58 (203):317–343.

Hinton, Leanne, Johanna Nichols, and John Ohala, eds.
    1994.   Sound Symbolism. Cambridge: Cambridge University Press.

Hirschfelder, Arlene, and Beverly Singer, eds.
    1992.   Rising Voices: Writings of Young Native Americans. New York: Ivy Books.

Hofling, C. Andrew.
    1987.   Discourse Framing in Itzá Maya Narrative. Anthropological Linguistics 29(4):478–488.

Hofling, C. Andrew with Felix Fernando Tesucun.
    2000.   Itzaj Maya Grammar. Salt Lake City: University of Utah Press.

Hoijer, Harry.
    1939.   Chiricahua Loan Words from Spanish. Language 15:110–115.
    1945.   The Story of the Navajo Hail Chant. International Journal of American Linguistics 11(2):123–125.
    1951.   Cultural Implications of Some Navaho Linguistic Categories. Language 27:111–120.
    1953.   The Relation of Language to Culture. *In* Anthropology Today. A. L. Kroeber, ed. Pp. 554–573. Chicago: University of Chicago Press.
    1971.   Patterns of Meaning in Navaho. *In* Themes in Culture. Maria Zamora, J. M. Mahar, and Henry Orenstein, eds. Pp. 227–237. Quezon City, Philippines: Kayumanggi Publishers.

Holiday, Marvin.
    1994.   Aheeh Hwiinidzin. The Navajo Times, December 15, A-7.

Holm, Wayne, and Agnes Holm.
    1995.   Navajo Language Education: Retrospect and Prospects. The Bilingual Research Journal 19(1):141–167.

House, Deborah.
    2002.   Language Shift Among the Navajos. Tucson: University of Arizona Press.

Hunn, Eugene.
    1996.   Columbia Plateau Indian Place Names: What Can They Teach Us? Journal of Linguistic Anthropology 6(1):3–26.

Hunter, Linda, and Chaibou Elhadji Oumarou.
    1998.   Towards a Hausa Verbal Aesthetic: Aspects of Language About Using Language. Journal of African Cultural Studies 11(2):157–170.

Hymes, Dell.
    1960.   Phonological Aspects of Style: Some English Sonnets. *In* Style in Language. Thomas Sebeok, ed. Pp. 107–131. Cambridge, MA: MIT Press.
    1979.   How to Talk Like a Bear in Takelma. International Journal of American Linguistics 45(2):101–106.
    1981.   In Vain I Tried to Tell You. Philadelphia: University of Pennsylvania Press.
    1990.   Thomas Paul's Sametl: Verse Analysis of a (Saanich) Chinook Jargon Text. Journal of Pidgin and Creole Language 5(1):71–106.
    2000.   Sung Epic and Native American Ethnopoetics. *In* Textualization of Oral Epics. Lauri Honko, ed. Pp. 291–342. Berlin: Mouton de Gruyter.
    2003.   Now I Know Only That Far. Lincoln: University of Nebraska Press.
Irvine, Judith.
    1990.   Registering Affect. Heteroglossia in the Linguistic Expression of Emotion. *In* Language and the Politics of Emotion. Lila Abu-Lughod and Catherine Lutz, eds. Pp. 126–161. Cambridge: Cambridge University Press.
Irvine, Judith, and Susan Gal.
    2000.   Language Ideology and Linguistic Differentiation. *In* Regimes of Language. Paul Kroskrity, ed. Pp. 35–83. Santa Fe: School of American Research Press.
Iverson, Peter.
    1998.   We Are Still Here. Wheeling, IL: Harlan Davidson.
    2002.   Diné: A History of the Navajos. Albuquerque: University of New Mexico Press.
Jackson, Jason.
    2005.   Yuchi Ceremonial Life: Performance, Meaning, and Tradition in a Contemporary American Indian Community. Lincoln: University of Nebraska Press.
Jakobson, Roman.
    1960.   Concluding Statement: Linguistics and Poetics. *In* Style in Language. Thomas Sebeok, ed. Pp. 350–373. Cambridge, MA: MIT Press.
Jameson, Fredric.
    1979.   Marxism and Historicism. New Literary History 11:41–73.
Jett, Stephen.
    1995.   Navajo Sacred Places: Management and Interpretation of Mythic Places. The Public Historian 17(2):39–47.

2001. Navajo Placenames and Trails of the Canyon de Chelly System, Arizona. New York: Peter Lang.

Jim, Rex Lee.
1989. Áhí Ni' Nikisheegiizh. Princeton: Princeton Collections of Western Americana.
1995. saad. Princeton: Princeton Collections of Western Americana.
1998. Dúchas Táá Kóó Diné. Beal Feirste, Ireland: Au Clochan.
2000. A Moment in My Life. *In* Here First. Arnold Krupat and Brian Swann, eds. Pp. 229-246. New York: Modern Library.
2004. Coyote Stories. *In* Voices from the Four Directions. Brian Swann, ed. Pp. 317-326. Lincoln: University of Nebraska Press.

John, Hershman.
2007. I Swallow Turquoise for Courage. Tucson: University Arizona Press.

Johnson, Broderick, ed.
1973. Navajo Stories of the Long Walk Period. Tsaile: Navajo Community College Press.

Johnstone, Barbara.
1996. The Linguistic Individual. Oxford: Oxford University Press.
2000. The Individual Voice in Language. Annual Review of Anthropology 29:405-424.

Kan, Sergei, and Pauline Turner Strong, eds.
2006. New Perspectives on Native North America. Lincoln: University of Nebraska Press.

Kari, James, and Bernard Spolsky.
1974. Athapaskan Language Maintenance and Bilingualism. *In* Southwest Areal Linguistics. Garland Bills, ed. Pp. 35-64. San Diego: San Diego State University Press.

Keane, Webb.
1997. Signs of Recognition. Berkeley: University of California Press.

Keller, Robert, and Michael Turek.
1998. American Indians and National Parks. Tucson: University of Arizona Press.

Kelley, Klara, and Harris Francis.
1994. Navajo Sacred Places. Bloomington: Indiana University Press.
2005. Traditional Navajo Maps and Wayfaring. American Indian Culture and Research Journal 29(2):85-111.

Kita, Sotaro.
1997. Two-Dimensional Semiotic Analysis of Japanese Mimetics. Linguistics 35(2):379-415.

Klain, Bennie, and Leighton C. Peterson.
 2000. Native Media, Commercial Radio, and Language Maintenance: Defining Speech and Style for Navajo Broadcasters and Broadcast Navajo. Texas Linguistic Forum 43:117–128.
Kluckhohn, Clyde.
 1960. Navaho Categories. *In* Culture in History. Stanley Diamond, ed. Pp. 65–98. New York: Columbia University Press.
Kluckhohn, Clyde, and Dorothea Leighton.
 1962. The Navajo. New York: Doubleday.
Kohn, Eduardo.
 2005. Runa Realism: Upper Amazonian Attitudes to Nature Knowing. Ethnos 70(2):171–196.
Kroskrity, Paul.
 1992a. Arizona Public Announcements: Form, Function, and Linguistic Ideology. Anthropological Linguistics 34(1–4):104–116.
 1992b. Arizona Tewa Kiva Speech as a Manifestation of Linguistic Ideology. Pragmatics 2(3):297–309.
 1993. Language, History and Identity: Ethnolinguistic Studies of the Arizona Tewa. Tucson: University of Arizona Press.
 2000a. Identity. Journal of Linguistic Anthropology 9(1–2):111–114.
 2000b. Regimes of Language. Santa Fe: School of American Research Press.
 2004. Language Ideologies. *In* A Companion to Linguistic Anthropology. Alessandro Duranti, ed. Pp. 496–517. Malden: Blackwell Publishing.
Kuipers, Joel.
 1998. Language, Identity, and Marginality in Indonesia: The Changing Nature of Ritual Speech on the Island of Sumba. Cambridge: Cambridge University Press.
Kwachka, Patricia.
 1992. Discourse Structures, Cultural Stability, and Language Shift. International Journal of the Sociology of Language 93:67–73.
Lamphere, Louise.
 1977. To Run After Them. Tucson: University of Arizona Press.
Landar, Herbert.
 1961. A Note on the Navaho Word for Coyote. International Journal of American Linguistics 27(1):86–88.
 1985. Navajo Interjections. International Journal of American Linguistics 51(4):489–491.

Lanoue, Guy.
    1991. Language Loss, Language Gain: Cultural Camouflage and Social Change Among the Sekani of Northern British Columbia. Language in Society 20:87–115.

Leap, William.
    1993a. American Indian English. Salt Lake City: University of Utah Press.
    1993b. Written Navajo English: Texture, Construction, and Point of View. Journal of Navajo Education 11(1):41–48.

Lee, Lloyd.
    2006. Navajo Cultural Identity: What Can the Navajo Nation Bring to the American Indian Identity Table? Wicazo Sa Review 21(2):79–103.
    2007. The Future of Navajo Nationalism. Wicazo Sa Review 22(1):53–68.
    2008. Reclaiming Indigenous Intellectual, Political, and Geographic Space. American Indian Quarterly 32(1):96–110.

Lee, Tiffany.
    2007. "If They Want Navajo to Be Learned, Then They Should Require It in All Schools": Navajo Teenagers' Experiences, Choices, and Demands Regarding Navajo Language. Wicazo Sa Review 22(1):7–33.

Lee, Tiffany, and Daniel McLaughlin.
    2001. Reversing Navajo Language Shift. *In* Can Threatened Languages Be Saved? Joshua Fishman, ed. Pp. 23–43. Tonawanda, NY: Multilingual Matters.

Le Page, Robert, and Andre Tabouret-Keller.
    1985. Acts of Identity: Creole Based Approaches to Language and Ethnicity. Cambridge: Cambridge University Press.

Linford, Laurence.
    2000. Navajo Places: History, Legend, Landscape. Salt Lake City: University of Utah Press.

Link, Martin.
    2001. The Long Walk and Academic Freedom. The Navajo Times, April 5, 2001, A-4.

Lockard, Louise.
    1995. New Paper Words: Historical Images of Navajo Language Literacy. American Indian Quarterly 19(1):17–30.

Makihara, Miki.
    2007.   Linguistic Purism in Rapa Nui Political Discourse. *In* Consequences of Contact: Language Ideologies and Sociocultural Transformations in Pacific Societies. Miki Makihara and Bambi Schieffelin, eds. Pp. 49-69. Oxford: Oxford University Press.

Martineau, LaVan.
    1973.   The Rocks Begin To Speak. Las Vegas: KC Publications.

Matthews, Washington.
    1894.   Songs of Sequence of the Navajos. Journal of American Folklore 7 (26):185-194.
    1994.   Navaho Legends. Salt Lake City: University of Utah Press.
    1995.   The Night Chant. Salt Lake City: University of Utah Press.
    1997.   The Mountain Chant. Salt Lake City: University of Utah Press.

McAllester, David.
    1954.   Enemy Way Music: A Study of Social and Esthetic Values as Seen in Navajo Music. Papers of the Peabody Museum of American Archaeology and Ethnology, Harvard University. Cambridge: Peabody Museum.
    1980a.   The First Snake Song. *In* Theory and Practice: Essays Presented to Gene Weltfish. Stanley Diamond, ed. Pp. 1-27. New York: Mouton.
    1980b.   Hogans: Navajo Houses and House Songs. Middletown: Wesleyan University Press.

McCarty, Teresa.
    2002.   A Place to Be Navajo. Mahwah, NJ: Lawrence Earlbaum Associates.

McDonough, Joyce.
    2003a.   The Navajo Sound System. Dordrecht: Kluwer Academic Publishers.
    2003b.   The Prosody of Interrogative and Focus Constructions in Navajo. *In* Formal Approaches to Function in Grammar. Andrew Carnie, Heidi Harley, and Maryann Willie, eds. Pp. 191-206. Amsterdam: John Benjamins.

McLaughlin, Daniel.
    1992.   When Literacy Empowers: Navajo Language in Print. Albuquerque: University of New Mexico Press.

McNeley, James.
    1981.   Holy Wind in Navajo Philosophy. Tucson: University of Arizona Press.

Meek, Barbra.
- 2006. "And the Injun Goes 'How!': Representations of American Indian in English in White Public Space." Language in Society 35:93–128.
- 2007. Respecting the Language of Elders: Ideological Shift and Linguistic Discontinuity in a Northern Athapascan Community. Journal of Linguistic Anthropology 17(1):23–43.

Meek, Barbra, and Jacqueline Messing.
- 2007. Framing Indigenous Languages as Secondary to Matrix Languages. Anthropology and Education Quarterly 38(2):99–118.

Milton, John R., ed.
- 1974. Four Indian Poets. Vermillion: University of South Dakota Press.

Mirkowich, Nicholas.
- 1941. A Note on Navajo Place Names. American Anthropologist 43(2):313–314.

Mitchell, Blackhorse.
- 1968. The New Direction. The Navajo Times, Centennial Issue, B8.
- 1969. Miracle Hill. In The American Indian Speaks. John R. Milton, ed. P. 110. Vermillion: University of South Dakota Press.
- 1972a. The Four Directions. In The Whispering Wind. Terry Allen, ed. P. 95. New York: Doubleday.
- 1972b. The Path I Must Travel. In The Whispering Wind. Terry Allen, ed. P. 94. New York: Doubleday.
- 1972c. Talking to His Drum. In The Whispering Wind. Terry Allen, ed. P. 96. New York: Doubleday.
- 2004. Miracle Hill: The Story of a Navajo Boy. Tucson: University of Arizona Press.

Mithun, Marianne.
- 1982. The Synchronic and Diachronic Behavior of Plops, Squeaks, Croaks, Sighs, and Moans. International Journal of American Linguistics 48(1):49–58.

Moore, Robert.
- 1988. Lexicalization Versus Lexical Loss in Wasco-Wishram Language Obsolescence. International Journal of American Linguistics 54(4): 453–468.

Morgan, William.
- 1949. Coyote Tales. Lawrence, KS: Bureau of Indian Affairs, Haskell Institute.

Morris, Irvin.
- 1997. From the Glittering World. Norman: University of Oklahoma Press.

Moshi, Lioba.
- 1993. Ideophones in Ki-Vunjo-Chaga. Journal of Linguistic Anthropology 3(2):185–216.

Mould, Tom.
- 2003. Choctaw Prophecy: A Legacy for the Future. Tuscaloosa: University of Alabama Press.

Mphande, Lupenga.
- 1992. Ideophones and the African Verse. Research in African Literature 23(1):117–129.

Murray, David.
- 1989. Transposing Symbolic forms: Actor Awareness of Language Structures in Navajo Ritual. Anthropological Linguistics 31:195–208.

Myers, Fred.
- 1991. Representing Culture: The Production of Discourse(s) for Aboriginal Acrylic Paintings. Cultural Anthropology 6:26–62.
- 1994. Culture-Making: Performing Aboriginality at the Asia Society Gallery. American Ethnologist 21:679–699.
- 2002. Painting Culture: The Making of an Aboriginal High Art. Durham: Duke University Press.

Neundorf, Alyse.
- 1982. Terminology Development in Navajo. International Journal of American Linguistics 48(3):271–276.
- 2006. Navajo/English Dictionary of Verbs. Albuquerque: University of New Mexico Press.

Newcomb, Franc, and Gladys Reichard.
- 1937. Sandpaintings of the Navajo Shooting Chant. New York: J. J. Augustin.

Nevins, M. Eleanor.
- 2004. Learning to Listen: Confronting Two Meanings of Language Loss in Contemporary White Mountain Apache Speech Community. Journal of Linguistic Anthropology 14(2):269–288.
- 2008. "They live in Lonesome Dove": Media and Contemporary Western Apache Place-Naming Practices. Language in Society 37(2):191–215.

Nevins, M. Eleanor, and Thomas Nevins.
- 2004. He Became an Eagle. *In* Voices from the Four Directions. Brian Swann, ed. Pp. 283–302. Lincoln: University of Nebraska Press.

Noss, Philip K.
  2001.   Ideas, Phones and Gbaya Verbal Art. *In* Ideophones. F. K. Erhard Voeltz and Christa Kilian-Hatz, eds. Pp. 259–270. Philadelphia: John Benjamins Publishing.
Nuckolls, Janis.
  1992.   Sound Symbolic Involvement. Journal of Linguistic Anthropology 2(1): 51–80.
  1995.   Quechua texts of perception. Semiotica 103(1/2):145–169.
  1996.   Sounds Like Life: Sound Symbolic Grammar, Performance and Cognition in Pastaza Quechua. London: Oxford University Press.
  1999.   The Case for Sound Symbolism. Annual Review of Anthropology 28:225–252.
  2000.   Spoken in the Spirit of Gesture: Translating Sound Symbolism in a Pastaza Quechua Narrative. *In* Translating Native Latin American Verbal Art. Kay Sammons and Joel Sherzer, eds. Pp. 233–251. Washington, DC: Smithsonian Press.
  2006.   The Neglected Poetics of Ideophony. *In* Language, Culture, and the Individual. Catherine O'Neil, Mary Scoggin, and Kevin Tuite, eds. Pp. 39–50. Muenchen, Germany: Lincom Europa.
O'Grady, William, John Archibald, Mark Aronoff, and Janie Rees-Miller, eds.
  2005.   Contemporary Linguistics: An Introduction. Boston: Bedford/St. Martin's.
O'Neill, Sean.
  2008.   Cultural Contact and Linguistic Relativity Among the Indians of Northwestern California. Norman: University of Oklahoma Press.
Parman, Donald.
  1994.   Indians and the American West in the Twentieth Century. Bloomington: Indiana University Press.
Pavlik, Steve.
  1992.   Of Saints and Lamanites: An Analysis of Navajo Mormonism. Wicazo Sa Review 8(1):21–30.
Peterson, Leighton C.
  2006.   Technology, Ideology and Emergent Communicative Practices among the Navajo. Ph.D. dissertation. Austin: University of Texas at Austin.
Pye, Clifton.
  1992.   Language Loss Among the Chilcotin. International Journal of the Sociology of Language 93:75–86.

Reichard, Gladys.
    1944.   Prayer: The Compulsive Word. American Ethnological Society Monograph 7. Seattle: University of Washington Press.
    1945.   Linguistic Diversity among the Navaho Indians. International Journal of American Linguistics 11:156–168.
    1947.   Reply to Hoijer's Review: The Story of the Navajo Hail Chant. International Journal of American Linguistics 13(3):193–196.
    1948.   The Significance of Aspiration in Navaho. International Journal of American Linguistics 14:15–19.
    1950.   Navaho Religion: A Study of Symbolism. New York: Bollingen Foundation.
    1997.   Spider Woman. Albuquerque: University of New Mexico Press.
Richland, Justin.
    2007.   Pragmatic Paradoxes and Ironies of Indigeneity at the "Edge" of Hopi Sovereignty. American Ethnologist 34(3):540–557.
Ridington, Robin, and Jillian Ridington.
    2006.   When You Sing It Now, Just Like New: First Nations Poetics, Voices, and Representations. Lincoln: University of Nebraska Press.
Rumsey, Alan.
    1990.   Wording, Meaning, and Linguistic Ideology. American Anthropologist 92:346–361.
    2000.   Agency, Personhood and the "I" of Discourse in the Pacific and Beyond. Journal of the Royal Anthropological Institute 6(1):101–113.
    2006.   The Articulation of Indigenous and Exogenous Orders in Highland New Guinea and Beyond. Australian Journal of Anthropology 17(1):47–69.
Rushforth, Scott.
    1992.   The Legitimation of Beliefs in a Hunter-Gatherer Society: Bearlake Athapaskan Knowledge and Authority. American Ethnologist 19(3):483–500.
    1994.   Political Resistance in a Contemporary Hunter-Gatherer Society: More about Bearlake Athapaskan Knowledge and Authority. American Ethnologist 21(2):335–352.
Samarin, William.
    1970.   Field Procedures in Ideophone Research. Journal of African Languages 9:27–30.
    1971.   Survey of Bantu Ideophones. African Language Studies 12:130–168.

1991. Intersubjective and Intradialectal Variation in Gbeya Ideophones. Journal of Linguistic Anthropology 1(1):52–62.

Samuels, David.
 2001. Indeterminacy and History in Britton Goode's Western Apache Placenames. American Ethnologist 28(2):277–302.
 2004a. Language, Meaning, Modernity, and Doowop. Semiotica 149(1/4):297–323.
 2004b. Putting a Song on Top of It. Tucson: University of Arizona Press.
 2006. Bible Translation and Medicine Man Talk: Missionaries, Indexicality, and the "Language Expert" on the San Carlos Apache Reservation. Language in Society 35(4):529–557.

Sapir, Edward.
 1921. Language. New York: Harcourt, Brace.
 1927. Speech as a Personality Trait. American Journal of Sociology 32:892–205.
 1929. The Status of Linguistics as a Science. Language 5(4):207–214.
 1932. Two Navajo Puns. Language 8:217–219.
 1938. Why Cultural Anthropology Needs the Psychiatrist. Psychiatry 1:7–12.
 1985. Culture, Language, and Personality, Selected Essays. David G. Mandelbaum, ed. Epilogue by Dell H. Hymes. First paperback ed. Berkeley: University of California Press.

Sapir, Edward, and Harry Hoijer.
 1942. Navaho Texts. Iowa City: Linguistic Society of America.

Saussure, Ferdinand de.
 1966 [1916]. Course in General Linguistics. New York: McGraw-Hill.

Saville-Troike, Muriel.
 1974. Diversity in Southwestern Athabaskan: A Historical Perspective. Navajo Language Review 1(2):67–84.

Schaengold, Charlotte.
 2003. The Emergence of Bilingual Navajo: English and Navajo Languages in Contact Regardless of Everyone's Best Intentions. In When Languages Collide. Brian Joseph, Johanna DeStefano, Neil Jacobs, and Ilse Lehiste, eds. Pp. 235–254. Columbus: Ohio State University Press.
 2004. Bilingual Navajo: Mixed Codes, Bilingualism, and Language Maintenance. Ph.D. dissertation. Columbus: Ohio State University.
 2006. Navajo Language: Purity and Survival. In Diné Bi'e'el'įį Baa Hane' Baa Náhát'į: Selected Papers from the 11th through 13th Navajo

Studies Conference. June-el Piper, ed. Pp. 29-33. Albuquerque: Navajo Studies Conference.

Schieffelin, Bambi, Kathryn Woolard, and Paul Kroskrity, eds.
    1998.   Language Ideologies. Oxford: Oxford University Press.

Schiffrin, Deborah.
    1987.   Discourse Markers. Cambridge: Cambridge University Press.

Schlafly, Phyllis.
    2002.   Foreign Language Ballots are a Bad Idea. http://www.eagleforum.org/column/2002/aug02/02-08-28.shtml.

Schwarz, Maureen.
    1997.   Modeled in the Image of Changing Woman. Tucson: University of Arizona Press.
    1998.   Holy Visit 1996: Prophecy, Revitalization, and Resistance in the Contemporary Navajo World. Ethnohistory 45(4):747–793.
    2003.   Blood and Voice: Navajo Women Ceremonial Practitioners. Tucson: University of Arizona Press.

Scollon, Ronald.
    1976.   The Framing of Chipewyan Narrative Performances: Titles, Initials and Finals. Working Papers in Linguistics, Department of Linguistics, University of Hawaii 7(4):97–107.

Scollon, Ronald, and Suzanne Scollon.
    1981.   Narrative, Literacy, and Face in Interethnic Communication. Norwood, NJ: Ablex.

Scott, James.
    1990.   Domination and the Arts of Resistance. New Haven: Yale University Press.

Seaburg, William.
    2007.   Pitch Woman and Other Stories: The Oral Traditions of Coquelle Thompson, Upper Coquille Athabaskan Indian. Lincoln: University of Nebraska Press.

Shaul, David Leedom.
    2002.   Hopi Traditional Literature. Albuquerque: University of New Mexico Press.

Sherzer, Joel.
    1978.   "Oh! That's a Pun and I Didn't Mean It." Semiotica 22(3/4):335–350.
    1987.   A Discourse-Centered Approach to Language and Culture. American Anthropologist 89:295–309.
    1990.   Verbal Art in San Blas. Cambridge: Cambridge University Press.
    1994.   The Kuna and Columbus: Encounters and Confrontations of Discourse. American Anthropologist 96(4):902–924.

2002. Speech Play and Verbal Art. Austin: University of Texas Press.

Shonerd, Henry.
    1990. Domesticating the Barbarous Tongue: Language Policy for the Navajo in Historical Perspective. Language Problems & Language Planning 14(3):193–208.

Silverstein, Michael.
    1979. Language Structure and Linguistic Ideology. *In* The Elements. Paul Clyne, William Hanks, and Carol Hofbauer, eds. Pp. 193–247. Chicago: Chicago Linguistic Society.
    1981. The Limits of Awareness. Sociolinguistic Working Papers, No. 84. Austin: Southwest Educational Development Laboratory.
    1994. Relative Motivation in Denotational and Indexical Sound Symbolism of Wasco-Wishram Chinookan. *In* Sound Symbolism. Leanne Hinton, Johanna Nichols, and John Ohala, eds. Pp. 40–60. Cambridge: Cambridge University Press.
    1998. Contemporary Transformations of Local Linguistic Communities. Annual Review of Anthropology 27:401–426.
    2000. Whorfianism and the Linguistic Imagination of Nationality. *In* Regimes of Language. Paul Kroskrity, ed. Pp. 85–137. Santa Fe: School of American Research Press.
    2003a. Indexical Order and the Dialectics of Sociolinguistic Life. Language & Communication 23:193–239.
    2003b. The Whens and Wheres—As Well as Hows—of Ethnolinguistic Recognition. Public Culture 15(3):531–557.
    2005. Axes of Evals: Token versus Type Interdiscursivity. Journal of Linguistic Anthropology 15(1):6–22.

Slate, Clay.
    1993. On Reversing Navajo Language Shift. Journal of Navajo Education 10(3):30–35.

Sorensen, Barbara.
    1996. Hasht'e' Sooké. The Navajo Times, June 6, A-7.

Spicer, Edward.
    1962. Cycles of Conquest. Tucson: University of Arizona Press.
    1971. Persistent Cultural Systems. Science 174(4011):795–800.
    1975. Indian Identity versus Assimilation. An Occasional Paper of the Weatherhead Foundation. Pp. 29–54. New York: New York.

Spolsky, Bernard.
    2002. Prospects for the Survival of the Navajo Language: A Reconsideration. Anthropology & Education Quarterly 33(2):139–162.

Swann, Brian, ed.
- 1994. Coming to Light. New York: Vintage Press.
- 2004. Voices from the Four Directions. Lincoln: University of Nebraska Press.

Tapahonso, Luci.
- 1987. A Breeze Swept Through. Albuquerque: West End Press.
- 1993. Sáanii Dahataał: The Women are Singing. *In* Sun Tracks. Vol. 23. Tucson: University of Arizona Press.
- 1997. Blue Horses Rush In. Tucson: University of Arizona Press.
- 2008. a radiant curve. Tucson: University of Arizona Press.

Taylor, Charles.
- 2006. An Issue About Language. *In* Language, Culture, and Society. Christine Jourdan and Kevin Tuite, eds. Pp. 16-46. Cambridge: Cambridge University Press.

Tedlock, Dennis.
- 1983. The Spoken Word and the Work of Interpretation. Philadelphia: University of Pennsylvania Press.
- 1999. Ideophone. Journal of Linguistic Anthropology 9(1-2):118-120.

Tedlock, Dennis, and Bruce Mannheim, eds.
- 1995. The Dialogic Emergence of Culture. Urbana: University of Illinois Press.

Thornton, Thomas.
- 2008. Being and Place Among the Tlingit. Seattle: University of Washington Press.

Toelken, Barre.
- 1971. Ma'i Joldloshi: Legendary Styles and Navaho Myth. *In* American Folk Legend. Wayland Hand, ed. Pp. 203-211. Berkeley: University of California Press.
- 1987. Life and Death in Navajo Coyote tales. *In* Recovering the Word. Brian Swann and Arnold Krupat, eds. Pp. 388-401. Berkeley: University of California Press.
- 2002. Native American Reassessment and Reinterpretation of Myths. *In* Myth: A New Symposium. Gregory Schrempp and William Hansen, eds. Pp. 89-103. Bloomington: Indiana University Press.

Toelken, Barre, and Tacheeni Scott.
- 1981. Poetic Retranslation and the "Pretty Languages" of Yellowman. *In* Traditional Literatures of the American Indians. Karl Kroeber, ed. Pp. 65-116. Lincoln: University of Nebraska Press.

Tohe, Laura.
    1999.   No Parole Today. Albuquerque: West End Press.
    2002.   In Dinétah. *In* Sister Nations. Heid Erdrich and Laura Tohe, eds. Pp. 100–106. St. Paul: Minnesota Historical Society Press.
    2005.   Tséyi': Deep in the Rock. Tucson: University of Arizona Press.
    2007.   Hwéeldi Bééhániih: Remembering the Long Walk. Wicazo Sa Review 22(1):77–82.

Towner, Ronald, ed.
    1996.   The Archaeology of Navajo Origins. Salt Lake City: University of Utah Press.

Urban, Greg.
    1989.   The "I" of Discourse. *In* Semiotics, Self, and Society. Benjamin Lee and Greg Urban, eds. Pp. 27–51. Berlin: Mouton de Gruyter.
    1991.   A Discourse-Centered Approach to Culture. Austin: University of Texas Press.

Urciuoli, Bonnie.
    1996.   Exposing Prejudice. Boulder: Westview Press.

Uyechi, Linda.
    1990.   Navajo Fourth Person: The Ji-/Ha- Alternation. Journal of Navajo Education 7(3):3–12.

Van Vleet, Krista.
    2008.   Performing Kinship: Narrative, Gender, and the Intimacies of Power in the Andes. Austin: University of Texas Press.

Voeltz, F. K. Erhard, and Christa Kilian-Hatz, eds.
    2001.   Ideophones. Philadelphia: John Benjamins Publishing.

Walton, Eda Lou.
    1930.   Navajo Song Patterning. Journal of American Folklore 43(167):105–118.

Watch Tower Website.
    2006.   Jiihóvah Yádahalne'í Bibee Bóhólníihii biWeb Site. http://www.watchtower.org/nv/index.html (accessed April 8, 2008).

Watson, Richard.
    2000.   A Comparison of some Southeast Asian Ideophones with Some African Ideophones. *In* Ideophones. F. K. Erhard Voeltz and Christa Kilian-Hatz, eds. Pp. 385–405. Philadelphia: John Benjamins Publishing.

Webster, Anthony.
    1999.   Sam Kenoi's Coyote Stories: Poetics and Rhetoric in some Chiricahua Narratives. American Indian Culture and Research Journal 23(1):137–163.

2004. Coyote Poems: Navajo Poetry, Intertextuality, and Language Choice. American Indian Culture and Research Journal 28(4):69–91.

2006a. From Hóyéé to Hajinei: On Some Implications of Feelingful Iconicity and Orthography in Navajo Poetry. Pragmatics 16(4):535–549.

2006b. Keeping the Word: On Orality and Literacy (with a Sideways Glance at Navajo). Oral Tradition 21(2):295–324.

2006c. The Mouse that Sucked: On "Translating" a Navajo Poem. Studies in American Indian Literature 18(1):37–49.

2008a. "To All the Former Cats and Stomps of the Navajo Nation": Performance, the Individual, and Cultural Poetic Traditions. Language in Society 37(1):61–89.

2008b. "To Give an Imagination to the Listener": The Neglected Poetics of Navajo Ideophony. Semiotica 171(1/4):343–365.

In press. John Watchman's Ma'ii dóó Gólizhii. In Inside Dazzling Mountains. David Kozak, ed. Lincoln: University of Nebraska Press.

Wheeler, Lesley.
2008. Voicing American Poetry: Sound and Performance from the 1920s to the Present. Ithaca: Cornell University Press.

Whitehurst, Lindsay.
2007. More Local Chapters Using Navajo Names. Farmington Daily Times, May 22, 2007. http://www.daily-times.com/news/ci_5963257.

Williams, Raymond.
1977. Marxism and Literature. Oxford: Oxford University Press.

Willie, Mary Ann, and Eloise Jelinek.
2000. Navajo as a Discourse Configurational Language. In The Athabaskan Languages. Theodore Fernald and Paul Platero, eds. Pp. 252–287. Oxford: Oxford University Press.

Wilson, Alan.
1970. Laughter: The Navajo Way (with Gene Dennison). Gallup, NM: University of New Mexico, Gallup Branch.
1995. Navajo Place Names. Guilford, CT: Jeffrey Norton Publishers.

Witherspoon, Gary.
1977. Language and Art in the Navajo Universe. Ann Arbor: University of Michigan Press.

Woodbury, Anthony.
    1987.   Meaningful Phonological Processes: A Consideration of Central Alaskan Yupik Eskimo Prosody. Language 63(4):685–740.
    1993.   A Defense of the Proposition, "When a Language Dies a Culture Dies." Texas Linguistic Forum 33:101–129.
    1998.   Documenting Rhetorical, Aesthetic, and Expressive Loss in Language Shift. *In* Endangered Languages. Leonore Grenoble and Lindsay Whaley, eds. Pp. 234–258. Cambridge: Cambridge University Press.

Woody, Everrick.
    1994.   Aheeh Hwiinidzin. The Navajo Times, December 15, A-7.

Woolard, Kathryn.
    1998.   Language Ideology as a Field of Inquiry. *In* Language Ideologies. Bambi Schieffelin, Kathryn Woolard, and Paul Kroskrity, eds. Pp. 3–50. Oxford: Oxford University Press.

Yazzie, Evangeline Parsons.
    2005.   Dzání Yázhí Naazbaa': Little Woman Warrior Who Came Home. Flagstaff: Salina Bookshelf.

Yazzie, Evangeline Parsons, and Margaret Speas.
    2007.   Diné Bizaad Bínáhoo'aah: Rediscovering the Navajo Language. Flagstaff: Salina Bookshelf.

Young, Robert.
    1989.   Lexical Elaboration in Navajo. *In* General and Amerindian Ethnolinguistics. Mary Ritchie Key and Harry Hoenigswald, eds. Pp. 303–320. Berlin: Mouton de Gruyter.
    1993.   The Evolution of Written Navajo. Journal of Navajo Education 10(3):46–55.
    2000.   The Navajo Verb System. Albuquerque: University of New Mexico Press.

Young, Robert, and William Morgan.
    1987.   The Navajo Language. Albuquerque: University of New Mexico Press.

Young, Robert, and William Morgan, with the assistance of Sally Midgette.
    1992.   Analytical Lexicon of Navajo. Albuquerque: University of New Mexico Press.

Yurth, Cindy.
    2006a.   Panel Wants Tséyi' Back in Navajo Hands. The Navajo Times, April 6, A1.
    2006b.   Storm Clouds over Tséyi': Canyon Residents Clash with U.S. Park Superintendent. The Navajo Times, February 16, A1.

Zachary, Mary-Kathryn.
    2005.   More Than the Law: Perspectives on an English-Only Case in Navajo Country. Labor Law Journal 56(1):5–29.

Zepeda, Ofelia.
    1982.   O'odham Ha-Cegitodag/Pima and Papago Thoughts. International Journal of American Linguistics 48(3):320–326.
    1997.   Jewed 'I-hoi: Earth Movements. Tucson: Kore Press.
    2000.   Autobiography. *In* Here First. Arnold Krupat and Brian Swann, eds. Pp. 405–420. New York: Modern Library.

Zolbrod, Paul.
    1984.   Diné Bahane. Albuquerque: University of New Mexico Press.
    2004.   Squirrel Reddens His Cheeks: Cognition, Recognition, and Poetic Production in Ancient Navajo Stories. Journal of the Southwest 46(4):679–704.

INDEX

Abasta, Rick, 111; *TerraIncognita: An Alternative Dine' Zine*, 111
Aberbach, David, 164, 182, 239
aesthetics, 2, 47, 70, 75, 79, 82, 247
affective display, 22
Agha, Asif, 82, 239; metasemiotic stereotypes, 15, 82–83, 92, 99, 119, 121, 185, 213, 217, 223, 237
Aheedlíinii, Curly Tó, 42, 61–66
Ahlers, Jocelyn, 186–87, 194, 239
Alaska, 10, 266. *See also* Woodbury, Anthony
Albuquerque Indian School, 125, 135, 137, 144, 145, 150
alienable/inalienable nouns, 19, 103
Allen, Terry, 110
American Indian Movement, 143
Anderson, Benedict, 36, 120, 239
Anderson, Myrdene, viii, 180
animacy, 53–54
Aoki, Haruo, 55, 239
Apache, 9–10, 57, 62, 96, 104, 106, 123–24, 127, 142, 198–99, 203, 240, 249, 257, 260
Apachean languages, 10
Apachean poetics, 123
Apaglish, 104
Arapaho, 199, 214, 244
Ashley, Rutherford (Ford), viii, 111–14, 116, 120, 132, 207, 227, 239;

Heart Vision 2000, 112–14, 227, 239
Athabaskan/Athapaskan language family, 10, 13, 51, 85, 100, 231, 265
Athabaskan Language Conference, 13
Auden, W. H., 1, 239
Austin-Garrison, Martha, viii, 56, 75, 240
Australian Aborigine art, 147, 187
Australian languages, 55
Axelrod, Melissa, 51, 57, 240; Koyukon, 57

Bahe, Maggie, 40–41, 240
Bahr, Howard, 13, 240; multiplying glimpses, v, 13, 218–25, 240
Bakhtin, Mikhail, 45, 80, 99, 119, 125, 163, 166, 240
Baldinger, Jo Ann, 95, 240
Bartelt, H. Guillermo, 10, 103, 240
Basso, Keith, 23, 32, 45, 62, 96, 123–27, 142, 166, 198–99, 234, 240
Basso, Keith, and Nashley Tessay Sr., 125, 240
Bauman, Richard, 9, 45, 98, 123, 126, 129, 163, 240; Iceland(ic), 98; performance-centered perspective, 9; traditionalization, 98, 119, 167, 224; verbal art as performance, 9, 240
Bauman, Richard, and Charles Briggs, 117, 123, 241

269

Bauman, Richard, and Joel Sherzer, 241
Beauty (*hózhǫ́/hózhǫ́ǫgo*), 29, 45, 169
Becker, Alton, 125, 241
Begay, Elsie May Cly, 23, 221, 231
Begay, Leandra, 155; "Heritage," 155
Begay, Lydia Fasthorse, 25, 74, 241
Begay, Shonto, viii, 130–31, 171, 227
Belin, Esther, viii, 3, 32, 35, 47, 81, 112–13, 115, 116, 130, 132, 148, 158, 163, 166, 174, 177, 218, 220, 227, 241; "Check One," 47; *From the Belly of My Beauty*, 3, 227, 241; "On Telly Biliizh," 112
Benally, AnCita, viii, 10, 241
Benally, AnCita, and Denis Viri, 10, 17, 20, 56, 241
Benally, Timothy, 132
Benally, Zoey (Twyla Zoann), viii, 6, 224
Bender, Margaret, 232, 241
Berglund, Jeff, 163
Bidtah, Minnie, 72–74
Binder, Wolfgang, and Helmbrecht Breining, 44, 241
Biolsi, Thomas, 186, 241
Bitsui, Sherwin, viii, 3, 11, 130, 132, 177, 220, 227, 237, 242; "Northern Sun," 3
Blommaert, Jan, 8–9, 242
Blot, Richard, 128, 242
boarding school, 46, 124–26, 130–31, 137, 142, 148, 190, 218, 236; Carlisle Institute, Carlisle, PA, 235
Boas, Franz, 7, 242
borrowing/loanwords, 85–86, 117
Bosque Redondo, 154. See also *Hwéeldi*
Bosque Redondo, Treaty of, 157–58, 174
Bosque Redondo Memorial, 23, 167, 221
Brenneis, Donald, and Alessandro Duranti, 123, 242
Briggs, Charles, 23, 68, 120, 242; Warao (Venezuela), 23

Briggs, Charles, and Richard Bauman, 163, 242
Bright, William, 242
Brill de Ramirez, Susan, 16, 90, 97, 111, 117, 242
Browne, Vee, viii, 8, 227, 242
Bruchac, Joseph, 166, 171, 242
Brugge, David, 173, 243
Bsumek, Erika, 85, 117, 218, 243; cultural borrowers, 117
Bunte, Pamela, 66, 243
Bureau of Indian Affairs (BIA), 24, 79, 88, 222; *Arrow*, 88
Butterfly Mountain (*K'aalǫ́gii Dził*), 171

Casuse, Larry, 150
Canfield, Kip, 80–81, 100–101, 103, 108, 243
Canyon de Chelly, 142, 163, 191, 199–202, 207, 214–15, 252. See also *Tseyi'*
Carbondale, IL, ix, 163, 186–200, 213–14, 231; Indigenous Peoples' Day, 187–89
Carson, Kit, 153–54, 160–61, 166–72
Casaus, Bernice, 72, 243
Chafe, Wallace, 234, 243
chantways, 27, 29, 43, 45, 84, 169, 181, 234
Chee, Melvatha, Evan Ashworth, Susan Buescher, and Brittany Kubacki, 86, 243
Chee, Norla, 19, 33, 94, 112–16, 120–30, 227; "A Navajo Sing," 94; "Shí Buddy," 19, 114, 116
Cherokee, 170, 232, 241
Chief Barboncito, 173
Chief Manuelito, 173
Childs, G. Tucker, 52–53, 55, 58, 77–78, 243; Meso-American languages, 55; Zulu (Africa), 53, 58, 78

INDEX   271

Chinese, 55, 246
Chipewyan, 10, 244, 261
Chuska Mountains, 33
clans, 21, 148, 162, 191–93, 213, 237
Claw, Eugene, 25
Clifford, James, 153, 182, 219, 243
clitic, 81, 104
Cly, John Wayne, 231
code-mixing, vii, 6, 80, 100–101, 104, 113, 243
code-switching, 6, 18–19, 26, 48, 89, 101, 111, 128, 188
Code Talkers, 162, 173, 194–95, 197, 236
Coleman, Steve, 164, 243
Collins, James, 19, 37, 177, 196, 244; indigenous articulations, 151–84, 219; Tolowa, 10, 19, 177
Collins, James, and Richard Blot, 133, 156, 244
Cool Runnings, 111, 207, 220
Cook, Eung-Do, 231, 244
Cowell, Andrew, 198–99, 214, 244
Coyote (*Mąʼii*), 113, 115–16, 149, 242, 253, 263, 265
Coyote narratives, 19, 30–48, 61–68, 113–16, 149, 222, 249, 250, 252, 256
Craig, Vincent, 19, 102–3, 116, 244
Crawford, James, 194, 244
creaky voice, 23
Cruikshank, Julie, 147, 149, 157, 168, 174, 187, 198, 216, 244
Csordas, Thomas, 163, 244

Dawn Songs, 68
DeLisle, Helga, 55, 245
Deloria, Philip, 186, 245
Denetdale, Jennifer Nez, 4, 10, 23, 92, 120, 127, 141, 153–54, 156–57, 163–67, 183, 218, 224, 236, 245
Deschenie, Tina, viii
Dick, Galena Sells, 17, 20, 49, 224, 245

Dick, Galena Sells, and Teresa McCarty, 17–18, 20, 245
Diné ("the people") v. Navajo, 25, 81–99, 120, 123, 126, 134–51
Diné békeyah, 153
Diné bizaad, 22, 84, 94–99, 106, 197, 211, 223, 241, 243, 266. *See* Navajo language
Dinétah, 35–45, 91–92, 155–83, 264
Diné Teacher Education Program, 74
Dinwoodie, David, 187, 198, 214–15, 232, 238, 245
discourse marker, 30, 43, 93, 261
discourse routine, 21, 47
Doke, Clement, 52, 245
Domenici, Senator Pete, 23, 221
Donovan, Bill, 156–57, 246; *Gallup Independent, The*, 156
Dooley, Sunny, 95
Dreamings, The, 187
Dunn, Cynthia, 165
Durbin, Marshall, 54–55, 246

Edmo, Ronald Snake, 232, 246; Shoshoni, 232
Emerson, Gloria, viii, 11, 24, 71, 76, 130, 207, 219, 222, 227, 246; *'Ahwééh/Gohwééh* coffee shop, 224; in *The Indian Historian*, 24, 246
enclitics, 29–32, 57, 69, 104–6, 110, 114–15, 120, 232
English-language poetry, 2–4, 6, 8, 10–51, 228
Erdrich, Heid, 158, 174, 246
Erdrich, Heid, and Laura Tohe, 158, 190, 227, 246
Erickson, Kirstin, 127, 153–54, 246; Yaqui, 153–54
Errington, Joseph, 5, 128, 216, 246
ethnopoetics, vii–viii, 1, 7–9, 50, 122–26, 184, 222, 242, 251

Evers, Terry, 110, 227, 246
Evers, Terry, and Felipe Molina, 237, 246

Fabian, Johannes, 148, 246
falsetto (vowel quality), 23
Farella, John, 45, 165, 231, 246
Faris, James, viii, 27, 34, 84, 218, 234, 247
Farnell, Brenda, 234, 247
Fast, Robin Riley, 90, 111, 247
Feld, Steven, 9, 23, 63, 174, 247; Kaluli (PNG), 9, 23
felt pragmatic iconicity, 221
Field, Margaret, viii, 13, 17, 21–22, 27, 47–49, 93–94, 101–2, 247
Field, Margaret, and Taft Blackhorse Jr., 28, 45, 55, 180–81
"First Woman," 113–16, 241
Fitzgerald, Colleen, 232, 247
Fort Sumner, 154–56, 174–83, 204. *See also* Bosque Redondo; Hwéeldi
Foster, Susan, Gloria Singer, Lucy Benally, Theresa Boone, and Anne Beck, 101, 109, 247
four, rhetorical uses of the number, 22, 33, 38, 42, 47–48, 60, 163–67, 176, 180–81, 233
framing devices, 16, 29–34, 43–48, 92. *See also* Hofling, C. Andrew; Scollon, Ronald
Francisco, Nia, 2, 24, 77, 88, 110, 130, 132, 150, 170, 177, 227, 247; "Naabeeho Woman Poet," 77; in *College English*, 24, 88
Frank, Della, and Roberta Joe, 227, 248
Friedrich, Paul, 6–9, 50, 122–26, 248; poetic indeterminacy, 6, 9
Frisbie, Charlotte, viii, 27, 34–35, 63, 68, 71, 248

Gal, Susan, and Judith Irvine, 83, 85, 118–19, 248; Macedonia, 119

Glittering World, 158, 164–65, 172. *See also* Morris, Irvin; Navajo, origins of the
Goffman, Erving, 44, 141, 248
Goode, Britton, 104, 198
Goodfellow, Anne, 22, 248; Kʷakʷʼala, 22
Goossen, Irvy, 60
Gorman, Howard, 171
Graham, Laura, 174, 187, 216, 248; Yanomami, 187
Greenfeld, Philip, 125, 144, 249

Haile, Fr. Berard, 31–33, 42–43, 61, 64, 66, 77, 249
Hale, Ken, 54, 249
Hamill, James, 41, 249; Navajo syllogism, 41
Hane' (stories), 1, 29–46, 61, 75, 92, 130, 155, 162–65, 219, 225; *Hane' naachʼąąh* ("designed stories"), 1
Hanks, William, 152–53, 157, 249
Hataal (chants), 27
Hill, Jane, 82–83, 249; Mexicano, Spanish, 83
Hill, Jonathan, 156–57, 216, 231, 249
Hill, W. W., 75, 117, 249
Hill, W. W., and Dorothy Hill, 41, 250
Hinton, Leanne, Johanna Nichols, and John Ohala, 52, 56, 250
Hofling, C. Andrew, ix, 29, 55, 250; Mayan, 55
Hoijer, Harry, 27, 31–33, 39, 54, 62, 66, 85, 169, 232, 233, 250, 260; Chiricahua Apache, 10, 62, 250, 265
Holiday, Marvin, 114, 250
Holliday, Billie, 46, 179; "Strange Fruit," 46, 170
Holm, Wayne, and Agnes Holm, 17, 194, 250
Hopi, 173, 208
House, Deborah, 4, 12, 17–18, 48, 85, 123, 148, 190, 207–8, 250; "Narratives

of Navajoness," 123, 128, 151–84; *Language Shift among the Navajo*, 12, 250
Hózhǫ́/hózhǫ́ǫgo/hózhóón (Beauty), 28, 45, 112, 233
Hubbard, Marilyn, 74; "*Pe'sii Laanaa* (I want Pepsi)," 74
Hunn, Eugene, 250
Hunter, Linda, and Chaibou Elhadji Oumarou, 52, 250
Hausa (Africa), 52
Hupa, 10
Hwéeldi, 39, 153–55, 172–78, 203–4, 236
Hymes, Dell, 7–8, 41, 52–54, 123–26, 223, 251; providential world, 41; ways of speaking, 21

icon (of identity), 5, 23, 46, 54, 63, 80–121, 178, 185–87, 199, 202, 211–13, 222–23, 233–34
identity, 4, 26, 49, 77–83, 122, 127–40, 149–55, 173–94, 213–25. *See also* icon; index
ideophones/ideophony, 22, 44, 51–79, 188, 222, 234. *See also* sound symbolism/forms
index (of identity), 5, 8, 14, 32, 46–48, 77–121, 128, 140–41, 149, 165–71, 180, 185–88, 193, 203–5, 213–17, 232, 237
Indians at Work, 24
indigenous people, 5, 10, 146, 200, 220
intercultural performances, 185–217. *See also* Cruikshank, Julie
intertextuality/intertextual reference, 15, 46–53, 71, 93, 116–19, 152–80, 200, 224
Irvine, Judith, 98, 237, 251; affective register, 98, 237
Irvine, Judith, and Susan Gal, 100, 118–19, 251

Iverson, Peter, 10, 125, 131, 154, 168, 235, 251

Jackson, Jason, 98, 251
Jakobson, Roman, 6–8, 79, 180, 251; expressive alignment, 6; poetic function of language, 6, 79
Jameson, Fredric, 149, 251
Japanese, 55, 236
Jehovah's Witnesses, 107
Jesusgo Shí Doo (I'd rather have Jesus), 106
Jett, Stephen, 191, 198–200, 215, 251
Jicarilla Apache, 10, 57
Jim, Rex Lee, viii, 2–4, 8, 11, 25–29, 32–36, 47–48, 68–77, 95–97, 112, 130–33, 139, 177, 212–16, 222, 227, 252; *Tó Háálį́* ("Spring"), 95
Jiní ("they say," quotative), 165–66
John, Hershman, viii, 88, 93, 228, 252; "The Dark World," 92
Johnson, Broderick, 154, 171, 252
Johnstone, Barbara, ix, 122–29, 150, 252; linguistic individual, 129, 150

K'aalǫ́gii Dził (Butterfly Mountain), 171
Kan, Sergei, and Pauline Turner Strong, 186, 252
Kari, James, and Bernard Spolsky, 117, 252
Keane, Webb, 44, 252
Keller, Robert, and Michael Turek, 215, 252
Kelley, Klara, and Harris Francis, 32, 191, 198, 215, 252; wayfinding, 32
Kita, Sotaro, 52, 252
Klain, Bennie, viii, 23, 231, 237, 253; *The Return of Navajo Boy*, 23, 231
Klain, Bennie, and Leighton C. Peterson, 102, 108–9
Kluckhohn, Clyde, 27, 38, 56, 61, 84, 253
Kluckhohn, Clyde, and Dorothea Leighton, 167, 182–83, 212, 231

Kohn, Eduardo, 53, 253
Kroskrity, Paul, ix, 5, 80–86, 94, 118, 253; Arizona Tewa, 84, 128, 253; linguistic conservatism, 118; pervasive principles, 84
KTNN, 20, 27, 81, 97, 102, 108–9, 118, 130, 139, 141, 215, 238
Kuipers, Joel, 5, 128, 253; Indonesia, 128
Kwachka, Patricia, 21, 253

Lamphere, Louise, 37, 70, 253
Landar, Herbert, 48, 57–58, 68, 253
language loss, 22–23, 143
language maintenance, 20, 83
language persistence, 2, 17, 49, 109, 219. *See also* Shonerd, Henry
language play, 202, 216, 222. *See also* Sherzer, Joel
language shift, 47, 50, 56, 90, 102, 128, 151, 166, 185, 194–97, 217, 222
Lanoue, Guy, 231, 254
Latter Day Saints, Church of, 60
Leap, William, 10, 103, 254, 261
Lee, Lloyd, 120, 219, 224, 254
Lee, Tiffany, 10, 109, 120, 164, 254
Lee, Tiffany, and Daniel McLaughlin, 17–18, 20, 254
Le Page, Robert, and Andre Tabouret-Keller, 127, 254
lexico-grammatical code, 22, 47
"LINEbreak," 26, 87–88
line structure (poetry), 65, 68, 133
Linford, Laurence, 62, 254
Link, Martin, 156–57, 254
linguistic ideologies, 13–14, 40, 77–121, 156, 203, 214, 222
linguistic purism, 14, 83–84, 121. *See also* Hill, Jane; Makihara, Miki
Lockard, Louise, 18, 254
Long Walk, 4–5, 15, 151–84, 203, 236

Mą'ii (Coyote), 30–31, 41–48, 61–65, 231–32
Makihara, Miki, 83, 109, 255; linguistic syncretism, 83; Rapa Nui, 83, 109
Māori, 8
Martineau, LaVan, 155, 255
Matthews, Washington, 18, 27–29, 45, 67–68, 255
McAllester, David, ix, 27, 35, 55, 68, 89–90, 255
McCarty, Teresa, 139, 255; Rough Rock Demonstration School, 139
McDonough, Joyce, 3, 133, 233, 255
McLaughlin, Daniel, 12, 18, 81, 105, 108, 114; special diglossia, 12
Meek, Barbra, 214, 231, 256
Meek, Barbra, and Jacqueline Messing, 119, 256
metalinguistic commentary, 15, 89, 94, 185, 217
metapragmatic ideal, 94
metasemantic commentary, 91
metasemiotic stereotypes, 15, 82–83, 92–99, 119–21, 185, 213, 217, 223, 237. *See also* Agha, Asif; Silverstein, Michael
Milton, John, 110, 228, 256
Mirkowich, Nicholas, 85, 92, 233, 256
missionaries, 23, 77–78
Mistic, 155, 183; *Tribal Scars*, 155, 183
Mistic and Shade, 155
Mitchell, Blackhorse, 110, 130, 132, 146, 167, 177, 207, 216, 220, 256
Mitchell, Charlie, 165
Mithun, Marianne, 55, 256
Moore, Robert, 18, 48, 81, 256
Morgan, Lawrence, 205
Morgan, William, 30–42, 56, 58, 256; "Origin of the Night Chant," 32
Morris, Irvin, 132, 164–65, 172, 177, 210–11, 256; *From the Glittering World*, 164–65, 210–11

Moshi, Lioba, 52, 257
Mould, Tom, 168, 257
Mowrer, Priscilla, 23
Mphande, Lupenga, 53, 78–79, 257
Murray, David, 35, 257
music festivals, 131–32, 139–48
Myers, Fred, 147, 174, 187, 216, 257
myth, 8, 17–18, 32–34, 61, 90, 115–16, 156, 165–66, 167, 181–88, 202, 215

Native American Student Organization, SIUC, 188–89
Navajo, bilingual, 15, 22–25, 80–121, 171, 197, 227, 236
Navajo, origins of the, 10–11, 92–93, 164. *See also* Dinétah; Glittering World
Navajo Chapters, 205
Navajo Education, Journal of, 75
Navajo expressive culture, 70
Navajo history, 4–5, 92, 153–57, 169, 173–83; Historic Preservation Office, vii
Navajoland, 32, 168
Navajo language: as threatened/endangered, 1, 10–12, 17, 49, 98; morphology, 69, 86, 104, 115; perfective/imperfective, 39, 59, 63, 92; pronominal argument language, 60, 133; SOV language, 133; triadic directive 21, 49, 101; verb-based language, 60, 133, 210–11
Navajo Language Academy, 132, 177
"Navajo Language page," 74, 114–15
Navajo literacy, 11–12, 18–20, 25–26, 47, 72–76, 96, 105, 114–16, 130–33, 156
Navajo literature, vii, 61, 79, 110
Navajo Nation, location of, 10–11
Navajo Nation Historic Preservation Office, viii; Maldonado, Ronald P., vii
Navajo Nation Museum, 27, 131, 143, 176–78, 229

Navajo poetry, history of, 24–27
Navajo rap, 155. *See also* Mistic; Mistic and Shade
Navajo Studies Conference, 12
Navajo Times, 23–27, 74, 110, 113–15, 141, 155–56, 215; "Poet's Corner," 25; "Navajo Page," 25, 28
Navajo worldview, 9, 206–8. *See also* Witherspoon, Gary
Navglish/Navlish, 24, 80–81, 94, 103–8, 119–20
Neundorf, Alyse, viii, 60, 85, 132, 234–35, 257
Nevins, M. Eleanor, 198–99, 203, 231, 257; Western Apache, 199
Nevins, M. Eleanor, and Thomas Nevins, 125, 258
Newcomb, Franc, and Gladys Reichard, 32, 257; symbolism of locality, 32
Northern Athabaskan, 51, 147
Northwestern Ethnographic Language Field School, 13
Noss, Philip, 52–53, 258; Gbaya (Africa), 53
noun-based language (English), 211
Nuckolls, Janis, ix, 36, 52–55, 67, 78, 258; metanarrative exhortation, 42, 47, 64; Runa (Pastaza Quechua, Ecuador), 53, 67, 78; "sound symbolic involvement," 53, 61

O'Grady, William, John Archibald, Mark Aronoff, and Janie Rees-Miller, 51, 258
Ó hAirtneada, Mícheál (Hartnett, Michael), 164, 249; *A Farewell to English*, 164; Gaelic, 164
O'Neill, Sean, ix, 48, 258
onomatopoeia, 35–43, 51–76. *See also* ideophones/ideophony
onomatopoeia, ritual uses of, 55
oral narratives, 16–50

oral traditions, 1, 15–25, 45–50, 71, 119, 149–152, 158, 168, 182–85, 219
orthographic/written poetry, 16–50

parallelism, 27, 43
Parman, Donald, 10, 154, 258
performance focus, vii, 5–15
Peterson, Leighton C., ix, 1, 231, 234, 258
phonological iconicity, 75, 198, 200–202, 211
pitch, 38, 65, 132, 211
place-names, 14–15, 38–43, 62–77, 91–104, 119, 124–27, 143, 149, 165–67, 181, 185–91, 198–205, 213–16, 233, 238
poetics, 51–79
proper speech, 40, 92–96
Proposition 203, 22–23, 106, 141, 197, 216, 221
puns/punning, vii, 6, 10, 54, 75, 99, 104, 107, 112, 117, 146, 199–203, 212–16, 222, 234
"purist" Navajo, 14, 80–83, 108–20
Pye, Clifton, 231, 258

quoted speech, 37, 41, 116, 200

Reichard, Gladys, 27, 32, 38, 54–56, 63, 66, 68, 84, 99, 118, 165–66, 233, 259; sound power, 54–55
repetition, 22, 27–29, 38, 45–47, 67, 166, 176, 180, 209
resistance, 14, 54, 78–79, 107, 169, 203, 222
Richland, Justin, 208, 259
ritualized wailing/weeping, 23–24, 167, 179, 220–21, 231; ingressive airstream, 23; Walker, Nicole, 167, 221
Roessel, Monty, 131–32, 139, 174
Rumsey, Alan, 81, 153, 180, 259; Ku Waru, 153
Rushforth, Scott, viii, 147, 259

Sa'ąh Naagháí Bik'eh Hózhóón (SNBK), 18
sacred mountains, 32, 33, 38–48, 92, 159–81; *Dibé nitsaa* (assoc. with Hesperus Peak), 38, 40, 92, 159; *Dook'o'oosłííd* (assoc. with San Francisco Peaks), 38, 39, 92, 159; *Sisnaajiní* (assoc. with Blanca Peak), 38–39, 159; *Tsoodził* (Mount Taylor), 39, 159, 166–67
Salina Bookshelf, 60
Samarin, William, 52, 259; Gbeya (Africa), 52
Samuels, David, ix, 9, 54–55, 77–78, 98, 104–6, 122–25, 150, 198–203, 260; emotional attachment, 9, 124; feelingful iconicity, 9–23, 52, 61, 122–51, 166, 180–82, 221–22; reference-centric view of language, 54
Sapir, Edward, 7–9, 16, 30–33, 51–53, 77, 260; Slavey (Canada), 10, 51, 77; Nootka, 52
Sapir, Edward, and Harry Hoijer, 61, 232, 260
Saussure, Ferdinand de, 130, 260
Saville-Troika, Muriel, 99–100, 118, 260
Schaengold, Charlotte, 80–81, 100–109, 260
Schiffrin, Deborah, 132, 261
Schlafly, Phyllis, 214, 261
Schwarz, Maureen, 95, 165–68, 261
Scollon, Ronald, 29, 261
Scollon, Ronald, and Suzanne Scollon, 218, 238, 261
Seaburg, William, 10, 261
Shaul, David Leedom, 30, 261
Sherzer, Joel, viii, 5, 7, 55, 119–27, 142–43, 153, 185, 234, 261; discourse-centered approach, vii, 5, 9–10, 123, 128, 185, 223 (*see also* Urban, Greg); Kuna (Panama), 5; play (language play), 142

Shonerd, Henry, 17, 84, 262
Shootingway, 32, 68
Silverstein, Michael, 35, 78–83, 118–27, 154, 165, 180, 186–87, 212, 262; emblematic identity displays, 128–29, 186
sin (songs), 27
Slate, Clay, viii, 17–18, 48, 262; nexus of Navajo, 17
sociolinguistic diversity, 83, 117, 119
Sorensen, Barbara, 74, 262
sound symbolism/forms, 14, 35, 48, 51–57, 68, 77–78, 224–25, 234. *See also* ideophones/ideophony; Nuckolls, Janis; Samuels, David
Southern Illinois University at Carbondale, 186, 189, 231
Spanish, 83–86, 198–200, 214, 233
Spicer, Edward, 4, 11, 117, 127–29, 153, 155, 262; persistent identity systems, 4–5
Spider Woman, 165
Spolsky, Bernard, 11, 17–20, 117, 262
stance, 93, 101, 133, 171, 222–23
storytelling, 1–6, 33–35, 46–47, 127, 130, 151, 187, 220
syntax, 25, 82–90

Tapahonso, Luci, 248, 263; "Hills Brothers Coffee," 87–89, 133, 199, 203; "In 1864," 171; "Leda and the Cowboy," 8; "They are Silent and Quick," 91; *A Breeze Swept Through*, 87, 228; *Blue Horses Rush In*, 87, 228; *Sáanii Dahataał: The Women are Singing*, 87, 228
Taylor, Charles, 9, 263
Tedlock, Dennis, 7, 52, 55, 126, 263; Zuni, 55
Tedlock, Dennis, and Bruce Mannheim, 223, 263
Thornton, Thomas, 198, 200, 263

Titla, Boe, 150; "Mathilda," 150
Toelken, Barre, ix, 30, 232–34, 263
Toelken, Barre, and Tacheeni Scott, 22, 34, 42, 61–64, 125, 132, 233, 263
Tohatchi School, New Mexico, 24, 81; "If I Were a Pony," 24
Tohe, Laura, viii, 26–49, 155, 122–50, 227–28, 233–38, 264; "Cat or Stomp," 15, 122–50; "Deep in the Rock," 76, 228; "Female Rain," 236; "Gallup Ceremonial," 236; "In Dinétah," 43–45, 91–92, 157–63, 174–83; "*Niłtsą́ Biką́*"/"Male Rain," 236; "Our Tongues Slapped into Silence," 49; "Poem about You," 236–37; "Sometimes Those Pueblo Men Can Sure Be Coyotes," 37–38; "The Names," 49; *No Parole Today*, 130–40, 146, 228; poetic language, Navajo as, 209; *Tseyi': Deep in the Rock*, 190, 200
Towner, Ronald, 163, 264
Trahant, Mark, 131
Trail of Tears, 161, 170, 236
transfer/transference/translation (across languages), 7, 14–50, 77, 90, 210
Tseyi' (Canyon de Chelly), 76, 163, 191, 200–205, 212–16, 228
Twin Heroes, 158–59, 165

Urban, Greg, 5, 23, 123, 128, 180, 264
Urciuoli, Bonnie, 17, 216, 264
Uyechi, Linda, 34, 264

Van Vleet, Krista, 5, 127, 223, 264
Voeltz, F. K. Erhard, and Christa Kilian-Hatz, 58, 264
vulgar language, 95–97

Walters, Anna Lee, 110, 228
Walton, Eda Lou, 27, 264
Watchman, John, 30, 61, 65, 232

Watson, Richard, 78, 264
Wauneka, Dr. Annie, 78, 173
Webster, Anthony K., 265; Coyote poem, 47; feelingful iconicity, 9–11, 70, 79, 98, 122–51, 166, 180, 182, 221; felt attachment, vii, 1, 2, 9, 11, 14, 22, 54, 129, 151, 207, 209, 216, 221–22; felt pragmatic iconicity, 61, 221, 234
we-ness, 151, 159, 170, 173–81, 196
Wheeler, Lesley, 224, 265
White, Orlando, viii, 11
Whitehurst, Lindsay, 212, 265
White Shell Woman, 158, 162, 165, 173
Williams, Raymond, 85, 265
Willie, Mary Ann, and Eloise Jelinek, 60, 265
Wilson, Alan, 62–63, 75, 92, 265
Witherspoon, Gary, 27, 45, 54–55, 84, 208, 210, 231–34, 266
Woodbury, Anthony, viii, 21–22, 52, 66, 70, 266; form-dependent expression, 7; secured domains, 17

Woody, Everrick, 266; *"Veterans Day-go,"* 113–14
Woolard, Kathryn, 81, 266
World War II, 178, 195, 236; Hitler, Adolph, 170, 177–78

Yazzie, Evangeline Parsons, 171, 266
Yazzie, Evangeline Parsons, and Margaret Speas, 58–60, 76
Yazzie, Venaya, viii, 158, 163, 174, 220, 228
Yeats, William Butler, 8, 164, 182; "Leda and the Swan," 8
Young, Robert, 60, 80, 85, 210, 266
Young, Robert, and William Morgan, 56, 58, 65–66, 100, 233–34, 266
Young, Robert, and William Morgan with Sally Midgette, 58, 62, 266
Yurth, Cindy, 215, 266

Zachary, Mary-Kathryn, 17, 84, 216, 267
Zepeda, Ofelia, 232, 267
Zolbrod, Paul, 48, 164–65, 234, 267

www.ingramcontent.com/pod-product-compliance
Lightning Source LLC
Chambersburg PA
CBHW020641230426
43665CB00008B/267